A Spoonful
of Sugar

Brenda is 91 years old and lives near Milton Keynes. She worked as a Norland Nanny for over 60 years and loved every minute of it.

BRENDA ASHFORD

A Spoonful of Sugar

A NANNY'S STORY OF HARD TIMES,
LOVE AND HAPPINESS IN WARTIME ENGLAND

HODDER

First published in Great Britain in 2012 by Hodder & Stoughton
An Hachette UK company

First published in paperback in 2012
1

A CIP catalogue record for this title is available from the British Library

ISBN 978 1 444 73986 2

Typeset by Hewer Text UK Ltd, Edinburgh
Printed and bound by CPI Group (UK) Ltd, Croydon, CR0 4YY

Hodder & Stoughton policy is to use papers that are natural, renewable
and recyclable products and made from wood grown in sustainable
forests. The logging and manufacturing processes are expected to
conform to the environmental regulations of the country of origin.

Hodder & Stoughton Ltd
338 Euston Road
London NW1 3BH

www.hodder.co.uk

Publisher's Acknowledgement

With thanks to the Hothfield History Society, Geoff Webb, author of *A Redbourn Commoner*, Michael Anderson of the Bookham History Society and Katherine Stone of the War Studies Department, Kings College London, Penelope Stokes, author of *Norland – The Story of the First One Hundred Years 1892–1992*, published by the Norland College 1992, Susan Briggs, author of *Keep Smiling Through the Home Front 1939–1945*, Richard Holmes, author of *Tommy* and Kevin Telfer, author of *The Remarkable Story of Great Ormond Street Hospital*.

Picture Acknowledgements

Most of the photographs are reproduced courtesy of the author. Additional sources: *The Daily Herald*/Mirrorpix, Getty Images, Great Ormond Street Hospital, the archives at Norland College, Geoff Webb Redbourn Collection.

Contents

Foreword

THIS BOOK came about (out of the blue) via the Norland College, at a time when I was getting very tired of being confined to my flat following a hip operation. I was asked if I was interested in writing about my time as a Norland Nurse before and after the Second World War. My immediate reaction was one of excitement, but I also felt very daunted at the prospect. I needn't have worried. Kate Thompson, whose help has been invaluable, came to see me soon afterwards, bringing her baby son Stanley, who was six weeks old. I had the privilege of nursing him throughout our first meeting. Right from the start Kate and I got along so well together and my sincere thanks go to her for the hard work, research and dedication to the making of the book. I am truly indebted to her.

I am grateful to my two brothers Christopher and David who have been so encouraging all along, and to the friends who have allowed me to write about the time spent with them and their families. We have changed names and some locations for confidentiality.

My sincere thanks go to my agent Diane Banks and the editors of Hodder and Stoughton. Also the Norland College, for all their help, encouragement and friendliness throughout the writing of this book. Without them it would never have made it into print.

Lastly, but not least, I would like to thank the warden Julia, and my friends in sheltered accommodation where I now live, also my many friends in the Baptist Church where I worship, for their prayers, encouragement and support.

Above all I thank God for his love and care for me throughout my 91 years.

Brenda Ashford

1

Recipe for a Happy Home

Lullaby, lullaby, hasten away
Little pink pilgrims till dawn of the day
Slow swings the cradle, but swift is the flight
Lullaby, hushaby, baby good night
            English nineteenth-century lullaby

I HAVE sung this lullaby thousands of times throughout my life and each time is as sweet as the last.

In 62 years of being a nanny I have lost count of the number of children I have cared for, but it must be approaching 100. Which means I am inordinately proud to say that, despite never having given birth, I have 100 children and my families are spread far and wide.

Children are born uniquely vulnerable and with a need for love that they never outgrow. A baby has a special way of adding joy every single day and can flood your heart with love like nothing else. They say you can never truly love a child that is not your own, but that goes against every instinct that runs through me. For I have loved children born to other women all my life and every child that I have ever cared for, I've adored with all my heart. Many I would have laid down my life for, in fact on some memorable occasions when I fled to air raid shelters clutching my charges to my chest, I very nearly did.

The outbreak of the Second World War catapulted me headlong into some of the most bewildering, exhausting, frightening and challenging moments of my career but I, like every sensible British woman I knew, never allowed terror to take hold. We had no choice but to go about our business; running the home, shopping, cooking and keeping the nation's children happy, healthy and as well fed as rations allowed, while chaos erupted around us.

There is little I haven't come up against in the years since I began my training as a Norland Nanny in 1939. Bombs, rockets, Spitfires battling German planes above my head, freezing winters, disease, adultery, deserters, scandal, inspiring evacuees and their memorable cockney mothers: all have conspired to make my life interesting. I know that few people get to experience the adventures I've had in my life, and I'm very grateful for the cards that were dealt to me.

When you've trained under the doyenne of Britain's oldest nanny school and the draconian matrons of 1930s hospital wards, Hitler and his army hold no fear. Every fibre of my being was focussed on the welfare of the children in my care. Nothing was more important than being the most loving and professional nanny that I could possibly be.

Britain has changed much since the Second World War ended, and the dangers facing our children today have drastically altered. Back then it was bomb blasts and malnutrition. Now there are the threats posed by the internet – things that we could never have imagined. But I believe that the fundamentals for bringing up happy children haven't changed.

I don't intend this book to be a childcare manual. I doubt I should even have the brains to qualify as a Norland Nanny today and I haven't a clue what childcare trends are in vogue;

but I do know this. If your heart sings with love for little children you can't go far wrong.

Where does this all-consuming love come from, in my case? A question I have asked myself on many an occasion, I think it stems from the moment I met my baby brother when I was nine years old.

The sense of excitement was tangible in the air at Hallcroft House in Lower Farm Road, Effingham, Surrey.

Every corridor, nook, cranny and crevice in the vast house hummed with quiet anticipation. Our cleaner, Winnie, an ageless, round woman who sang as she worked, had come up from the village and polished and scrubbed the house until every surface sparkled like a new penny.

Winnie was flushed red from her efforts.

'Got to get everything just right for the new arrival,' she'd said, winking, when she'd spotted me watching her.

Winnie had done us proud. The oak floors gleamed like freshly churned butter. Every room smelt of lavender polish and carbolic soap, the leather thong handles on the doors glistened with beeswax, and pretty pink roses had been picked from the garden and dotted round the house in glass vases.

King George V himself, who was on the throne at the time, wouldn't have got such a rapturous reception had he showed up at Hallcroft that sunny spring morning. Little wonder the birth of my baby brother or sister was more exciting than every birthday and Christmas rolled into one.

My poor mother. From the moment she first told me she was expecting, I had pestered her on a daily basis.

'Is the baby coming today? Where is she, she's taking so long.'

I said *she* because I was certain the baby would be a girl, a real life doll for me to dress up in pretty dresses and push around in my pram alongside my favourite actual doll, Constance.

And now the great moment was here.

I had been sent off to stay with my aunt Jessie. My elder sister Kathleen and my younger brothers Michael, Basil and Christopher had been packed off to various other relatives, but now, finally, the call had come to say the baby had arrived and my mother, Doris, was at last ready for our return home.

My father Arnold was duly dispatched to collect us all and bring us home.

As was customary in 1930, my mother was expected to give birth at home. That was quite the norm in those days. The poorest of the poor right up to aristocracy and royalty made their entry into the world in the surrounds of their own home, attended by a local maternity nurse.

If that sounds backwards to you I should put it in context. The Midwives Act had only been passed in 1902, after a group of pioneering and inspiring women fought to have midwifery and antenatal care recognised as a profession. Prior to that, any woman, or for that matter man, could deliver a baby.

Usually babies were delivered by a woman from the local community called the handy woman. Some were good at their job, others less so; some were apparently prostitutes who were reputedly paid in gin.

Fortunately the Act became law, the Royal College of Midwives was born, birthing standards soared and infant deaths dropped.

When you consider that in the year I was born, 1921, there were 700 deaths per 100,000 births and that I came unannounced, it is exceedingly lucky I am writing this book at all!

There was no time for pain relief for her, not that it would have helped that much in any case. The only respites from the agony of childbirth were chloroform and forceps to speed things up if the baby got stuck.

Goodness only knows what pain my mother suffered giving birth. Not that she would have discussed it with us, or anyone else. What went on in her bedroom remained strictly between herself and the maternity nurse, with Father banished downstairs to avoid the gruesome reality, and us children packed off to stay with a relative.

Back in those days, women were confined to bed for at least ten days after giving birth. This was known as the lying-in period. I still find it hard to believe that some women are now discharged from hospital just 48 hours after giving birth. Don't they deserve more time to rest?

After ten days' bed rest and recuperation for Mother, we were finally allowed to come home.

The door to my parents' bedroom swung open as I pushed it and my excitement bubbled over. 'Where's the baby?' I gasped, in a fever pitch of emotion.

An angry face loomed into view. Nurse Evans the maternity nurse. She was a short dumpy woman in her fifties wearing an apron and hat, and radiating disapproval.

'Hush child,' she hissed. 'You'll wake the baby.'

But her words were lost on me.

Because there, nestled in his wicker Moses basket lined in mauve cotton and organza with delicate mauve bows, was quite simply the most exquisite thing I had ever set eyes on.

'Oh,' I breathed in wide-eyed wonder.

'She is a he,' said my mother, smiling, when she spotted my face.

'Meet your baby brother David.'

The world turns on tiny things. It's not so much the outstanding events that have influenced my life. It may sound absurd but, though hearing we were at war with Germany, witnessing the devastation of the Blitz and the jubilant crowds on VE Day were all moments I shall never forget, the most life-altering of all was when I set eyes on baby David.

I swear my heart skipped a minute's worth of beats.

My other brothers' arrivals simply didn't make the same impact on me because I had been too young to remember or to help out. But now I was old enough to see clearly what a miracle I was witnessing.

He was just a tiny little scrap of a thing, dressed in a white cotton gown, no bigger than a porcelain doll.

Any lingering disappointment I may have had over not having a baby sister melted away when he snuffled and sleep-ily opened his eyes. The little creature fixed his dark blue eyes on mine and I was done for, hook, line and sinker.

'Can I hold him?' I asked, utterly mesmerised.

A thunderous voice piped up from the corner of the bedroom.

'NO! He's not to be woken,' Nurse Evans muttered through thin lips.

But even a cranky old nurse couldn't stem the unspeak-able joy that flooded through me. Was it his dark lashes that swept over creamy cheeks, the little murmurs and sighs he made when he slept?

Or was it the way his tiny fingers curled round mine and the beautiful musky smell that filled my nostrils when I kissed his soft downy hair.

No, the thing I loved most about David, and every baby I cared for after him, was his heartbreaking innocence and vulnerability.

Adults are complicated, contrary beings, capable of hurt-ing or betraying you. But babies are simple, sweet and full of love.

Many great things were invented and created in 1930, the year David was born: helicopters, FM radio broadcasting, the jet engine and the world's first antibiotic to name but a few; but to my mind the greatest creation ever was my baby brother.

Today my baby brother David is 83 and we still share a bond that I know was created in those precious early days.

From that moment on I cared for David as if my life depended on it. My mother had only to issue a simple request and I was there. Nothing was too much trouble.

I fed him his bottles, helped bathe him, changed his cloth nappies, sterilised his glass feeding bottles and spent hours singing him lullabies.

When he cut his first tooth I helped the pain of teething by giving him an ivory ring to chew or dashing to the shops to buy him Allenburys rusks. When he was ready to be weaned it was usually me gently feeding him gruel, or porridge, as we know it now.

Most of all, I loved gently picking him up out of his warm, cosy nest to feed him his evening bottle. He was so sweet and drowsy that his little rosebud lips would begin sucking before the bottle was anywhere near them. Then, like a little lamb, he would hungrily latch on and suckle. I witnessed a small miracle every evening at 6.00 p.m.

That little boy flooded my heart with love every time he nestled into my chest and fell asleep on me and when I gently put him on my shoulder to wind him and he gave a soft milky burp it did so make me chuckle.

Those days exist in my memory as a warm and rosy glow, and little did I know it then, but they sparked a life-long love for children.

Every day was filled with magic and promise . . .

If home is where the heart is then at the heart of my home were my parents. You'd be hard pressed to find a more devoted couple than Doris and Arnold Ashford. I often wonder what was the secret to their success but all I know is that in 45 years of marriage they could hardly bare to leave each other's side.

My mother was a gentle soul, a quiet loving woman devoted to her husband and six children. Women had only won the right to vote seven years after my birth in 1928, and traditional attitudes towards women prevailed. Married women were not expected to work. It never occurred to any of us that Mother should leave the home and actually get a job. Nor to my mother either I suspect.

She was never happier than on the Saturday afternoons we spent sitting round a crackling coal fire in the sitting room, with Henry Hall's BBC dance orchestra playing on the gramophone accompanied by the clicking of her knitting needles.

My mother had six children pretty much one after the other so she seemed to me to be constantly either pregnant or nursing a baby. But every so often my father would insist on sweeping my mother to her feet so they could dance round the sitting room.

'Dance Bobby?' he'd enquire, gathering her in his arms.

I often wondered why he called her Bobby. It was only years later I discovered that Mother had contracted Spanish flu before she had us children and was really rather ill. The flu hit England in 1918, just after the end of World War One. It was a worldwide pandemic and 50 million people died, making it one of the deadliest natural disasters in human history.

Poor Mother was so ill all her hair fell out and after that it never grew past her shoulders so she always wore it in a bob, hence the nickname. I thank goodness she was strong enough to survive. She was one of the lucky ones.

Maybe this made Father love and cherish my mother all the more. Their eyes would lock and they would smile tenderly at each other, it was a secret little smile of understanding and it left me breathless with wonder.

It saddens me a little to think that I never found that love for myself, but I don't dwell on it. I prefer to think instead that the love they gave to me enriched my whole life. Besides, I was too busy with my babies.

Doris and Arnold were so potty about one another they insisted on having every Sunday afternoon by themselves, with us children packed off to the garden. We knew better than to try to disturb them. I wasn't short of playmates, though. Besides me there were my elder sister by 13 months, Kathleen, and my four younger brothers: Michael, Basil, Christopher and baby David.

The whole essence of my childhood and, in my opinion, the key to any happy childhood is simplicity.

I have never forgotten reading the following passage in *Etiquette for the Children*, published in 1901:

> *The simpler the life led by children the happier they will be. Simple meals, regular hours and plenty of healthful exercise should be the keynote of the regime for both nursery and schoolroom.*
>
> *How pleasant it is to see the enjoyment of children so brought up at the most simple treats and pleasures.*
>
> *They are real children in every sense of the word and in later life they will have none but happy recollections of a childhood past in this way.*

I passionately believe those words to be true.

Because my days weren't filled with television, computer games and constant activities, my siblings and I learnt to use our imagination. Sometimes children need to be bored in order to stimulate themselves. Except with five siblings for company, life was anything but boring.

Michael was the musical one, always tinkering around on an instrument. His hard work paid off as in later life he became a stage manager for the musical *Oliver!*

Poor Christopher and Kathleen always suffered with their health, so they seemed to spend a lot more time inside, with Mother fussing over them. I did so feel for my siblings. They were wrapped in cotton wool and had cod liver oil rubbed on their chests daily by Mother. It seemed like a simply horrible thing to be so weak. I was so robust and untroubled by illness, and looking back, I'm sure I took my good health for granted.

That left me, Basil and as soon as he could run, David, to charge around the garden with. I begged my only sister to join us in our adventures but she always had her head stuck in a book.

'Oh, do come outside,' I urged one day. 'We've got a wizard game of hide and seek going on.'

Kathleen stared at me from over the top of *What Katie Did Next*.

'Can't you see I'm busy reading?' she sniffed.

'Suit yourself,' I said, and grinned, galloping out the door and down the stairs. I couldn't for the life of me see what was more fun than hide and seek. Books were dull. The real adventures were to be found outside in the fresh air.

Try as I might I just never could apply the same tight restrictions and self-control that Kathleen governed her life with.

Books and study weren't my bag, oh no. If there was a tree to be climbed, a stream to be waded through or a field to be explored you could bet I'd be there, in the thick of it with my brothers, flushed with excitement. Why should boys get to have all the fun?

While Kathleen was losing herself in literature I was usually to be found tearing through the vegetable patch with a headdress on my head, whooping at the top of my voice and pretending to be an Indian or a cowboy. Kale, cabbages and carrots were trampled underfoot as I ran hollering after my little brothers.

I loved our house, but as a child the garden was one giant adventure playground, designed to feed my vivid imagination.

The rockery in the front garden, which was usually ablaze with colour, was not simply a place to cultivate alpine flowers. To me it was a mountain to be scaled, an ideal look out for a surprise enemy attack. The kissing gate at the end of a path lined with lavender was the perfect spot to launch an ambush on an unsuspecting little brother. The rose garden in the back garden? Why a training camp for spies, of course. And the fields, or roughs as we called them, which backed onto our house, they were a wild territory to roam for hours on end, with streams to dam, blackberries to pick and frontiers to conquer.

My mother never worried about us when we played out there, sometimes for a whole day. In fact she would make us some cheese sandwiches and pack us off out to the roughs. Out there we could be anyone we wanted to be, an explorer, a nurse, a train driver . . .

But the delicious smell of Mother's homemade Queens Pudding, my favourite confection of breadcrumbs baked with jam and meringue, would creep out from the kitchen, over the fields and soon have us haring for home . . .

Poor Mother. Six grubby children would tear into the kitchen like a giant whirlwind clutching all manner of treasures, from sheep's wool we'd collected from the fences, to acorns and sticks.

'Eurgh,' she'd cry when she spotted the wool. 'Dirty things full of maggots and lice.'

I did little to trouble my mother; we left that to Basil, the naughty daredevil of the family. If there was mischief to be found, Basil would be there, in the thick of it.

It was Basil who coined the rhyme for little Bobby Penfold the washerwoman's son, who would bring back our freshly laundered clothes each week, wheeling them up the drive in a baby's pram.

Washing's in the pram, baby's in the bath, Bobby pushes it up the hill, how it makes us laugh.

It was also Basil who wrote 'bomfers' on the coalhouse door. Bomfers was just a silly word that made us children roar with laughter, as we imagined it to be something rather naughty. Whatever it meant, it earned Basil a clip round the ear. If you heard a distant cry of alarm from somewhere in the house you could bet Basil had jumped out, shouted 'boo' and run away laughing.

We once had a French au pair for the summer. I didn't know her name, we just called her Mademoiselle. She was terribly lazy and often when she should have been tending to us she would sit reading the paper.

On one memorable occasion she was sitting by the gas fire, reading, with Basil at her feet. I looked up to see her engrossed in an article on sewing with flames licking up the bottom of the paper.

'Fire,' I gasped.

She looked up, startled, then . . .

'Le feu, le feu!' she screamed, leaping to her feet with a red-hot copy of the *Telegraph* burning in her lap. Adds a new meaning to hot off the press.

Mother dashed in and put her out with a wet cloth and no harm done, but mademoiselle pointed the finger at Basil. He could be a bit mischievous at times but I never thought him capable of setting fire to a French au pair. She left shortly after.

Nowadays they'd label Basil as having attention deficit disorder or some such nonsense. I like to think he was just high-spirited.

Hallcroft, our childhood home, was a beautiful idyll that father had worked hard to create.

Arnold Ashford was a six-foot-tall bear of a man. With his cheeky crooked grin, pointed ears and striking blue eyes that sparkled with fun, I worshipped him. His slight stutter and lisp just endeared him to me more.

From Monday morning to Saturday afternoon Father worked in Regent Street in London, running a business selling ladies' and children's knitwear that supplied grand stores like Harrods. With six mouths to feed he was no stranger to hard work, but he earned enough to design and have built his dream home.

Father was typical of many men of his era. During World War One he was a lieutenant in the army. He was even awarded the Military Cross for his courage and skill in leading his platoon at one of the bloodiest battles of the war, at Hill 60, or as it was nicknamed, 'Hell with the lid off'.

Millions of boys died for their country during that dreadful war.

Those poor young men, if they had known at the start of the conflict what they were facing, would they have signed up? Probably. If the famous poster of Lord Kitchener pointing out of the frame with the words 'Your country needs you' didn't get them, then they would have been made to feel like cowards by the women who handed out white feathers to men who didn't join up. If they ever felt like deserting, which surely some must have, then the punishment – death by firing squad – would have acted as a deterrent.

My father may have talked to those comrades that survived Hill 60, but he never uttered a word to me about the horrors he must have witnessed, or what he did to earn his Military Cross. Part of me wishes I knew what his exact role was, but maybe he was right not to divulge it to us. He wanted to preserve our childhood and keep it as innocent as possible, hopeful that we wouldn't be touched by the horrors of war.

Apart from the mental scars he must have carried with him he also had a piece of shrapnel lodged in his shoulder. Years later and suffering with pain in his thigh he went to the doctors who discovered that the same piece of shrapnel had worked its way from his shoulder down to his leg.

I often wonder how a man can witness such atrocities and misery, then bury them away so deep they can't touch them. Did he have nightmares, flashbacks and panic attacks as a result of his time at Hill 60? If he did he never revealed them to his children. Even his medal was hidden away in a drawer. It only came out on Armistice Day to be worn with pride. It's a wonder he didn't go insane, I suspect I would have. Perhaps the only way his body betrayed him was a slight stammer in his gentle rumbling voice.

Mother was certainly no shrinking violet when it came to war efforts either. Because of her love of children she had always longed to train as a Norland Nanny, but in the 1920s, childcare wasn't considered a 'respectable' career for a young woman of the upper middle classes. There were really only two options for a woman of my mother's social rank: teaching as a governess or nursing. Like me, my mother showed no academic prowess so she opted to train as a nurse, which was thought less intellectually demanding.

During World War One she became a VAD nurse, or Voluntary Aid Detachment nurse. VAD nurses were usually from genteel backgrounds, largely because only really wealthy women could work for free and fund the training required. One of the most famous VADs was Agatha Christie, who dispensed drugs.

During the war my mother worked in hospitals dressing wounds and tending to the injured. For a woman unaccustomed to hardship this must have come as some shock. Nursing plunged her and many other well-to-do young women into life-altering adventures and exposed them to horrors they could never have imagined.

Whilst many VADs served tea and sterilised equipment, they were just as likely to be asked to hold down the exposed intestines of a mortally wounded soldier.

Before she began her training, Mother was confined by the Victorian belief that a woman should know nothing of a man but his face and clothes until marriage, so her work tending to wounded soldiers must have been an eye opener. I read later that she would have witnessed amputations, deaths and cleaned up rivers of blood.

Mother and Father rarely discussed the awful things they had seen, nor would they ever dream of discussing any problems or disagreements they may have had in front of us children. Throughout their entire marriage I didn't hear a single word uttered in anger between them. They set a marvellously good example by never ever quarrelling in front of us. They exercised extreme self-control and courtesy. You must remember, and this is something my parents knew, of course, that in little ones the imitative faculties are highly developed. A child's character will receive lasting impressions from those with whom they interact.

In later life, if I ever heard one of the families I worked

for bickering I was horrified. Why would you fill your home with anger and subject your children to disharmony? It remains a mystery to me today.

Maybe this is another reason I never married; how could any relationship match up to my parents'? My father's eyes shone with love whenever he talked of my mother and she in turn devoted her life to him and us children. This intense love just made the powerful tragedy that occurred later all the more painful.

Work may have claimed my father for most of the week but come midday Saturday he was all ours. As soon as we heard his key in the lock we ran to the door and jumped all over him like excited puppies. His smart tailored navy wool suit, tie, trilby hat and briefcase would soon be discarded in favour of fawn flannels and a cotton shirt . . . then the fun would begin.

'What have you brought for us, Daddy?' we'd cry.

'Close your eyes and hold out your hands,' he'd say, in a voice rich with fun and laughter.

Eagerly, I'd squeeze shut my eyes and stick out my hands.

Just the rustling of a brown paper bag was enough to make my mouth water.

'No peeking,' he'd warn. As if I'd want to spoil the magic of the moment.

Seconds later a pear drop or some other tasty morsel would be deposited in our outstretched palm. Mother was always rewarded with a bag of sugared almonds and a kiss on the cheek.

For taste buds unaccustomed to really sweet things, the tangy, acidic burst of sugar on my tongue was like nectar. Pear drops were my favourite and always made a Saturday but if it weren't those it would be bullseyes, which we'd take out to the roughs and suck until our tongues were purple.

Sometimes Father brought Pontefract cakes, small liquo-rice disks, but I never understood how anyone could like liquorice.

In the 1930s, sweet shops were all the rage and popping up all over London. It was a very productive decade for Rown-tree. For a small child, imagining where the sugary delights came from was a constant source of wonder. After incessant begging from us children, Father finally told us.

'There's a little place I go to just off Regent Street,' he said, his voice dropping to a whisper, 'with a bell on the door that jingles as you enter and a lady older than your mother wear-ing a housecoat who appears with a metal scoop to weigh out your sweets . . .'

'Tell us about the sweets, Daddy,' I interrupted.

Father smiled and paused for dramatic effect.

'Row upon row upon row of shiny glass jars crammed with sweets,' he said eventually.

My eyes were as a big as bullseyes as he went on.

'Every kind of sweet you can imagine . . . lollipops, liq-uorice bootlaces, gobstoppers, peanut brittle, toffees, walnut whips, cherry lips, coconut mushrooms, Uncle Joe's mint balls, pineapple chunks.'

I glanced over at Basil. He was virtually drooling.

'And on the counter, chocolate, glistening fudge, ginger-bread men, sugared plums.'

It was almost too much. Our palates weren't much troubled by unusual flavours in those days and food largely consisted of some sort of meat, potatoes and vegetables such as turnips or carrots from the garden, with suet or steamed sponge pud-ding for dessert. To hear about these exotic sounding treats was to be transported to food nirvana. It's no wonder sweet o'clock, midday Saturday, was the most hotly anticipated time of the week.

I must confess, Father's treats left me with a lifelong sweet tooth. If you were to visit me in my flat today you would find a good number of chocolate biscuits stacked in my cupboards. One bite of heavenly chocolate and if I close my eyes I am transported back to my childhood.

Our Saturday fun didn't stop there. Whilst some fathers may have retired to the study with a paper and strict instructions not to disturb, ours adopted a more hands on approach.

We loved sitting at his feet as he read Rupert the Bear to us and supped stout from a large brown bottle. For us children it was a cup of hot cocoa in winter or a glass of the milk that was delivered weekly by a milkman on a horse-drawn float and sold by the jug from a stainless steel milk churn.

On one day I'll always remember, Father spent hours in the garden plotting a surprise. When we children were finally allowed outside the suspense was killing us.

Father stood in the middle of the lawn to the side of the house that had always been earmarked for use as a tennis court, with a smile a mile wide.

'What is it, Daddy?' I piped up, puzzled.

'Look down,' he said, and winked.

Father had mowed lines in the garden to look like railway tracks and up and down the tracks he'd placed 'signals' that he'd made in the shed and that he operated with a string pulley system.

'Who wants to play trains?' he bellowed.

Did we ever? Every Saturday afternoon after that was spent hurtling up and down the tracks on our trains, which to the untrained eye might have looked like bicycles.

Mother and Father's unashamed love of children, enthusiasm for life and sense of fun made our childhood that much richer. Thanks to their efforts I realised subsequently that becoming a mother or father doesn't automatically make you a good parent. You have to learn and work hard at family life, a lesson I hope I have instilled in my many charges.

The only blot on my heavenly childhood was the time I got it into my head that I must have been adopted and didn't really belong to my family.

Shortly after David turned one I was marvelling at his beautiful head of blonde curly hair. It occurred to me that Basil had beautiful soft curls, as did Michael, Christopher and Kathleen. By contrast my own hair was poker straight, not so much as a wisp of a curl.

Quite suddenly, in the middle of the night, it came to me. It was so obvious . . . why hadn't I seen it before?

I was adopted.

Marching through to my parents' room I let out an anguished wail.

Mother was sitting up in bed knitting and Father was reading the *Telegraph*.

'I don't belong to this family,' I sobbed. 'Look at my hair, it's all wrong!'

My parents stared at me, shock written all over their faces.

'W . . . what darling?' stuttered my mother eventually. 'Of course you do, sweetheart. You are our blood and we love you very much. There's nothing at all wrong with your hair.'

Suitably reassured, I allowed my mother to tuck me back under my eiderdown. The next morning she got out some rags and used them to twist my hair into beautiful corkscrew curls.

'There,' she said, tenderly stroking my cheek. 'Now we're all the same.'

Over the years I have treasured that memory and used it to remind myself many times that children, whilst they may come across as bold, bouncy and robust, suffer the same irrational and nameless fears and anxieties that us adults do. Children, no matter how stable and happy their upbringing, need constant love and reassurance.

My heritage assured, I would quite happily never have left Hallcroft, but two events necessitated leaving the house.

The first was our annual visit to Norfolk to see Granny Brown for a fortnight during the summer holidays. We would travel by train from Liverpool Street to Yarmouth with my heart sinking as the fields turned to broad salty marshes. I did so dread our visits to see my mother's mother. We used to be sent there once a year on 'holiday,' and probably to give Mother a much-needed break.

Granny Brown was from the Victorian era and clung to the rigid disciplines of her day. She certainly didn't share our father's hands on approach to child rearing. Not for Granny Brown the sugary delights of hidden pear drops and running amok in the vegetable patch. Like most Victorian people, she believed that children should be seen and not heard and expected docility and obedience at all times.

She had been raised and had raised my mother to be a mini adult. Discipline was harsh and often intent on breaking the spirit of the child. By withholding affection from their children when they were young and then attempting to control their behaviour well into adulthood, Victorians both suppressed childhood and made it last for ever.

From virtually the minute she emerged from the womb, Granny Brown was expected to be obedient, dutiful, honest, hard-working, stiff-upper-lipped and emotionally self-contained.

And by golly she was all these things.

Little wonder when you consider her childhood reading. Whilst I was raised on Enid Blyton, Granny Brown would have read something far more fear-inducing. Literature of the time included a popular poem, 'The Dreadful Story of Pauline and the Matches', a cautionary tale about a little girl who failed to heed her mother's advice not to play with matches.

> *But Pauline would not take advice,*
> *She lit a match, it was so nice!*
> *It crackled so, it burned so clear,*
> *Exactly like the picture here*
> *She jumped for joy and ran about,*
> *And was too pleased to put it out.*
> *Now see! Oh see! What a dreadful thing*
> *The fire has caught her apron string,*
> *Her apron burns, her arms, her hair,*
> *She burns all over everywhere.*
> *So she was burnt with all her clothes*
> *And arms and hands, and eyes and nose*
> *Till she had nothing more to lose*
> *Except her little scarlet shoes*
> *And nothing else but these were found*
> *Among her ashes on the ground.*

Ghastly, isn't it. Poor Granny Brown. With bedtime reading like this it's no wonder she turned out the way she did.

Her routine crushed the joy of childhood and made our days with her full of fear, respect and conformity to adult values and attitudes. Little wonder I dreaded visiting her town house and when her black door swung open my heart dropped to my boots.

A short, austere woman who wore her hair tightly scraped back in a bun, she'd fix me with her beady eyes. The thing that always struck me most was the thick determined set of her jaw. It was so strong you could have bounced a penny off it. No kisses or hugs from Granny Brown, just a curt nod.

Our days were rigid in their routine. Fresh air on the beach was followed by lunch of watery mince or a lump of cod boiled to within an inch of its life, followed by junket pudding that stuck in my gullet.

Yarmouth bloater, a smoked herring, was the only thing she served up that tasted of anything.

Aunt Muriel, Mother's unmarried sister, lived with Granny Brown. Poor Aunt Muriel. One of five girls, she was the only one unmarried and childless after some chap cruelly let her down, so it was left to her to look after Granny Brown. I expect she found this a deeply frustrating situation. She was nice enough to us but I suspect not particularly interested in engaging with her nieces.

Perhaps that's why after lunch she and Granny Brown insisted we lie very still on the cold bare parlour floorboards and rest, whilst they got on with their sewing or knitting. We were expected not to move an inch and not to utter a word.

'The rest will do you good,' said Granny Brown.

Kathleen lay still and did all that she should, but I was a proper fidget pants.

'Lie still, child,' Granny barked at me. 'Look how well Kathleen does it.'

Of course she did. Kathleen, clearly Granny Brown's favourite, was good at keeping still. For me it was agony and within minutes my leg would be twitching involuntarily.

'Stop fidgeting,' hissed Kathleen out the corner of her mouth.

'I can't,' I blurted.

'Silence, Brenda,' boomed Granny Brown.

Oh, why couldn't I be more like Kathleen at times like these? I could never lie as still as Granny Brown wanted. To an excitable child who just wanted to be running free this was nothing short of agony.

The only time a frenzied burst of activity was acceptable was when the national anthem came on the wireless and we were expected to leap to our feet, with the command 'show some respect and stand to attention.'

Granny Brown's life ended in a very sad way. She developed dementia and when Aunt Muriel could no longer manage, was looked after by a companion in Putney, south west London. Late one evening she was found wandering up Putney High Street, naked save for a fur coat. For a woman whose life was governed by self-control and discipline, this was indeed a tragic end.

Looking back at the childhood my parents had, it is nothing short of a miracle that they turned out so full of love. Or maybe that's why my childhood was so joyful and full of fun. Did you know that the end of the Victorian period coincided almost exactly with the invention of psychoanalysis? I'm fairly sure that my parents never went in for any of that but perhaps they made an unconscious decision not to replicate their own childhood in the way they brought up their own offspring.

One tradition that was most certainly passed down was that of a boarding school education. Aged 11, in 1932, I was sent to Courtfield Gardens School for girls in Bognor Regis.

The boys were all sent to boarding schools on the Isle of Wight and Kathleen had gone to Courtfield Gardens the year before me. She was sent there because she had always been a sickly child. After contracting glandular fever as a small girl she had suffered with her health and it was believed the fresh sea air would be a tonic.

Having been duly equipped with the correct green school uniform, I prepared to set off with my father, who was to drive Kathleen and me with our trunks and tuck boxes containing a few sweets, down to Bognor.

It was only 50 miles, but I may as well have been travelling to the moon. Apart from our trips to Norfolk to see Granny Brown and short excursions into the village, I had scarcely left Hallcroft. I was desolate to leave David, who was coming up to two, but I accepted my fate. Girls from my background were always sent to boarding school to be educated.

Nevertheless, it was a big change for an eleven-year-old. Parting from the warmth and security of my family was agony.

As Father loaded our trunks into the car, Mother stood on the doorstep, clutching little David to her chest. His chubby little arms pumped with excitement when he saw the car. He loved cars almost as much as he loved my kisses. Already I knew big changes would take place in my absence. Every day he'd pick up a new word, toddle that bit further up the garden, embark more boldly on life's journey . . . and I wouldn't be there to witness any of these new milestones.

Sadness gripped my heart.

'Be good my little angel,' I whispered in his ear, as I planted a soft kiss on his jam-smeared face.

Sensing my sadness, Mother scooped me into her arms.

'I'm so proud of you, Brenda, now you do me proud.'

She kissed me and my cheek tingled where her soft, downy cheek had touched mine. Her skin was as warm as toast and she smelt of lemony soap.

I gulped back my tears and nodded my head vigorously. 'I will, Mother,' I whispered.

In the car Kathleen stared out the window lost in her own thoughts so I was left quite alone in my misery. I could still smell Mother's sweet soapy-smelling kiss in the air and a small tear trickled down my cheek. As every mile passed I longed for Father to turn the car around. But of course he didn't, and by the time we pulled up in front of Courtfield Gardens my head was spinning.

The driveway was full of parents unloading trunks, excited girls hugging each other and babbling away ten to the dozen, anxious mothers and fathers checking their watches. You could spot the new girls a mile off, they looked as bewildered as me.

I stared at the older girls and felt utterly overwhelmed. Would I ever share their breezy confidence?

Father smiled and crouched down to our level.

'D . . . do . . . do me proud my darlings,' he stuttered, hugging us both close.

My lip wobbled as I watched him turn and stride to the car. *Don't cry Brenda, don't cry, not here, not now.*

And then he was gone, and I was sucked into the regime that is boarding school life.

Kathleen, being in her second year, was in a different part of the school and there was barely time to say goodbye before I was marched off to my dormitory by an efficient school secretary.

Courtfield Gardens was a rambling old mansion house with ten or so dormitories sleeping five girls each. The deputy matron slept in her own room on the same floor as us girls, with the headmistress, one Miss Morehouse, occupying her own room on the ground floor.

Our routine was similar to most boarding schools. The day started at 7.30 a.m. when the deputy matron came to wake us. There was only one bathroom, which could accommodate a dormitory at a time, so we waited our turn to wash. After that we dressed and stripped our beds, folding our blankets and sheets neatly at the end of our beds.

Mother was always very proud of the fact that she had taught all her children how to correctly make a bed. Some of the girls in my dorm had never made a bed before. No such shame for me.

We waited for the bell to ring, which was the signal for quiet while we said our prayers, then filed to the dining room for a breakfast of porridge with hot milk, brown sugar and bread, butter and marmalade.

Then we filed to our classrooms for whatever lesson we had that morning. Lunch was always at 12.45 p.m. and was always a hot course, a roast or similar with tonnes of vegetables and gravy, followed by a hot steam sponge pudding or my favourite, spotted dick and custard.

More lessons in the afternoon were followed by tea at 4.15 p.m., which was usually bread and butter, and a cup of tea.

Supper at 6.30 p.m. consisted of bread, butter, jam and more tea. Our day finished with one hour's prep between seven and eight o'clock.

Occasionally I saw Kathleen in the dining hall but our lives were still very separate; she had her friends and I had mine. Mind you, she still managed to impact on my life.

Formal education in those days was focussed on the Three Rs: reading, writing and arithmetic, but there was also an emphasis on good manners, discipline and how to behave as a member of society.

If you weren't living up to the teachers' expectations you were informed in no uncertain terms.

One morning, during a particularly complex lesson on algebra, I found myself completely dumbfounded. No matter how hard I tried I just couldn't grasp it. The letters and numbers swam in front of my eyes like a foreign language.

'Why can't you get it Brenda?' snapped the teacher. 'Your sister Kathleen can do it.'

Annoyance prickled inside me. I was hopeless, totally hopeless at numbers and as soon as the teacher started making comparisons to Kathleen, something inside me just shut down even more.

I wasn't Kathleen. I was me. Brenda Ashford.

That moment lodged in my mind. Throughout my career I have never, ever drawn comparisons between children in order to humiliate them. Each child is a unique individual with their own skills and talents.

Outside of classes, the deputy matron was always on hand to supervise the bedtime routine. We waited for the bell to sound for prayers, then we took it in turns to wash and then we tucked up in bed for lights out at nine o'clock.

There was a strange sense of comfort in the unchanging daily routine but even so, boarding school was a bewildering place with many unspoken rules to learn and observe. As a spirited girl you could be sure I was always in trouble, even if it was more Enid Blyton's Malory Towers than St Trinian's. I was always one for fun and doing things I shouldn't, especially when I fell under the spell of a beautiful but mischievous Egyptian girl called Leilah. In our dorm of five girls, as soon as lights went out the high jinks began – midnight feasts, dares and the like.

Leilah was forever issuing me dares and, not liking to let her down, I always obliged. I wasn't always successful in my endeavours, though.

'I dare you to run out to the fire escape without getting caught,' she whispered wickedly one blustery winter's night after lights out.

I didn't need any encouragement, and a minute later, having snuck past Matron's bedroom, I found myself clinging to a fire escape on the side of the school, shivering while the freezing wind whipped in off the channel and up and under my nightie.

Once I had fulfilled my dare and stayed out there the necessary five minutes I started to creep back to our dorm, but to my horror, I saw Matron's door swing open. I nipped into the toilet as fast as a rat up a drainpipe.

Matron had clearly cottoned on. She placed herself directly outside the toilet door and settled herself in for a long wait. I could just see her brown wool stockinged feet from under the door. You didn't mess with her.

I waited in that dark, damp, toilet for what felt like hours. It became a Mexican stand off.

'I know you're in there, child,' she said eventually. 'Are you ill?'

Finally, my legs and bum were numb and aching and I was forced to admit defeat and come out. Naturally I didn't breathe a word when she questioned me. Matron concluded I must have some difficulties in the toilet department and my little stunt earned me a big helping of syrup and figs but what did I care? I was the heroine of the dorm after that.

Emboldened by my new status as a daredevil I felt my confidence growing. I began to see how the thrill of getting caught and being a bit naughty would have driven my younger brother Basil to acts of daring.

Every Sunday morning the whole school would walk to church. I looked forward to and dreaded these trips in equal measure. There would be boys there. Actual boys! They may only have been choirboys but they were the opposite sex and this was cause for much interest amongst us girls. For an eleven-year-old at an all girls' boarding school, they may as well have been aliens from Mars. Judging by the nudging that went on when we filed into church they were equally fascinated by us.

I was fixated. The way their tiny Adam's apples bobbed when they sang, the little sideways glances they shot me when they walked past, the frisson of excitement if their robes touched my leg . . . It was utterly thrilling.

But even the possibility of the briefest of brushes with a choirboy couldn't dull the dread I felt at getting dressed for church.

It was always such a rigmarole. As well as all the usual under-garments we were expected to wear, which consisted of stays (a kind of soft corset) that buttoned onto a garter belt, which in turn buttoned to wool stockings, voluminous bloomers and petticoats, we had to make an extra special effort on a Sunday. For church visits we were required to wear a smart dress, a green coat and a pudding basin hat, brown leather boots that took an age to lace up with a hook, as well as gloves. We must have looked a strange sight, like mini adults trotting along the road in pairs in a crocodile formation.

By the time you took your pew you felt half suffocated. The Anglican parish church where we took weekly mass was a high church and senior members of the congregation would walk up the aisle swinging incense. The intoxicating scent from the incense coupled with our stifling undergarments and the thrill of being in such close proximity to choirboys had a somewhat restrictive effect on the lungs. On more than one occasion a schoolgirl would suddenly slump forward in her seat, her head hitting the pew in front.

One day, this gave me an idea. What a perfect way to be excused from mass.

'Pretend to faint,' I hissed out the corner of my mouth to Leilah who was sitting next to me.

Her eyes gleamed with mischief and she dazzled me with one of her ravishing but naughty smiles.

Leading by example I slithered forward in my seat until my head came to rest on a bible. Leilah followed, then the girl next to her. Down we went, one by one, like dominoes, until a whole row of schoolgirls were slumped over. And then I felt it, Leilah's shoulders shaking with laughter next to me. I suppressed a giggle. But suppressed giggles just seemed to double the fun. The harder I tried the more it threatened to bubble over and burst out.

Must not laugh. Must not laugh.

I bit my lip until it nearly bled. How I didn't scream out loud I'll never know. It was agony.

No one even raised an eyebrow.

I suppose a whole pew of fainting girls was perhaps not very subtle. Either that or one of my giggles escaped despite my best efforts. In any case, they rumbled we were faking it, and the incense carried on being swung, hymns carried on being sung and our headmistress stared resolutely ahead.

Only outside did she fix us with a glacial stare and say very slowly, 'Now we won't do that again, will we girls.'

Suitably chastised, we filed back to school.

Granny Brown would probably have been thrashed soundly for such a wilful act of subordination. I'm glad we weren't punished. To suppress a child's sense of mischief is to crush the joy out of their lives. While caring for children I am always mindful not to be too strict on harmless acts of mischief and be tolerant of their short attention spans!

Mother wrote me lovely, long letters and I still missed Hallcroft dearly but thanks to the new friendships I'd formed, my homesickness eased. By the end of first term the fear and loneliness I experienced on my first day were already long forgotten. Even so, when Christmas came around and Father collected us for the hotly anticipated holidays, I couldn't wait to get home. I tore up the drive like a tornado and covered Mother and David's faces in a flurry of kisses.

Soon, Kathleen, David and I were joined by Basil, Christopher and Michael, back from their school on the Isle of Wight. The house was a riot of noise and laughter as stories, escapades, acts of bravery and tall tales were swapped.

Kathleen shook her head in despair when I told everyone how I sneaked out onto the fire escape. She would never have dreamt of such an act of mischief.

In the middle of it all, like a beacon of warmth and quiet strength, stood Mother, stirring beef stew on the stove, a look of peace and happiness shining in her eyes.

When we returned to Courtfield Gardens after the Christmas break the journey seemed to pass in the blink of an eye and I hummed as I unpacked my trunk in the dorm. Catching sight of Leilah I shrieked with excitement and laughter. Although I missed home, it was good to be back.

As winter gave way to spring we were told we would be spending more time outdoors on physical activities, which was music to my ears. I was always looking to get outside. Long dreary lessons on algebra bored me to tears, I lived for lacrosse and outdoor pursuits. What I loved more than anything was when us girls were taken out for our constitutionals, swimming in the channel from the beaches of Bognor.

Our swimming excursions were always hugely exciting. We walked along the seafront in the customary crocodile, dressed in our all-in-one, long-sleeved cotton swimsuits and ghastly rubber hats.

There were always boys on the seafront, which for girls approaching puberty with no access to the opposite sex made swimming a thrill indeed. What's more these weren't choirboys, they were local lads. Rough, bawdy and with considerably more hair. There would be winks and whistles, which left us girls in a state of near hysteria.

Bognor was quite the place to be in those days and was rivalling neighbouring Brighton for popularity. Sir Billy Butlin, who went on to establish Butlin's holiday camps after the war, had just arrived in the resort and opened the town's first amusement arcade on the seafront, and a small fairground. No one, least of all us, had witnessed anything like it. We were dazzled by the laughing clowns, the clanging and ringing of the slot machines and amazed at the sight of a mirror maze. The combination of the intense noise of the fairgrounds, the presence of the opposite sex and the sea air was a heady mix.

'Eyes ahead and look where you are going!' boomed our headmistress if she felt the sight of all the boys, balls and bells was proving too distracting.

A short sharp swim in the waters of the freezing channel was usually enough to blast away the cloud of hormones that followed us around.

We girls were in good company with our weekly swims. Royal company no less. Three years earlier, in 1929, his Majesty King George V's physicians had selected Bognor as the venue for his convalescence from a chest infection, and apparently he enjoyed repeated visits to the resort. His granddaughter Elizabeth, our future Queen, made sandcastles while the old king sat in a bath chair in the sunshine, covered in rugs, watching her.

We never did spot His Majesty or Elizabeth in her swim-mies on the beach, and if he ever spotted a gaggle of giggly schoolgirls, he certainly never made his presence known!

As the story goes, when he was petitioned to rename the town Bognor Regis as a mark of his visits, the King, known for his fruity language, remarked, 'Bugger Bognor.'

I never felt quite that strongly about the place, though I was certainly relieved when summer term ended. I couldn't wait to be allowed home to Hallcroft House. Finally, I would cuddle my beloved David and roam free on the roughs. But in my absence there had been a dramatic chain of events that was to impact my life greatly.

Father collected Kathleen and I in his Austin, as usual. No

sooner had he loaded our trunks into the boot than I was rat-tling off questions like machine gun fire.

'How's David, is he walking, do we have any strawberries yet, can we play charades?'

But Father seemed more subdued than usual.

'D . . . d . . . David is fine,' he said eventually.

I noticed his stutter had grown worse over the last six months, and there was something else. Something different about him I couldn't quite put my finger on. He seemed deflated, broken, weary. His blue eyes had lost their sparkle. I wasn't sure how to question my father about any of this, though. All I could do was wait.

The minute the car pulled up outside Hallcroft I was racing up the familiar drive and bursting in through the door.

'Mother, David,' I shouted. 'We're home.'

Mother came rushing into the hall. I noticed her slight hands were nervously ringing a tea towel. She had faint black circles under her eyes and a vein twitched in her temple.

What had gone on since I was at school?

And then I noticed. *Everything* was different. The hall was piled up with brown packing boxes, the windows had no curtains and even the ceiling lights were just bare bulbs.

I ran from room to room, tears blurring my eyes. Each and every room had been stripped bare of its belongings. The bedroom we had all been born in looked vast and empty. Even the air felt thinner. I felt as if someone had sucked the air from my lungs.

Shivering, I returned to the hall where Kathleen and mother stood looking bewildered.

'What's going on?' I asked.

'I'm afraid we are moving, girls,' said Mother. Her voice was no louder than a whisper.

And that was all that was said on the matter. Neither

Mother nor Father elaborated any further. In those days you simply never questioned your parents. When we are small we accept life and events as they come.

Years later I learnt the truth about why we had to leave Hallcroft that fateful summer morning. Father's business partner had done the dirty on him.

For years my father had been asking to see the books and his partner had been fobbing him off. Father looked after the manufacturing side of things and his partner did the accounting and finance, but when he finally got his hands on the books, my father was horrified to see the company was in debt. Bad debt, that his unscrupulous partner had run up against the business. Then the scoundrel did a runner to America, leaving Father to face the music. The wholesale ladies' and children's knitwear business with its grand Regent Street premises was forced into bankruptcy.

Mother's brother, our Uncle Jeffrey, came to the rescue and gave Father enough money to rent a small bungalow in Bookham in Surrey, but the business was closed and Hallcroft had been sold.

All this while I had blissfully whiled away the last year in Bognor Regis.

Can you imagine the shame of bankruptcy for a man like my father? A man with high morals, decorated for his bravery during the war. He had survived the trenches only to be destroyed by an enemy closer to home.

It must have been a savage blow.

Father had a hand in everything that had gone into Hallcroft, right down to those leather thong door handles. He had designed it and overseen the building of it. It was the pinnacle of everything he had achieved and his lifeblood pulsed through every oak staircase and floorboard. He had been so proud of that house.

Now there would be no more travelling to Regent Street to work, no more grand home, no more private education for his children, and to our agony, no more Saturday afternoon sweets. The train tracks Father had mown into the lawn would be turfed over to make way for the next occupants' tennis courts, and some other lucky children would have the rambling garden as their playground.

It could have been worse. I am sure he was eternally grateful to his brother-in-law's generosity. After all, who knows what would have happened had he not come to the rescue? Workhouses had only officially been abolished two years previously in 1930, but the reality was that many didn't really close until years later. We could so easily have ended up there, with the family split up, and forced into a punishing, spirit-breaking regime of hard work and cruelty.

Still, to lose the house and the business he had built left Father a broken man. I don't think he was ever truly the same again.

But the human spirit is nothing if not resilient and to us children it was merely a blip. We might no longer have our glorious home to run through but we still had each other. Our family. Mother and Father were the heart of the home and to me it didn't matter where we slept at night as long as I had them. So in the summer of 1933 we found ourselves living at Amberley bungalow in Bookham, Surrey.

I was absolutely flabbergasted to hear recently that Hallcroft House is now worth in the region of £1.35 million. I wonder what my father would make of that. He bought the site for a few pounds in 1929.

Over the eighty years since we left our beloved home I have moved many times and I do so without a backward glance.

Trading down taught me an important lesson. Never let a house define you. You can make a home anywhere, from an air raid shelter to a shed, if you have to. Riches and wealth don't matter a jot. You can be happy anywhere so long as you have love and family in your life. I may never have had much money but I have always been rich in love.

That first night, as I snuggled down in a shared room with Kathleen and listened to the boys' soft breathing in the room next door, I looked forward to the next adventure in my life.

2

The Calling

Dear heart
And soul of a child,
Sing on!
'The Poet', Enid Blyton

THE WIND of change was heady in the air. King George V
had died and his heir to the throne, Edward, was causing
shockwaves throughout the country with his determination
to marry scandalous American divorcee, Wallis Simpson.

To a fifteen-year-old girl not schooled in the ways of
love this seemed simply outrageous. How could he court
a woman who had cheated on her husband, and expect us
to accept her as our Queen? Preposterous. It wasn't only
schoolgirls who felt that way, mind. I didn't meet a single
person who didn't think it was wrong. Looking back, the
vilification of Wallis Simpson was probably over the top, but
in those innocent yet judgmental times their love seemed
destined to fail. In the end, Edward chose love over duty,
whereas I have always chosen duty over love. Would I have
been happier had I opted for marriage rather than life as a
nanny? I very much doubt it.

I remember sitting with my parents and siblings to listen to
the coronation of the reluctant King, George VI, on 12 May
1937 on the wireless.

The BBC was six months old when it broadcasted the ceremony, not that we got an opportunity to watch as barely anyone had television sets in those days.

I gasped as a fanfare of trumpets sounded out over the wireless. None of us uttered a word, you could have heard a pin drop. No-one listened quite so nervously as Father though.

Father had a stammer, like King George VI, and he knew better than anyone the sheer agony of terror that the King must have been experiencing that day. Mother reached over and squeezed Father's hand as we waited. Suddenly there was his voice, hesitant and slow.

'It is with a very full heart I speak to you tonight. Never before has a newly crowned King been able to talk to all his people in their . . . o . . . own homes on the day of . . . h . . . his coronation. Never has a ceremony itself had so wide a significance, for the dominions are now free and equal p . . . partners in this ancient kingdom and I felt this morning that the whole empire was gathered within the walls of Westminister Abbey. I rejoice that I can now speak to you all, where ever you may be.'

Father was on tenterhooks throught the speech and I suspect he was almost as relieved as the King himself when it was all over. Everyone knew that George VI had never expected to be King, and that he battled with a stammer; we all wished him well and there was a tide of good feeling and respect towards our new King.

I think Father always felt a special affinity with our King. They had both served in World War One and both fought private demons over their speech. We always listened to his addresses to the nation, on the wireless. It was almost as if he were in our living room with us.

There was change in my life too, albeit on a smaller scale.

Our reversal of fortune meant no more smart boarding school for me. Instead, the local county school in Epsom beckoned Kathleen and I.

As for my brothers, Father had made a gentlemen's agreement with the headmaster of their boarding school on the Isle of Wight that they could stay on, and eventually all four would be schooled there, on the proviso he could have two boys educated for the price of one. It was only later when the bill for the school fees came in that he realised the headmaster had reneged on his agreement and charged Father the full cost for all their board and education. This was a fresh blow for my father, who was struggling financially.

In many ways Father was naïve, he just accepted what everyone told him as gospel. He simply saw the best in people and never had a bad word to say about anyone. I hope I have inherited these traits. Sadly, people with personalities such as ours will never grow rich, but at least we know we will always do right by others.

It was with this attitude that I marched into my first day at my new school.

As I walked into the classroom, I felt all eyes swivel and turn to rest on me. I could see all the girls taking in my freshly pressed and starched uniform, gleaming white socks and plimsolls. We may not have had much money now but my mother was a proud woman and wouldn't have dreamt of having her children leave the house looking anything less than immaculate.

Nervously I took my seat as the others girls tittered and nudged each other. Listening to them talk, I was amazed. I had led a sheltered life and these girls were street smart.

'Ere,' hissed the girl next to me, elbowing me sharply in the ribs. 'Ainch ya that girl what lost all 'er money?'

I swallowed back my tears and tried to ignore her.

In playground at lunchtime it was more of the same. They pushed their noses up and marched past me cackling.

'Stuck up cow,' one laughed. 'Who does she fink she is.'

I didn't think I was anyone. I just wanted friends to play with.

It was a miserable time and I hated it. My old, safe, comfortable world seemed a million miles away. By the time the first school term ended I was in a state of despair. I had made no real friends, showed no aptitude for learning and was at a loss to know what to do with my life. Why couldn't I be a clever bookworm like Kathleen?

'I don't belong,' I wailed to Mother and Father one night as they attempted to explain a mathematical formula for what felt like the one hundredth time. 'I don't understand it and I hate school.'

My head slumped into my hands as I sobbed.

'I'm just a stupid, stupid dummy.'

Mother was horrified. 'Of course you're not, my darling,' she soothed. Gently she cupped my face in her hands and looked me right in the eyes. 'You are different to Kathleen, it's true, but you are just as clever as her in different ways. You have very good practical skills.'

I loved my mother for trying so hard to console me, but her assurances did nothing to ease my loneliness and sense of isolation.

Fortunately Father knew the answer. We had the captain of the local Girls' Brigade living with us as a mother's help and she persuaded Father to let Kathleen and me join. It was run by the local Baptist church, where we worshipped every Sunday, and before long us girls were going along to the meetings every Saturday.

Here I was accepted.

The aim of the Girls' Brigade was to help its members to become followers of the Lord Jesus Christ and, through self-control, reverence and a sense of responsibility, find true enrichment of life.

Well, back then I didn't know much about the Christ part but I loved the sense of family and belonging that the brigade fostered.

I lived for the weekends when I could put on my smart navy uniform, knee-high white socks and little navy hat. It was such an innocent, jolly pastime and it filled my adolescent years with fun and happiness.

In the same year that Robert Baden-Powell was hosting his final world famous scouting jamboree, in 1937, the Girls' Brigade of Bookham, Surrey, were off on our own voyage of discovery to the Isle of Sheppey.

By day we went beach combing, caught crabs in the sea, rode donkeys on the beach and played hide and seek and catch in the sand dunes as the sun kissed our skins brown.

Come nightfall we would light campfires, drink Ovaltine or cocoa and sing songs or sit round listening to the captain of the brigade talk about spiritual matters. The flickering flames made my face rosy and sitting shoulder to shoulder with my new friends I felt waves of warmth and contentment wash over me.

I realise now that in some ways I was sad that my idyllic childhood was coming to an end. At 15 I was in that funny land straddling childhood and adolescence. Adulthood seemed like a bewildering, frightening place to be. Adults could lie to you, steal from you, march you into war then betray you. I longed to stay huddled by the campfire with my fellow brigades forever.

My elder sister Kathleen was also much moved by what she saw and heard and at the end of the camping trip, she invited the Lord into her life.

By now Kathleen had turned 17 and was so clever she

had just been accepted – a year early – to train as a nurse and midwife at Clapham Women's Hospital. At the end of the summer she would leave for London and start an exciting new chapter of her life. Perhaps all those days spent huddled in her bedroom with her books weren't so daft after all, I realised with a jolt.

For me the summer marked a different, but no less serious, milestone in my life. Back then I didn't know it, but the simple action of putting on the Girls' Brigade uniform was a powerful one. It transformed me from a lost teenager into a member of a larger family, someone with a duty to perform. But what purpose did I have in life? I wasn't like clever Kathleen with a career path all mapped out and a faith to cling to. What did my future hold?

Of that I wasn't yet sure but there was one thing I was certain of. I was going nowhere fast at the local county school. I was sick of feeling like the dummy, of being compared to my clever older sister, and tired of Father having to explain my homework to me over and over. By the time I went home from the camping trip I had made up my mind. I had turned sixteen by now, surely that meant I could decide my own fate?

I strode into school on Monday morning with fire in my belly.

Knocking on the headmistress's door I politely requested a meeting.

I sat down and drew in a deep breath. 'I think it's time I left school,' I said.

The headmistress looked at me through her half-moon glasses and not unkindly replied, 'But you have to take your exams, Brenda.'

Sitting up straight I coughed nervously. 'But what is the point? I don't think I'll pass.'

Headmistress sighed and removed her glasses.

'Well,' she said finally. 'I have to agree with you.'

What a blessed relief.

It was decided there and then that I should leave school with immediate effect. Walking out of the building, I felt an enormous burden lift from my shoulders.

Back at home, Mother wasn't cross, just concerned about what I would do with my life.

'Oh darling,' she sighed. 'I wish you'd stayed on to take your exams but I can't say I'm surprised. We need to find you a job.'

Mother had seen my despair building and I half wonder if a tiny bit of her wasn't relieved. She was practical and good with her hands like me and she could see I was drowning under all that homework.

But if I had thought I could sit around at home while I worked out what to do next, it seemed Mother had other ideas.

'I can stay here and help you look after David,' I protested.

'No,' she insisted, her voice turning a shade firmer. 'You need to work.'

All too soon she had lined me up with a job. I was to be a mother's help to Mrs Ravenshere who lived not far from us in a smart home in Byfleet in Surrey. She had two sons aged eight and eleven who attended Dulwich School as day boys. My duties included helping her to run the house, run errands and help look after the boys when they returned from school. For that I was paid the princely sum of ten shillings a week. A pittance really. I have never earned much money throughout my life, but then you don't go into childcare for the money, do you?

The lady of the house also had a number of horses and ponies including one mischievous little Shetland pony by the name of Jelly who would escape and rampage through the neighbours' gardens causing chaos.

After we had spent one afternoon chasing Jelly round the neighbourhood, Mrs Ravenshere and I sat down to tea.

'You know, Brenda, I've been thinking,' she said. 'Have you ever thought of training to be a Norland Nanny? You're good with children, they love you.'

Of course I had heard of Norland nannies. Everyone had. They were famous for only taking on smart young ladies of genteel birth and schooling them to achieve the highest standards of childcare for the offspring of the wealthy. Everyone knew it wasn't easy to earn the right to push those big coach prams round London's smartest postcodes.

I had seen pictures of them in my mother's *Nursery World* and *Good Housekeeping* magazines and admired their beautiful uniforms and capes but it was all far too grand for sixteen-year-old Brenda Ashford from Surrey. I was just a country girl.

Besides, Father had no money now; there was no way he could afford to send me to train with the Norland Institute. There was an entrance fee of one guinea and a year's tuition cost £132. On top of that, those beautiful uniforms cost £16 10s. It all added up to a small fortune, one I knew my father simply didn't have.

'But there could be a way round it,' insisted Mrs Ravenshere. 'Let me talk to your father.'

'No, please,' I pleaded. 'I don't wish to trouble him.'

Since the bankruptcy, Father was struggling to find work and set up in business again. I didn't want to add to his load by reminding him that he could no longer afford to have his children educated. Besides, I couldn't move all the way to London, by myself.

But the conversation left me feeling even more fretful about my future. What was my calling in life?

The answer came via a large black horse.

Later that day Mrs Ravenshere said she was sending me to the local stables, owned by a friend of hers, for a riding lesson round Byfleet common. As a horse lover, especially one for whom riding lessons had been consigned to my old life as just another unaffordable luxury, I was thrilled at the prospect. Mrs Ravenshere's friend even gave me a new pair of cream jodhpurs and a beautiful pair of shiny brown leather boots. They must have cost a small fortune. I hesitated to take such kind gifts but she insisted.

Then, out of the stables the instructor led the most magnificent horse I had ever seen. Jet was sixteen hands high and his well chiselled head, long neck and high withers told me he was a young and spirited thoroughbred. His black coat gleamed as he trotted round the yard tossing his mane this way and that.

I felt a ripple of excitement run through me as the instructor gave me a leg up. Soon Jet and I were trotting happily along the common. Didn't I feel grand and grown up, riding on such a beautiful creature in my new leather boots.

But as we trotted under a railway tunnel a train thundered overhead. Jet took fright, flared his nostrils and started to dance all over the path.

'Hold on tight, Brenda,' warned the instructor. 'I think he's going to bol . . .'

Her words were lost on the wind as Jet bolted. Hedges and trees flashed past in a blur of green as we galloped full tilt over the common.

Clinging on for dear life, my heart was in my mouth as we thundered down the path. Using all my might, I tried to pull his head up, but it was to no avail.

'Please stop,' I whimpered.

My weedy arms were no match for his powerful neck.

Just then I realised. *We were heading for the road.*

My knuckles were white with terror as we galloped full tilt towards the traffic.

No way was this horse going to send me flying into the path of a motorcar.

With an almighty grunt and a superhuman show of strength I pulled his head up and at the last minute we swerved out of the way of the road and slowed to a halt by a tree.

It was hard to say who was trembling more. Me or Jet. His flanks were coated in sweat and my hands were shaking so hard I could barely hold the reins.

Suddenly I experienced something else. Pure exhilaration. Grappling a runaway horse had sent my blood racing. By the time the instructor caught up with me I was laughing.

'I thought I was a gonner,' I said breathlessly.

'So did I,' she panted.

When we arrived back at the stables and Mrs Ravenshere heard of my adventure she was obviously impressed with my ability because she rewarded me with a cup of hot sweet tea and a slice of cake.

My brush with death made me appreciate something. There were no second chances in life and perhaps we should grab all that is put in our way.

'I was thinking,' I said between sips of hot tea. 'Perhaps you could speak to Mother about the Norland?'

'If you handle children as well as you handle that horse you will make an excellent nanny,' said Mrs Ravenshere, with a smile.

And so it was that my mother and I found ourselves some months later boarding a train bound for London Victoria.

The Norland interview, which my mother had arranged over the phone, had put me in a state of heightened excitement for weeks, and the night before I had barely slept a wink.

'Now remember, Brenda,' advised my mother as the train hurtled towards London, 'Don't talk too much, listen, nod your head politely and sit up straight.'

I don't recall much about that journey, what I wore, or what I'd eaten for breakfast. Just that my destiny was unfolding and everything hinged on this interview.

In London my senses were assaulted. I'd never been to the big city before and I was bewildered and excited by everything I saw.

Mother decided we should walk from Victoria to the home of Norland at Pembridge Square in London's Notting Hill. There was intense noise everywhere. Red buses whizzed past belching out clouds of smoke, the road seemed to be clogged up with motorcars and electric trolleybuses. We even passed an underground station where mother told me there was a train every ninety seconds. Unimaginable.

Me and My Girl was on at the theatre and street traders stood outside selling roasted nuts for a penny a bag.

'Keep up,' Mother ordered, as I slowed down to crane my neck upwards at the highest buildings I'd ever seen.

Suddenly I felt so small. Everyone seemed to be marching about with real purpose and a sense of determination.

I spotted a sweet shop much like the one Father must have bought our Saturday treats from. The glass jars lined up in the window glittered, tantalisingly close. But then I remembered, I was on a mission too. There was no time to dawdle.

Soon the crowded cobbled streets gave way to wider pavements and smart leafy squares. The Notting Hill and Ladbroke Grove area, which today is a buzzy multicultural place filled with bars, shops, restaurants and a yearly carnival, was very different seventy-three years ago.

Elegant, stuccoed facades looked out on a slow-moving world. Calm, peace and prosperity prevailed. Norland nannies and smart mothers pushed their fashionable black coach prams serenely in front of the imposing mansion houses. Little girls in smart smock dresses walked in a crocodile to school, boys in sailor suits ran along clutching boats to sail on the Serpentine in Hyde Park.

My mother stopped in front of one of the grandest homes I'd ever seen. It was far bigger than our little bungalow, bigger even than Hallcroft.

Numbers 7, 10 and 11 Pembridge Square, London, W2. Home of the Norland Institute Nurseries Ltd.

Suddenly I felt like a tiny little mouse on the doorstep. I'd never crossed the threshold of somewhere so grand.

Mother knocked on the imposing black door.

Looking back, it must have been a strange moment for her. She too had longed to train with the Norland but Grandpa Brown didn't consider it to be a suitable career choice for a young lady, and forbade it. Times had changed and now I was about to have the interview she had always longed to have.

Mother turned to me with a faraway look in her eyes. Excitement and something else, sadness perhaps, flickered over her beautiful face.

'I can't tell you how much I would love to have been a Norland Nanny, Brenda,' she said softly. 'I loved babies just as much as you.'

I didn't doubt it. She would have made a wonderful nanny; no one knew more about children than my mother.

She shook herself a little, as if to shrug off the ghosts of unchased dreams. 'Listen to me,' she snorted, as the door swung open. 'Silly old thing. I'm so thrilled for you, darling, let's show them what you're made of.'

Straightening out my coat and smoothing down a stray hair, she pushed me gently inside the impressive hallway.

A few chairs lined the black and white tiled corridor.

Mother and I sat down nervously. A large clock ticked ominously on the wall.

Finally a door was flung open and a tall, imposing woman whom I guessed was in her forties, towered over us. She was dressed immaculately in a dark-coloured dress with collar and cuffs trimmed in white lace.

Miss Ruth Whitehead. The principal, and to my young mind, a truly terrifying sight. This woman held the key to my future.

'I'll have a word with you now,' she said.

Mother and I leapt to our feet, scraping our chairs back and nervously straightening our skirts.

'Not you,' she said, fixing my mother with a penetrating gaze. 'You stay here.'

Mother sat down, well and truly put in her place.

My heart hammering, I followed Miss Whitehead into her office and sat down opposite her, on the other side of a grand mahogany desk.

On the wall above her head was a black and white photo of a regal looking lady, underneath the Norland motto, *Love Never Faileth*. She seemed to be staring straight at me.

Miss Whitehead noticed my gaze. 'That is Emily Ward (née Lord), she founded Norland.'

I nodded, unable to tear my eyes away from the photo.

'An exceptional woman in every way.'

She was indeed. I sat rapt as Miss Whitehead told me her story. Emily Mary Jane Lord, born in 1850 in Derby, was something of a pioneer. In 1850 Queen Victoria had already ruled for thirteen years and the nursery was a very different place. Nannies were a relatively new phenomenon, and occupied a social position somewhere between that of the lower servants and the master. Those parents of the higher social classes that could afford to employ a nanny spent perhaps only an hour a day with their children. The nanny was the children's constant companion and would nurture and shape their aspirations.

Obedience took precedence over affection. Children could expect to be flogged, caned, or thrashed with a slipper to have the sin beaten out of them. 'Spare the rod and spoil the child,' was the accepted thinking of the time. I hadn't grown up under such a regime, thank heavens, but my Granny Brown and Emily Lord had.

In her early twenties, Emily Lord joined the staff of Notting Hill High School, where she was assigned the infant school. At that time the classroom was an extension of the nursery, merely another place to forcibly shape children into miniature versions of their parents.

However, the alternative theories of a man named Friedrich Froebel were just starting to gain acceptance.

Born in 1782, Froebel had an unhappy childhood. In later life he came to believe that the development of children could be likened to plant growth. He saw teachers as gardeners who should provide a secure, loving environment in which to nurture children's talents and aspirations. Despite critics pouring scorn on his beliefs he coined the word 'kindergarten', designed educational play materials and insisted on the value of singing, dancing, gardening and self-directed play.

The first kindergarten was opened in England in 1851, with a timetable that has been acknowledged as a precursor of today's nursery school teaching pattern. The world had seen nothing like it. This man was a visionary and we owe him a huge debt of gratitude.

A young Emily Lord was as impressed as I later was, after she spent a summer in Geneva studying under one of Froebel's disciples.

Her ambition to open her school for nannies was fired by

a desire to put these principles into practice and to overturn the tyranny of the nursery.

In a climate of childhood repression, the Norland Institute was born in 1892. It offered the world's first formal training for 'women of genteel birth' to become nannies.

But like Froebel, Emily Lord also had her critics.

In late-Victorian Britain Nanny wielded power and it was a brave person who questioned her methods of childcare. She was feared and respected in equal measure, could be either kind or unkind, but was always dominant and strict.

Emily was struck by the oppressive methods of these nannies.

'They have no idea what it feels like to be a child,' she observed. She questioned the fitness of these women to rear other people's offspring. So the idea came to her of a training institute that would answer two pressing needs: a further career opportunity for genteel women, and enlightened and educated nannies for young children.

Critics poured scorn on her plans. 'Nobody would wish to train for such a menial task,' they said. 'No gentleman would employ educated young women from the upper middle classes as servants.' Even, 'So you plan to train our failures.'

But Emily Lord persisted and, despite fierce opposition, insisted that children needed gentle encouragement and nurturing from a professional. A Norland nurse would tread the fine line between master and servant, accountable to the mother but respected by the father. She should also have 'clever fingers and a love of children'.

Today, people would call it 'identifying a gap in the market', but back then it was simply a passion to improve baby care and make it child-centred, loving and nurturing.

Emily Lord rejected the need for smacking or spanking of children. She believed that they were not only born innocent but good, and that their attitudes and behaviour were shaped by their formative years and upbringing. In short, there was no sin to thrash out. Her beliefs were genuinely radical for the time and were underpinned by the Norland motto 'Love Never Faileth'.

Emily knew her ideas would need support from prominent members of society and set about with zeal, driving her plans forward. She hosted a series of drawing room meetings, as was the convention of the day, and invited thirty guests, including the legendary Miss Buss, who founded Cheltenham Ladies College. Miss Buss was equally pioneering in her determination to reform girls' education and establish it on a par with boys'.

Miss Buss's temperament was described as 'gunpowdery' and Emily's as 'hotheaded'. I would love to have been a fly on the wall of that particular drawing room.

Before long, Emily had drummed up enough support to finance the purchase of a London property and employ teachers for such skills such as needlework and physiology. A lecturer from the Buckingham Palace School of Cookery came in once a week to give lessons on how to cook, amongst other things, cheese straws and Swiss rolls. Emily Ward herself lectured on Froebelian principles.

When they moved in to numbers 7, 10 and 11 Pembridge Square, many Norland traditions were established. The conservatory was used to house all the prams and the billiard room became the workrooms where the uniforms were made.

Miss Lord considered the numbering of rooms to be soulless, so she named them after Victorian virtues such as Gratitude, Sincerity, Tenacity, Integrity and Patience. The Institute's first male accountant was assigned an office called Chastity.

Emily, now Emily Ward after a marriage to a retired tea merchant, also insisted on mothering her new recruits; her

ritual goodnight kiss after prayers was an institution. She even
found time to hand-trim all the uniform bonnets by hand.

One early student was typically gushing about her.

> *What a remarkable and gifted young woman she is and what a faith-*
> *ful steward of many talents. How many lame dogs and persons she*
> *helped over stiles; how many barriers she removed; how many paths*
> *she opened. How brave, original and unconventional and yet what*
> *an apostle of beauty, seemliness.*
>
> *She never seemed disheartened, depressed or weary. She was ready*
> *to open a fresh campaign before reaping the laurels of the last. As for*
> *resting on her laurels, the mere idea would have seemed contemptible*
> *to her.*
>
> *I was a shy, weak, unpractical bookworm but her strength never*
> *failed me. She transformed ugly ducklings into practical and useful*
> *swans. Hundreds are indebted to her and she has made the world a*
> *safer and better place to live.*

This great woman died on 15 June 1930, nine years before I
found myself staring in fascination at her portrait above Miss
Whitehead's head, but I felt her presence echo round the
walls of the beautiful office.

On hearing the inspiring story of Emily Ward's life's work,
my heart felt like it was about to burst. I practically shot out
my seat as excitement bubbled over.

But this was me . . . this was the way I felt about children and
babies.

I felt like the sun had just come out from behind the clouds.
The world was suddenly a far, far bigger place than Bookham.
Sitting in this smart London house I had an epiphany, a light-
bulb moment if you like.

This was my calling in life.

I wasn't clever enough to be a teacher or nurse like

Kathleen, but I did love babies and children. If Norland was a glove then it fitted me perfectly. I too could help bring the dreams of children to life.

Suddenly I felt better about the fact that I could no more do what Kathleen was doing than fly to the moon. To learn how to deliver a baby, change dressings, administer medicines and tend to the sick was out of my league, my head span at the mere thought; but place a baby in my arms and well, that was another matter. I could love, cherish, protect and care for a baby with more heartfelt passion than anyone I knew. To nurture a baby into a child and then help it on its journey into adulthood was an honour and a privilege as far as I was concerned.

This building whispered with the ghosts of legendary figures.

Friedrich Froebel, Emily Ward, Miss Buss. Between them they had discovered childhood, banished terror in the nursery, changed the face of childcare and put women's education on a level footing with men's. I so desperately wanted to make a difference like they had.

I thought of my poor mother sitting outside in the corridor, willing me on. She never got the chance to follow her dreams but I could do this, I could do this for me and for her.

Ignoring my mother's advice not to talk, I started to chatter away, ten to the dozen. When I get nervous I start to babble, and I was really, really nervous.

Don't say the wrong thing, Brenda.

'I love children, Miss Whitehead, I really do,' I blurted. 'I've helped raise my brother. I was no good at school, not at all clever . . . not like you. My father has no money, well he did have, but he lost it all you see. Then I nearly fell off a horse . . . we got the train up you know . . . terribly nervous.'

On and on I rambled.

Miss Whitehead raised one eyebrow a fraction and finally my voice trailed off to a whisper.

'. . . and so here I am.'

Silence.

'I see,' said Miss Whitehead in a clipped voice. 'We'll be in touch.'

That signalled the end of the interview. I slunk out the room to rejoin my mother.

'Well?' she said, on the edge of her seat.

'I don't suppose I shall get in,' I whispered, biting my lip to stop myself from crying.

I'd well and truly fluffed it.

The journey back to Amberley seemed to last forever. I gazed out the window so Mother couldn't see the tears threatening to spill down my cheeks. Despair gripped my heart. I'd let Mother and Father down. I'd let Mrs Ravenshere down.

But worst of all, I could see my dreams crumbling to dust . . .

3

Nannies in Training

Every baby born into the world is a finer one than the last.

Nicholas Nickleby, Charles Dickens

IT WAS Mother who opened the letter.

For days I'd been moping round the house like a wet weekend, utterly desolate and quite convinced I'd fluffed my interview.

We were sitting at the breakfast table drinking tea while Mother sifted through the morning's mail. I looked up when I noticed that she had frozen in her seat, staring intently at the letter in her hand.

'You've done it Brenda,' she cried, nearly knocking her teacup over with excitement. 'You've been accepted by the Norland.'

Father's face paled. 'But how darling, there's no money to train.'

'It's all right,' Mother went on, reading excitedly from the letter. 'Says here that at first you were considered for the maiden's scheme but upon reflection you are suitable to start immediately as a student, and the training will be funded with a bursary.'

'A what?' I asked, puzzled.

'It means they pay the cost of your training, darling,' she went on.

Euphoria fizzled up inside me. I'd done it. I'd really, really done it.

'Oh thank you, oh thank you,' I laughed, dancing round the kitchen kissing everyone in sight.

There was much rejoicing in the Ashford household that day.

'Just think,' said Father, kissing me on the head, 'our little Brenda's going to be a Norland Nanny. I'm proud of you, love.'

If he felt any shame at having his daughter's education means-tested and funded, he kept it to himself. He was a proud man but he only ever wanted the best for his children and could see I was over the moon.

I later found out what the maiden's scheme was. In 1904 Norland introduced the scheme to help those girls who were eligible but could not afford the fees. They were to give their services in domestic work for a year, and in return for cooking, cleaning and housework they would go on to receive the training and uniform for free. During their year of maiden's work they were required to forfeit their Christian names and agree to be known by the names of Honour, Mercy, Prudence and Verity. They would wear a special uniform whilst on duty and sleep in a cubicled dormitory on the top floor.

This may seem strange but the thinking was that when they had completed their year of work they could then begin their training, revert to their Christian name and be accepted on an equal footing by their fellow students. It was so popular a scheme that there was a waiting list.

Turns out I had narrowly escaped being named after a Victorian virtue. Miss Whitehead had decided I qualified for a bursary from the Isabel Sharman Fund. This was set up after the death of the Institute's first principal, to help fund training for suitable ladies of slender means.

And there was me thinking I'd fluffed the interview. I suppose I must have said something Miss Whitehead liked.

'We can't have our Brenda going up to that fine house looking scruffy, now, can we,' announced Father later that day. 'Mother, take Brenda up to London. I think she will need some new shoes.'

I saw Mother go to protest but my father silenced her with a wink. I knew that the train fare alone was a princely sum, never mind new leather shoes, but my father would work selling jumpers all night if it meant sending his Brenda off in fine style. He had a heart as soft as butter and I loved him all the more for it.

Travelling to London for a day out shopping gave me cause for delight and terror in equal measure. I loved London, the thrill, the buzz and the bustle of the big city, but it was also a place of hidden dangers. I had heard of young girls being abducted and shipped off to be sold into the white slave trade, never to be seen by their families again.

Only recently, a visit to the cinema to watch the new Shirley Temple film *Dimples*, had left me trembling with terror. I had gone alone, while Father concluded some business in town. He was busy again, re-establishing his knitwear company one sale at a time and we were all so proud of him.

I felt terribly grown up being allowed to go to London with Father. As on my previous trip to town with Mother for the Norland interview, the rules were just as strict. Don't speak to strangers, always be polite, and don't wander off.

Father's business would take a couple of hours so he took me to the cinema near Regent Street and paid for my ticket, with instructions to wait outside at the end of the film, for him to collect me.

What a joy. I loved Shirley Temple and watching the film

alone felt like a big adventure. Not long now and soon I would be living in London all the time! I tingled at the very thought of it.

While Shirley danced her way across the screen, her blonde curls bouncing, an old man in the row in front got up and came and sat next to me in the dark. As Shirley's dazzling smile filled the screen the man's knarled old hand came to rest on my knee.

My heart virtually pounded out of my chest.

When his hand started to slide up my thigh I leapt to my feet and ran out of that cinema like my feet were on fire.

Now, as Mother and I alighted from the train at Victoria, my fertile imagination buzzed with activity. I imagined men like Bill Sikes summoning me from dark cobbled alleyways. Every passerby was a potential pickpocket in my eyes.

Mother must have sensed my terror as she gripped my hand all the way through town.

I'd never seen so many motorcars whizzing over the cobbled streets, nor so many elegant ladies in fur coats and make-up.

When we reached the grand department store in Baker Street my fear subsided.

My eyes were out on stalks the minute the liveried door-man opened the door for us. It was sleek, elegant and like nothing I'd ever seen. Beautiful ladies who looked like Greta Garbo and Rita Hayworth stood in front of row upon row of rouge and perfumes.

Mother relaxed her grip. Nothing bad could ever happen here.

Dizzied by the smell of expensive French perfume, we stumbled to the shoe department.

'Oh, mother, look,' I gasped, spellbound. I have always loved shoes more than anything and this was a shoe shopper's paradise.

T-bar heels, black and white Oxfords and Mary Jane pumps jostled for space with red velvet, suede-soled swing shoes and black patent leather lace-up boots.

Heaven!

'And what would madam like?' enquired the sales assistant.

Madam would have liked the lot but sadly I plumped for a practical pair of chocolate-brown low-heeled leather lace-ups, as stipulated by the Norland.

'They're for my daughter's new job,' said Mother as the attendant wrapped the shoes. 'She's going to train with the Norland you know.'

I smiled shyly. She was enjoying this wonderful time every bit as much as me.

After that it was off for a look round Gamages of London, in Holborn. Gamages prided itself on being a cornucopia of essential and not so essential items. You could purchase everything here, from household goods to bathing tents, bee-keeping equipment and crocodile-hide trunks to meat juice extractors, sliced ox tongue, prawns in Aspic, fake beards and musical chairs.

Mother loved having a good rummage round Gamages. In particular we both loved the pram department. They stocked the latest in coach prams, roomy, well sprung, with leather upholstering and enormous wheels. They had names like The Burlington, The Wonder, The Newmarket, The Marmet and The Superbe. We could spend hours in there.

'Just think, darling,' murmured Mother, running her hands over the embroidered white cotton pram cushions. 'You'll be pushing some of these soon.'

No trip to London was complete without a visit to Lyons Corner House in Tottenham Court Road. To an impressionable eighteen-year-old this was a dazzling experience.

Once past the art deco gold lettered entrance you were whisked to your seat by a waitress otherwise known as a 'Nippie' in a black uniform, starched white apron and a frilly hat trimmed with a black velvet ribbon. Tea was served on bone china and brought to a fancy table covered in a white linen tablecloth. In the background men in tuxedos played in an orchestra.

I thought it just marvellous to be serenaded while you drank your tea. You wouldn't get that experience in Starbucks, now would you.

Mother treated me to an ice cream sundae with warm chocolate sauce and glacé cherries and I felt terribly grand and grown up eating it out of a long glass dish.

On the train home I was giddy with excitement. What a thrilling day. And not a child snatcher in sight! Satiated with warm chocolate sauce I promptly fell fast asleep on mother's shoulder.

Equipped with my brand new shiny shoes I was now ready to start. Three weeks later, the morning of 23 March 1939 dawned bright and clear. My first day at the Norland Institute. Today was the first day of the rest of my life and of one thing I was certain: I was going to be the best nanny I could possibly be.

Upon reporting to Pembridge Square, Mother left me at the doorstep. I could scarcely believe it. The last time I stood on these steps I was certain I was destined for failure. Now here I was. An actual Norland nurse. Well, a nurse in training.

My stomach was in knots.

'Well, darling,' said my mother, briskly drawing herself upright, I suspected to stop herself from crying. 'This is it. Do me proud.'

'Oh I'll try mother, I really will,' I said.

'I know you will, darling.'

She gave me a sweet, sad little smile, kissed me on the cheek, and then was gone.

Mother had the softest velvety down on her cheek and as she turned and walked up the road I could still feel its sweet sensation on my face. The smell of the Lux soap that she washed with hung in the air and I felt a lump form in my throat. Suddenly the enormity of my situation hit me. I was eighteen years old and all alone in The Big Smoke. I knew no one here except the terrifying Miss Whitehead.

I crept upstairs and nervously pushed open the door to my modest dorm room.

A girl stood unpacking.

'Hello,' I said timidly. 'I'm Brenda.'

'Mary Rutherford's the name,' barked the tall, confident brunette, bounding over to shake my hand enthusiastically.

'That's your bed over there. Look lively, we've to report to Miss Whitehead in the lecture room in five minutes.'

'Oh . . . oh right,' I said, impressed at Mary's efficiency. Wouldn't do to be late on our first day.

On my bed was an immaculately starched and folded bundle of clothes. My Norland uniform.

I changed into the fawn long-sleeved dress with stiff detachable white collars and cuffs, a white apron, Petersham belt and brown Petersham bow to tie at my neck.

I hung up my wool cloak and felt hat in the small wardrobe beside my bed. My real pride and joy, though, was a beautiful blue silk dress with a cotton apron with lace insertion across the bib and round the hem of the apron. The lace was specially made in Belgium. It was exquisite. No wonder it was for use on formal occasions and children's parties only.

'Rather special, isn't it,' said Mary, beaming as she watched me.

I took it out of the tissue paper like it was made of butterfly wings and hung it up carefully.

As I was smoothing down my skirt, two more girls came in as shyly as I had.

'Hi, I'm Joan,' said a young girl, blushing. 'I'm from Devon, my first time in London.'

Instantly I warmed to Joan. She was followed by a beautiful Scottish girl. Her kind green eyes twinkled beneath a halo of fiery red hair.

'I'm Margaret from Dumfries.'

Her warm Scottish accent endeared me to her instantly.

Margaret was followed by Yvonne. Yvonne was a very well-to-do French lady, which made her incredibly exotic in my eyes. Her dark eyes and shiny black coiffeured hair spoke money. She had the most exquisite clothes, all arranged beautifully in her leather case.

As she started slowly removing her things I noticed that she was utterly bewildered. She held up clothes like they were foreign objects and tugged at her bedside drawer like she'd never unpacked before.

It was then that I realised. She probably never had unpacked.

'We have servants who do this for us,' explained Yvonne, when she spotted me watching her.

'Come on, girls,' ordered Mary, rounding us all up. 'We can't keep Miss Whitehead waiting.'

Having helped Yvonne to unpack the last of her clothes, we all hurried downstairs to the main lecture room. The arctic blast of air hit us all at the same time.

'Gosh,' I said with a shiver. 'It's freezing in here.'

'Aye, not a patch on Dumfries,' said Margaret, grinning, 'but perishing all the same.'

Wanting to ingratiate myself with the twenty or so girls assembled in the room, I hurried over and shut the window.

Minutes later, Miss Whitehead marched into the room.

Some people have an air of authority about them that

commands respect. As soon as she strode purposefully to the front of the hall, twenty heads snapped to attention and you could have heard a pin drop.

Miss Whitehead, dressed immaculately in a navy dress with a white apron and white pleated cap, put down her books and looked long and hard at each of her trembling new recruits.

She took off her navy cloak lined in red silk and carefully and deliberately placed it over the back of her chair.

'Stand, please,' she ordered.

The sound of scraping chairs filled the room as we jumped to attention.

Her lips pursed disapprovingly.

'Your first lecture will be on hygiene,' she barked. 'Will the student at the back please open the window?'

I wanted the ground to swallow me up. Trust me to do the wrong thing on the first day.

Mary dashed to her feet and flung open the window.

'Fresh air makes for healthy living,' announced Miss Whitehead.

Never again would any of us dare to close a window.

Miss Whitehead quickly became a legendary figure in our eyes. She had been appointed principal four years previously in 1935, after working as a trained nurse and midwife, but was fast making her mark as a draconian guardian of the uniform. She was adamant that her nurses would only be seen as superior nannies if they were dressed and behaved impeccably at all times.

Gone with the Wind was playing at the cinema and was captivating audiences. All over London, women clamoured to dress like Scarlett O'Hara with romantic full-length skirts over crinoline. Others raised temperatures with silk stockings or were prone to lifting one perfectly groomed eyebrow from under a little velvet hat tipped over one eye, à la Greta Garbo in *Romance*. To get the Hollywood look women flaunted their assets by wearing brassieres that pushed their breasts up and out under tight sweaters and finished the look off with a slick of pillar-box red lipstick.

No such daring for us Norlanders. Miss Whitehead would have had a blue fit if we'd sauntered in wearing any such feminine outfits.

Inside these hallowed walls there was no room for silk stockings or make-up. Cosmetics were strictly banned from the nursery and stockings were made of a sensible and comfortable wool.

'I am a stickler for a properly worn uniform,' she went on, surveying us all as she spoke.

Immediately I looked down at my own and tried discreetly to straighten my skirt and smooth out the material under my belt.

'Mrs Ward once said, "It's such a pity that we could not give only the good nurses a uniform and take it away from the others," and I do endorse this. In fact,' she said, her voice rising an octave, 'I might think of having a Roll of Honour of the nurses who really do wear a properly kept uniform, but I am afraid it would not require a large frame.'

She paused to let her words sink in.

'You are given the uniform, having promised to wear it, that you may demonstrate to the world that you are a member of this Institute, which has the highest ideals. Among them is an awareness of the great responsibility it is to bring up little children to be true and good, to enable them to be men and women of the highest character.

'You have much to be thankful for. The first style with its long cloak finished just six inches from the ground. The fastenings were a hook and an eye at the neck and three tiresome little tabs to be buttoned. The summer cloak, which was a delicate grey, showed every mark. Next came cloaks with capes down to the wrists, and when the wind was frolicsome, the nurse was liable to be enveloped, and temporarily unable to see.

She paused again, positively aghast at such a notion.

An image of a poor Norland nurse fighting frantically with her cloak popped into my head and I suppressed a giggle. I had a feeling Miss Whitehead would not have been as tolerant of an impromptu fit of the giggles as my old boarding school teacher.

'Throughout these years, a white cambric tie was worn. Tying and retying it constantly made it apt to be much creased and the bonnet strings required frequent ironing to keep them looking fresh.

She paused again to let her words have maximum effect.

'How fortunate *you* are.

But Miss Whitehead wasn't finished with us yet.

'The rules for all Norlanders are these . . .

We braced ourselves.

'You will have one afternoon a week off. Outside these four walls you are a representative of this Institute, which means no smoking or gossiping on street corners like a park nurse, especially when with your charges. I have been known to cycle around these streets to ensure there are no Norlanders on parade engaging in these unsavoury activities.

'And no male visitors to this establishment under any circumstances.

I wondered briefly what the penalty was for any nurse caught smuggling a man into a dorm, but looking at Miss Whitehead now, I found it hard to believe anyone would dare try.

'Bedtime is 10.00 p.m. prompt and your dormitories are to be spotless at all times.

This was one doyenne not to be messed with! Every student in the room shifted uncomfortably.

'Finally,' she said shrilly, 'I would like to remind you that none of you are training to be nannies.

Every face in the room looked utterly baffled.

'You are nurses. The word nanny embodies the status and standards that Mrs Ward was determined to rise above.'

I don't remember much more of the rest of the lecture but when Joan, Margaret, Mary, Yvonne and I returned to our dorms we sank onto our beds quite exhausted. Just as well that it was supper, evening prayers then lights out 10.00 p.m. prompt as my head was swimming with exhaustion.

The next morning we were presented with our black leather-bound testimonial books. I opened mine gingerly, as if it were made of the most fragile lace, marvelling at the beautiful gold-embossed cover and marbled endpapers. I gasped. There was my photograph on the inside cover, followed by page after page of subjects to be studied just waiting for a grade to be marked against them. I swallowed hard. There was a lot of work ahead.

I read through the Institute's definition of my working conditions. *Do not ask your nurse to eat with your servants, nor to eat meals in her bedroom. She should not be expected to carry coal or scrub floors. She should be given time off to worship and take exercise.*

I hardly minded if they did ask me to carry coal or eat with the servants, so pleased was I to even be here!

We were to have three months' training at the Norland Institute, followed by three months' experience of living and working in a London hospital, after which we returned to Pembridge Square for another three months of lectures and practical domestic work. At the end of this we were to take written exams and our certificate was deferred until twelve months' satisfactory work had been completed in our first post.

'Your employers will be required to write you a written reference in your testimonial book,' our lecturer informed us. 'Forgery is an offence which will result in instant dismissal.'

After a punishing day of back-to-back lectures we returned to our dorm to prepare for supper.

No sooner had we stepped inside than Yvonne gasped. Her dark eyes flashed with anger.

'Mon Dieu,' she said, dropping her books on the floor with a thud.

All her bed linen had been stripped off and her drawers emptied.

'Who has messed up my bed?' she demanded. 'I made it this morning.'

It was a complete mystery.

'Perhaps someone broke in,' said Joan the country girl, instantly fearing the worst.

'Bally cheek,' blasted Mary. 'Who would do such a thing?'

All was about to be revealed.

In marched a senior lecturer, who turned on Yvonne.

'Your bed was a complete mess, child. Most irksome. You will learn to make your bed properly with the crease of the sheet to run in a straight line down the middle. The corners will be neatly tucked in. Your eiderdown will be turned down and drawn tight and neat, otherwise there will be a mark against your name,' she snapped. 'You will be required to make it again properly this time and every day from here on in.'

Yvonne's mouth was still flapping open and shut in shock as the lecturer disappeared in a cloud of disapproval.

Poor Yvonne. Servants made her bed every morning. She never learnt quite simply because she never had to.

I doubted that she had ever made her own cup of tea or cleaned a toilet in her life, either. At that moment I was so grateful to my mother for teaching me the importance of housewifery.

'Is like being in the army,' Yvonne grumbled.

I offered to help her redo it and showed her how. 'Let's all muck in together.'

It wasn't her fault she had led such a pampered, privileged life.

From then on, dorm inspection became a daily occurrence. Our rooms, beds and belongings had to be spotless, with not a thing out of place. Even our toothbrushes weren't allowed to have a trace of toothpaste on them!

But Yvonne wasn't the only student shamed by the Institute. The next day Margaret rushed into the room her eyes red and puffy and her face as white as flour. She threw herself onto her bed sobbing.

'What ever is wrong, Margaret?' I asked, alarmed.

'They want me to have elocution lessons,' she cried in her beautiful soft lilting Scottish accent. 'I have to learn to speak the Queen's English so employers can understand me better. I dinnae know there was anything wrong with the way I speak. They cannae do that . . . can they?'

It seemed that if Margaret wanted to be a Norland nurse they could and they would.

Poor Margaret. I felt so desperately for her and was quite certain that at some point I too would be called into the principal's office and informed I would need to improve my speech.

Of course I'm certain they wouldn't dream of doing such a thing now, it seems perfectly archaic, but back then, received pronunciation was quite the norm.

One thing was for sure. Us Norlanders were going to be whipped into shape pretty damn fast whether we liked it or not.

'Come on,' I said, putting my arm round Margaret. 'Let's go for dinner, things won't seem so bad on a full stomach.'

All the students and lecturers ate their meals in the same room on long scrubbed wooden tables, with Miss Whitehead and senior lecturers seated at a top table.

The maidens, in whose number I was so nearly included, served us our meals. I always made a special effort to be nice to them. I'm sure I didn't deserve to be served by them for one moment.

'Thank you very much.'

I smiled at the young maiden as she heaped a steaming pile of beetroot and spinach alongside my meat.

Mother and the rest of the family always called me the human dustbin for my seeming ability to eat whatever was put in front of me, but aside from junket, which was the devil's work as far as I was concerned, beetroot was the only food I truly loathed. How could anyone like something so slimy?

I wolfed down the meat and spinach but left the beetroot.

Suddenly an unmistakable voice boomed across the dining room. The infamous Miss Whitehead.

'Brenda Ashford. Rule one. Never leave anything on your plate. When you are in charge of children you have to lead by example. How can you expect them to eat everything if you do not? Now eat up.'

Flushing the same colour as my beetroot, I forced it down.

First the window, now the beetroot. Could I not do anything right?

The next day we began housewifery, taught by Miss Danvers.

She was lovely, softly spoken with a kind voice and a gentle manner. The good cop to Miss Whitehead's bad cop.

'Our first lesson, girls,' she said, smiling angelically, 'is to learn how to clean a toilet properly.'

Every girl in the room looked horrified. This wasn't why

we had come to the Norland. Where were the adorable children and the strolls in Kensington Gardens?

I could virtually hear Yvonne weighing up whether to call her mother now and get the chauffeur to come and collect her.

Instead she stayed glued to her seat as Miss Danvers handed each of us girls a bottle of Jeyes Fluid Disinfectant and a scrubbing brush and pointed us in the direction of the toilets with the command, 'Don't forget to clean under the rim.'

After that we learnt not to dare to complain and to do everything that was asked of us.

For three months we scrubbed toilets until they were so clean you could eat your dinner off them, polished shoes to such a high shine Miss Danvers could see her reflection in them when she came to do an inspection, and scrubbed all the Norland's Marmet coach prams down in the chilly stone basement until they gleamed.

Who knew there were so many cleaning instruments, all of which had to be identified correctly. For sweeping alone there was a stove brush, a cornice brush, banister broom, a whisk broom, carpet broom, and on the list went.

Pram parade was at 3.00 p.m. sharp every day. We had to line our polished prams up on the lawn outside in a semi-circle so Miss Danvers could conduct her inspection. She was the domestic equivalent of a drill sergeant! Every girl held her breath as she walked slowly past each pram, nodding and making notes.

The soft leather bonnet had to be well waxed with Johnson's Wax Polish, the high black sides shining, the white cushions and blankets in the pram spotless and plumped up and the wheels without a trace of dirt. Any unfortunate girl that failed pram parade was sent back to clean until the pram was up to Miss Danvers' exacting standards.

'Please don't let it be me today,' muttered Yvonne, under her breath, as Miss Danvers inspected the every nook and corner of her carriage.

'You bonnet is lacking shine,' she commented.

My turn. I held my breath as she cast a critical eye over my pram.

'Very good, Brenda,' she said finally. Phew. Another inspection passed.

It was backbreaking and exhausting work. It's amazing no one dropped out, though I am certain it must have crossed poor Yvonne's mind. The Norland might have required girls of a genteel background but they had better jolly well work like a soldier in His Majesty's army.

Soon I was so hungry I learnt to eat every last scrap on my plate, Yvonne was making beds like an expert and even poor Margaret was starting to sound like a southerner. I doubted her parents would even recognise her.

We fell into bed exhausted each night, our fingers virtually bleeding and our backs aching. I didn't even mind the freezing wind that blasted through the open dorm windows.

Slowly it began to dawn on me. I was having the time of my life.

I was learning a trade and I loved every second. I learnt how to sew, cross stitch, how to knit children's woollies, how to make a delicate smock dress out of the finest linen. Miss Danvers showed us how to do the most intricate needlework, and woe betide you if you didn't do it right; you would stay in that needlework room until you could show her the finished article.

What's more, I began to realise I was actually pretty good at it all.

'Very good, Brenda,' said Miss Danvers one morning as

she surveyed me embroidering a little pink cotton dress. 'You have a definite knack for this.'

I basked in the glow of her praise.

No one could compete with Mary, though. Her embroidery was a wonder to behold.

'Excellent, Mary,' said Miss Danvers, beaming. 'Really excellent.'

Mary wore a grin like the Cheshire cat for the rest of the day after that. One naughty wink from Joan was enough to get my mouth twitching.

There was one room we dreaded. The laundry.

The modern laundry is unrecognisable from those of yesteryear, or certainly the ones we worked in at the Norland.

Today's housewife enjoys a multitude of machines to make laundry work a thing of ease. She has a spin-cycle, a number of rinses and temperatures, all at the touch of a button, and even a machine to dry her clothes . . . not to mention an electric iron. Oh the luxury of an electric iron!

Back then all we had was vast stone sinks, a mangle, a packet of Lux and the dreaded flat iron.

As you can imagine, with a large house filled with women and children, there was an awful lot of laundry to be done and cloth nappies to wash.

Mary, Joan, Yvonne, Margaret and me would plunge our arms into the huge sinks of warm soapy water and scrub until our hands were numb.

The laundry room was fiercely hot and soon all our faces were flushed red from the heat. Three big copper boilers heated by a gas flame dominated the room and all the sheets, pillow cases, napkins, clothes and nappies went in there to be boil washed.

Nowadays I hear a baby needs anywhere between 6,000 and 8,000 nappy changes from birth until they are potty trained. Back then we used two dozen cloths per baby to see us through, all of which needed regular boil washing and soaking in a bucket of Lux.

We would scrub what couldn't be boil washed, by hand.

Afterwards the clothes had to be wrung on a giant mangle, which required the biceps of a sailor to turn. Then everything had to be hoisted up onto giant wooden maidens attached to the ceiling, so the clothes could be dried.

This was easy work in comparison to the ironing.

We worked beside a hot stove where, two, sometimes, three irons were heated before use. The knack was then to alternate the irons, moving them from stove to ironing table and back again in an endless cycle of heating, pressing and re-heating.

The irons were heavy too, and one had to press down with great force to get the immaculate result Miss Danvers required. But they also required great delicacy and care, because there were no controls, so it was easy to scorch fabrics. The irons had to be kept spotlessly clean with no trace of ash or dirt to soil the clean laundry.

It was hot, tiring, relentless work and it all had to be completed in our wool stockings, uniforms and aprons.

'No wonder Maman gets the butler to send ours to Whiteley's,' muttered Yvonne as she wrestled with the mangle.

Joan and I exchanged a little grin. Most families had no choice but to do their own, or send it out to a local washerwoman. For us girls, laundry work was deemed an important part of our training.

On more than one occasion one of the girls would collapse with exhaustion, close to fainting. Usually Yvonne.

'I can't do this,' she'd sob, when she got a burn mark on her sheet or the mangle got too much.

'Yes, you can,' I'd insist, helping her to her feet. 'Come on, I'll help you with the mangle.'

'Do tell us one of your stories,' shy Joan would say to me. 'That'll pass the time.'

Joan loved hearing about David, the dares I used to get up to at school or my naughty brother Basil's escapades.

Soon we were flushed with steam and laughter. The camaraderie between us girls was what got us through the long, hard days in the laundry room.

When we weren't scrubbing, cleaning, polishing, sewing, knitting or lining up for pram parade we would gather in the draughty, freezing cold lecture rooms for lectures on neatness, punctuality, speech and moral tone.

'Moral tone' sounds very pompous and outdated but in fact many useful things were conveyed to me in these lectures and have fared me well throughout the rest of my life.

Miss Whitehead took some of these lectures herself.

'The future is made by the children for whose characters and training you are responsible. Your contribution and examples are valuable,' was one of her favourite sayings.

The other thing that the Institution believed in more than any other was telling the truth. (Telling a little white lie to avoid ruining the fun of Christmas by saying that Father Christmas doesn't really exist, didn't count.)

We were taught the value of the tremendous force of absolute truthfulness.

'When your charges ask you where babies come from,' Miss Whitehead was fond of intoning, 'they do not appear under gooseberry bushes, neither are they parachuted in by an obliging stork. They come from mummy's tummy.'

To aid us in our journey to a higher moral ground we were given a poem to memorise, as a reminder of Norland's moral foundations and the importance of the virtues.

When Mrs Ward had well begun her new house to plan
She thought, 'Now these probationers I'll teach them one by one,'
And see if they don't run along the straight path very soon

I'll label wondering bedroom doors with words that much can teach,
And see if painted sentiment their hard heart cannot reach
And fast on Norland principles their stranded souls we'll beach

Whene'er the weekly candle died out on Tuesday night,
Whene'er with empty match boxes they fail to make a light,
That word upon their bedroom doors will rush upon their sight,
And teach them 'Thrift'

Whene'er Miss Barton comes along and says, 'Now tie it tight,'
Whene'er with wondering consciousnesses you duly answer, 'right'
And that domestic pudding gives even you a fright,
That word upon your bedroom door will burst upon your sight
And teach you 'Carefulness'

The poem went on to work through the virtues of honesty, punctuality and tidiness in their turn and was a distillation of everything we were taught to value. But even more important to remember were children's nursery rhymes, stories and prayers. I love nursery rhymes so for me this didn't even feel like work.

The lecturers would observe us as we recited poems and stories in front of class. I hated this part and always wished the ground would swallow me up. To help me, I'd close my eyes, think of David and suddenly I'd be back at Hallcroft.

Lullaby and goodnight,
Mummy's delight,
Bright angels around

My darling shall stand.
They will guard you from harms,
You shall wake in my arms.
They will guard you from harms,
You shall wake in my arms.

I could almost smell the sweet musky scent of his head as a baby, feel his little fingers curling round mine. I missed him fiercely.

Miss Danvers also took us for another element of domestic science: what to do with little children when they are ill.

Today we have plasters, Calpol, and no end of over the counter medications we can reach for when little heads are hurting, or knees are bleeding, but back then we had to be a little more resourceful.

The cupboards were groaning with items we had to learn how to use.

Olive oil had a multitude of uses. Rubbed into the scalp it was a cure for dandruff, or warmed and massaged into a baby's back and chest it was comforting and helped to fend off colds.

I learnt that an ounce of warm water will quieten a fretful baby and cure wind.

A handy recipe for diarrhoea? Take a cup of milk and two glasses of port wine, heat milk and add wine, bring to boiling point, stand till curd breaks, strain and give a tablespoonful to child.

A bath of bicarbonate of soda has a soothing effect on heat spots. Eucalyptus oil can be dropped in hot water and inhaled for colds and carrow oil makes an excellent dressing for burns.

There was bottle after bottle in Mrs Danvers' cupboards, all with some medicinal purpose. Brandy, dill water, borax, glycerine, ginger, camphorated oil, Dr Bow's liniment, castor oil, Gregory's Mixture and peppermint oil. Mrs Danvers elucidated in precise steps what purpose each could serve.

At this point you might be wondering where on earth all the children were. Just whose nappies were we washing and whose prams we were cleaning so diligently?

Norland *did* have resident children. No 11 Pembridge Square was converted into several nursery rooms, christened Spring, Dawn, Bluebell, Daisy and Forget-me-not. A quiet back garden led into Kensington Gardens.

The children who lived here were usually the offspring of civil service families posted abroad who didn't want to take their children with them for fear of illness or danger. The Institute also cared for children whose mothers died in childbirth and illegitimate children. It offered a continuous child care service at least until the age of seven, when the children were sent to boarding school. Their day-to-day care was in the hands of the trainees in their third term, not first-termers like me.

It was agony for a young girl who was itching to care for children. Mastering a flat iron was all well and good but when would we ever get to the real thing?

But rules were rules. First term was to learn moral qualities, housewifery and domestic science, second term was training in hospital and third term we would finally get to train alongside the children.

I would see them outside playing or being strolled out to Kensington Gardens. Occasionally their sunny laughter drifted up to the lecture rooms from the gardens. Joan loved children as much as I did and would sigh when their excited chatter carried through the walls.

I suppose in some ways this may have been an unusual childhood for these children. They were left in the care of strangers who used them as a sort of training ground; but they always seemed so happy and well cared for that no one thought it out of the ordinary.

They were taken for walks in the park, dance classes, trips to the zoo, the circus, shows, tea with friends and day trips to the seaside.

Smacking was forbidden by the nursery so punishment was to stand in the corner or the withdrawal of jam for tea. And of course, the children of the upper classes were almost always cared for by staff, so in that sense, there was nothing terribly peculiar about the arrangement.

As well as resident children there was also a day nursery school for local children from Kensington and Notting Hill.

Neither did Norland's connection to children stop at the offspring of wealthy Kensington inhabitants. The Institute also had an affiliation with the Bethnal Green Day Nursery in the East End of London and supported it with a mission fund donation of £100 a year.

When Norland was founded, Emily Ward had toyed with the idea of a day crèche to be run as a charitable venture for poor mothers. Such facilities were desperately needed for the poor working mothers who back then had no choice but to leave their young children and babies locked in a room all day while they went to work. It wasn't uncommon to see four- and five-year-olds wandering the streets. But there was no call for a crèche in the affluent streets of West London, so in 1915 Norland vowed to help Bethnal Green Day Nursery financially, and in any way we could. A lot of the woolies we knitted wound up on the children of the East End. It filled me with a lovely, warm glow to know I was doing my bit.

I remember reading a letter from Edith Taylor, who ran the nurseries.

I send you my very very great thanks for all you have sent to our babies. You have been as generous as ever.

We were also kindly sent forty tickets to see *Me and My Girl*. The entertainment was greatly enjoyed and we arrived back at Whitechapel at 9.20 p.m. with the mothers dancing 'The Lambeth walk' home. Also, through the generous proceeds of the Norland's toy sale, Miss Whitehead sent me a huge cheque, with the kind and sensible suggestion that each mother should receive 1 cwt. of coal. The mothers are most grateful. It is a pleasure to see any Norland Nurses who come to visit us.

I made a vow that one day I would make it to Bethnal Green to meet those children. Of course I had no idea how our worlds were fated to collide. Destiny had big plans for the children of the Bethnal Green nursery and me.

For now though, London's East End seemed a million miles from Pembridge Square. The furthest I had ventured thus far was Sunday morning worship at the nearest Baptist church, and Paddington Baths in West London for our weekly swimming lessons.

After learning to swim in the freezing waters off the coast of Bognor, these beautiful old baths were a real treat.

The swimming lessons were paid for by a wealthy family who had once employed a Norland Nanny. Whilst on holiday, the child of the family, a small boy, got into trouble swimming. Without hesitation, the Norland Nanny dived in and saved him from a certain death by drowning. So relieved and grateful were the family that they donated a large sum of money to the Norland on the proviso that the Institute used it to teach all new students to swim.

Well, I could already swim but I wasn't going to let that stop the enjoyment of splashing about with my new friends.

The baths were huge with tiled walls and our excited laughter echoed round the huge space. Best of all, there was an enormous diving board at least 50ft up at one end of the pool, that could only be reached by climbing three flights of stairs.

On one occasion, after we all tired of seeing who could hold their breath for longest under water, Margaret turned to me.

'Brenda,' she said with a wicked glint in her eye. 'I dare you to climb that diving board.'

'Yes,' egged on Yvonne. 'Do it, Brenda.'

'I don't know if that's such a good idea,' whispered Joan.

But the others' cheers drowned her voice out.

Well . . . how could I say no? I never was one to turn down a dare!

What an excellent opportunity to show off just a little.

Before I had a chance to change my mind I was out the water and scurrying across the tiled floor.

Up I climbed with my chest puffed out, swaggering with bravado. But then a strange thing happened. The higher I climbed the funnier I felt. My stomach seemed to stay on the ground as I climbed up and up . . . and up!

Hmm. I'm sure it didn't look this high from the ground.

Yvonne, Joan, Mary and Margaret looked like little Swan Vespa matches below with their skinny white bodies topped off with rubber swim hats.

Once at the top I paused and gulped.

It was an awfully long way down.

I thought about turning back, and then I looked at the girls grinning down below. Margaret gave me the thumbs up.

Oh crikey. I could no more turn back now than I could fly to the moon.

Here goes nothing.

'Geronimo,' I hollered, hurling myself off the board.

The smack of my tummy hitting the water must have been heard in neighbouring Notting Hill.

It was the mother of all belly flops and I was winded well into the next week but I didn't care. I hadn't been branded a wimp and to an eighteen-year-old girl, what was more important than that?

Soon after, and approaching the end of our first period of three-month training, Mary and I were summoned to Miss Whitehead's office.

Oh crumbs. I wondered whether she'd got word of my diving board stunt? But once inside the same office where I'd had my interview, I realised Miss Whitehead was actually smiling. At me!

'Well done, girls,' she said. 'I have been observing you both and it has become clear that you have excelled at your training and both have leadership potential.

I felt Mary swell with pride next to me.

'For devotion to duty and ability I am making you head girl, Mary and you are her second in command, Brenda. That is how you shall both be known henceforth. That is all. You may go back to your training now.'

I left Miss Whitehead's office feeling ten feet tall. We had done something to make Miss Whitehead pleased. My joy was only matched when I was handed my black testimonial book. Good, Very Good or Excellent in all my subjects.

I floated on air for the rest of the day. All was well in the world.

Or so I thought.

Far beyond the quiet gentility of Pembridge Square, where failing pram parade was the biggest possible scandal, dark forces were at work. Hitler was gathering his troops. War was brewing.

Ever since Hitler had become Chancellor of Germany in

1933, under his leadership the country had developed into a ruthlessly aggressive state. Democratic government and political opposition were swept away using coercion, repression and propaganda. The National Socialist party took their place and fixed world domination in its sights.

Unbeknownst to us students, Hitler had given the people of Germany back their sense of national pride. There was great bitterness in Germany after World War One, when it had been forced to pay huge damages and admit guilt for causing war. This had sowed the seeds of discord and we were about to pay the devastating price.

It may seem hard to believe that I didn't have the faintest clue that war was about to break out, but we had no papers, no wireless and no television set at Pembridge Square. We seldom left the Institute except to go to church or swim. It may as well have been 1839 not 1939. As long as prams were pristine, our uniforms impeccable and our moral tone and hygiene beyond question then that was all that mattered. I had vaguely heard of this Hitler chap, but he wasn't about to stop the pram wheels rolling!

My parents' letters from home were full of news of David falling out the apple tree and the first batch of blackberries being spotted on the hedgerow. Mother and Father would never discuss world politics and current affairs with me. It simply wasn't done.

Our first inkling that anything was wrong was when the chairman of Norland wrote in the *Norland Quarterly*.

The worst danger which threatens us from Central Europe is not so much the soldiers, the armaments, or the horrors that make this so called peace even more terrible than the war of 1914–1918. It is the hearts and minds of young people; brought up and educated for one thing only – War! And our defense is not anti-aircraft guns, shelters and gas masks, it is the hearts and minds of our children, the will to peace. This is the responsibility of parents and nurses, and it can only be fulfilled by us if we can turn our minds from the destruction of war to the construction of peace.

But alas, his words were falling on deaf ears. It was already too late for that. Little did we know it, but our comfortable, well-ordered world was already in peril . . .

4

The Matron

The best way to treat obstacles is to use them as stepping-
stones. Laugh at them, tread on them, and let them lead you
to something better.

Mr Galliano's Circus, Enid Blyton

As HITLER mobilised his troops I merrily moved on to the
second phase of my training in a state of blissful ignorance.

Second term was to be spent training on the wards of a
London hospital.

Emily Ward had had to work hard to get the matrons of
London hospitals to accept Norlanders. The matrons, quite
rightly, were less than keen to let a load of young, untrained
girls loose onto their rigidly controlled wards. Emily persisted, staunch in her belief that every Norlander should gain
an insight into the life and struggles of the poor and sick. She
typified the spirit of Victorian philanthropy that maintained
the rich had a duty to help the poor and suffering.

By 1939, thanks to the support of Sir Robert Hutchison,
an eminent paediatrician, there were a number of London
hospitals willing to take Norland students.

We were acutely aware to be on our best behaviour, particularly when Miss Whitehead sat us down in the draughty
lecture room before we left.

'Although you are trained to care for healthy children, some insight into the principles of sick nursing is of great value to those in charge of nurseries,' she said. 'This is a timely opportunity to remind ourselves of the traditions of the Norland. As well as maintaining high ideals and Christian beliefs, we are here to serve. Whilst at hospital you must forget yourselves. You are merely a pair of hands for service, to minister to the suffering children and make them as happy and comfortable as you can. You will learn that your lives during your career will be full of self-sacrifice, for the needs of your charges will call forth all your love, devotion, intelligence and watchful care. Remember our motto: 'Love Never Faileth'.

This was delivered in Miss Whitehead's usual commanding tone and it was a brave woman who would let her down.

We all duly trooped to the front of the lecture room to find out where we were to be dispatched. My eyes scanned the list.

Brenda Ashford . . . Great Ormond Street.

Great Ormond Street Hospital! How thrilled was I to be joining such an esteemed institution! Kathleen, my older sister, who was training to be a nurse at Clapham Women's Hospital, would be impressed.

'Lucky you,' boomed Mary. 'Jolly good hospital.'

And so on a sunny June morning in 1939 I bid Joan, Yvonne, Mary and Margaret a fond farewell and with Miss Whitehead's words still ringing in my ears, made my way with my trunk the short distance across town to Great Ormond Street Hospital.

As I sat in the taxi en route, the real reason my body was drumming with anticipation was because finally, finally, I could get to look after my beloved babies and children. Don't get me wrong, I loved needlework and nursery rhymes, but caring for children was the reason I had joined the Norland, after all.

Pulling up outside the hospital, dressed in my freshly pressed

Norland uniform and cape, I paid my fare then stopped to take in my new home. The magnificent red brick building soared into the sky, among a jumble of eighteenth- and nineteenth-century terraced homes.

Back then, before Hitler rained his bombs down on our heritage, London's skyline looked very different. Just like the Great Fire of London three hundred years before, the Blitz totally decimated parts of the capital.

But on that day the majestic building looked like a grand old dame, with the cluster of little houses, her charges, sitting at her feet.

Goodness gracious didn't I feel humble to be standing here.

I felt a strange kinship to this hospital. It was the first institute in Britain to provide specialist in-patient care to children only, and perhaps the oldest children's hospital in the English-speaking world. Their motto 'The child first and always' was inspiring and could have been written with me in mind.

The Hospital for Sick Children first opened its doors at 49 Great Ormond Street on Valentine's Day 1852, with ten beds. The medical staff consisted of two voluntary physicians, a surgeon and five nurses. Dr Charles West was the driving force behind its opening, driven by the shockingly high level of infant mortality in the capital.

The first in-patient was Eliza Armstrong from Lisson Grove, suffering from consumption, otherwise known as pulmonary tuberculosis, a rampant and often fatal disease in Victorian London. The first child admitted to Great Ormond Street Hospital as an outpatient was two-year-old George Parr, who had catarrh and diarrhoea – not serious by today's standards, but this was a time when one third of children born in London died before adulthood. Most of the hospital patients came from the notorious slum districts of Clerkenwell and Seven Dials, within a short walking distance.

Incidentally, both areas today are very smart, bulging with restaurants and bars. Ironic when you think that one hundred years ago, families of ten or more crowded into one room without so much as a crust of bread to go around.

These poor mites suffered enormously from extreme poverty and exploitation. Children as young as five worked in factories, mines and chimney sweeping, where their tiny little bodies allowed them access to small spaces. Heart-breakingly, they often worked naked because of the heat and to save their clothes.

Chimney sweeps, or climbing boys, as they were often known, had the worst jobs of all. The heat and dark of those tiny spaces must have been terrifying to a five-year-old boy. Often, callous employers would light a fire in the grate to send a blast of heat up the chimney and ensure they weren't slacking. My darling baby brother David, now nine, would already have been working for four or more years had he been born in the 1800s. An image of him shinning up a dark, hot dangerous chimney made me shudder with fear.

The boys who were sent to work underground in mines barely saw sunlight all year round and so vitamin D deficiency and rickets were rife, and the climbing boys could look forward to a life ruined by stooped backs and cancer of the scrotum.

The Industrial Revolution only made matters worse. Starving and exhausted children worked fourteen hours a day, six days a week in factories, with scarcely a break. They were considered the lucky ones for at least they had steady work. Poor children of London with no employment were forced to scavenge food from the streets.

It's almost impossible to imagine how dark, filthy, danger-ous and foggy those London streets looked to a child back then. Not that many would have survived long enough to see them. Mortality rates for babies in the slums were 50 per cent. In such a harsh and hopeless world, the horrors and disease of the workhouse were the best that a deprived child could hope for.

Those admitted to the workhouse were instantly separated from their families, held down by the workhouse master while they had their heads shaved, and forced into a punishing and thankless regime of work. Common tasks included picking oakum, which meant painstakingly picking the heavily coated tar from old rope, or crushing bones to make fertiliser.

In and out of the workhouse, disease was rife. Measles, whooping cough, tuberculosis, croup, rickets, lice and tapeworm spread through children like wildfire.

Dr Charles West saw all this and realised that a children's hospital was an innovation that was urgently needed in London.

Like Emily Ward, who banished fear in the nursery and Friedrich Froebel, who maintained that childhood should be a happy, carefree time, Dr West put children firmly at the heart of everything he did. He believed that love was amongst the most important attributes of nursing children.

Like Emily and Friedrich he overcame pressure, prejudice and adversity to open Great Ormond Street children's hospital, just a year after the first ever kindergarten was opened in the UK.

Thanks to these legendary figures, childhood was finally emerging as a stage of life with its own value. Most people don't even know the names of my heroes let alone of their achievements, but part of the fact that our children today have the right to a happy and healthy childhood is down to them.

The new hospital quickly attracted public support. Queen Victoria, Charles Dickens and J.M. Barrie, who donated the copyright of his famous play, *Peter Pan*, were among the first to pledge their support. That I, eighteen-year-old Brenda, was about to tread in the footsteps of such incredible figures in history was nothing short of a miracle.

Staring up at the imposing edifice, I felt honoured to be here.

Hadn't I already come a long way from my village? I was more determined than ever to make mother proud.

I and another three Norlanders who were also training at the hospital were instructed to report to the Matron's office.

Great Ormond Street Hospital was like nothing I'd ever seen before.

The doctors and surgeons – all male – swept imperiously along the long, tiled corridors. I virtually flattened myself against the wall and the lumpy old cast iron radiators as they swept by.

'Good morning,' I smiled at one important looking man in a white coat but he looked right through me, and the matron by his side glared at me. I was totally invisible to him, and to most of the countless nurses who bustled from room to room with their clipboards and air of authority.

Suddenly I felt quite small and alone, a tiny cog in a huge machine. But with all the optimism of youth, I felt sure it wouldn't be long before I fitted in.

Wards with high ceilings and high windows led off the long corridor. Every room felt slightly austere and forbidding, even the enormous open wards.

Every now and again I'd catch a glimpse of some poor little mite, laying still and pale against a pillow. But this was not a time to be sentimental. I couldn't keep matron waiting.

There was nothing to fear though, was there? I was a deputy head girl of my set at the Norland Institute. Surely that meant I would move into this world with seamless ease?

Finally, after navigating a maze of corridors, I saw a door with a sign on the front.

Matron's office.

Hurrah, I'd done it; better still, I was the first Norlander there. I congratulated myself, somewhat smugly, on a first job well done.

Drawing myself up straight I knocked on the door, fixed a smile on my face and then turned the handle.

'STOP!'

The sound boomed down the tiled corridor. I froze like a startled rabbit in headlamps, my hand still clamped to the doorknob.

'Do not go in there. Under no account are you to enter matron's office unless I announce you.'

The thundering voice belonged to the home sister. As she marched along the corridor, nearly 6ft tall in her stockinged feet, I shrank back.

'I'm s . . . sorry,' I stuttered like a fool, whipping my hand off the doorknob.

This was my first meeting with the home sister and unfortunately the impression I left on her was not a patch on the one she left on me.

She was a vision of starched efficiency, from her pleated white nurse's hat down to her sensible lace-up shoes.

I didn't know it back then but the nursing staff of this hospital were typical of the women of their era, a formidable breed in their own right. If I thought the Norland had strict rules and procedures in place, I was in for the shock of my life. Great Ormond Street in 1939 made the Norland look like a veritable playground.

There was a complex nursing hierarchy in place, with matron ruling supreme. Many exacting etiquettes governed the system.

Unfortunately not a single one was conveyed to me.

I quickly learnt that being a deputy head girl at Norland

counted for absolutely nothing at Great Ormond Street. I was firmly at the bottom of the pecking order. I had to learn by my mistakes and over the coming months be assured there were plenty.

Shortly after the dressing down from the home sister, I made the ultimate faux pas. I walked up the stairs in front of a more senior member of staff, a doctor. I'd been lost in a daydream and hadn't noticed, though I doubt if it would have made any difference if I had. You see, no one had told me I wasn't supposed to do this.

The sister witnessed my crime and oh boy did she give me a telling off.

'Ashford,' she barked at the top of the stairwell. 'Show some respect to your seniors.'

I scuttled back down those stairs, a picture of abject misery.

I was lost in a bewildering world. This was pre-NHS days, there was no such thing as staff rights or patient charters. The wards were governed with a rod of iron, and matron ruled. One sight of her white hat with the goffered edges and you better make sure your bedpans were sparkling and your beds made just so. Put one foot wrong and you would swiftly know about it.

That night, alone in my tiny room, I cried myself to sleep, loneliness and despair engulfing me in waves. My dream of overcoming the tyranny of the nursery seemed to grow more fragile with every passing day. I was like a fish out of water here. Why couldn't I do anything right?

The next morning I gave myself a talking to.

Come on Brenda. You can do this.

After a breakfast of porridge in the nurses' dining room, I reported for duty bright and breezy and presented myself to ward sister. Today was a new day.

Her eyes shot down to my wrists and anger flashed over her face.

Oh no. Not again.

You knew what was coming before she had even opened her mouth.

'Nurse Ashford,' she said in a clipped voice. 'In future you will not address me unless you are wearing your cuffs.'

Curses. I'd forgotten to take my frills off and put my cuffs on.

The frills were a piece of elasticated material that kept long sleeves up while working and we wore these over our Norland uniforms for the majority of the time, but the starched cuffs had to be worn before you addressed ward sister.

I suppose I should have counted myself lucky. Ward sister and matron's Victorian predecessors sounded even more terrifying.

One of the first matrons of Great Ormond Street was a formidable-looking woman by the name of Catherine Wood. In the photo that hung in the current matron's office, she was buttoned from head to toe in black, with barely an inch of flesh on show and wore a glare that could curdle milk at twenty paces.

She was well known on the wards for her severity, as she demonstrated in her book, the *Handbook of Nursing for the Home and Hospital*. 'The clever, bright attendant may succeed in hoodwinking the doctor,' she wrote in a disapproving tone. 'She has the sharpness to change her poultices just before the clinical rounds, to put on the clean linen for his visits; but the hot poultice and the clean sheets should be eyed with suspicion – for they are the marks of a gay deceiver.'

In fairness, she probably needed every ounce of her ferocity in order to push for the reform that was badly needed in nursing at that time.

Catherine was one of the earliest members of the Royal British Nursing Association and she laid the foundations for modern paediatric nursing and training. She died at a great age after lecturing in hygiene and nursing, writing a great many articles on nursing standards and a bestselling book, introducing a two-tier system of formal nursing, and training countless generations of nurses. Oh, and raising her dead brother's eleven orphaned children.

I rather suspect Matron Wood would have made mincemeat of me.

After the cuffs debacle my nerves were shot to pieces and my confidence at rock bottom. I tiptoed around the place like a nervous kitten. The funny thing is, as soon as you have done one thing wrong, disaster is attracted to you. I was forever dropping things and getting in the way.

I thought of my sister, training at Clapham Women's Hospital and, according to our mother, having the time of her life. Kathleen was obviously made of more robust stuff than me. I was too soft by half. Hospital etiquette combined with the sight of all those sick children reduced me to mush.

The children made for a pitiful sight and something inside my soul stirred when I saw them. Some suffered from rickets and their legs were so bowed they could scarcely walk, others, suffering from dyspraxia, were strapped to a bed with both legs in plaster. The children on the wards were being treated for everything from lupus, to rheumatism.

I hated to see their suffering.

Some were so ill and listless they could barely lift their heads from the pillow. Most of the poor scraps didn't even open their eyes much, but those that did wore little smiles that broke my heart.

Unwell children, unlike adults, do not feel sorry for themselves.

How could these beautiful and brave little children battling every day *not* affect me?

Walking through the wards was a truly humbling experience

that left me breathless with admiration. Too many adults busy in their everyday world sever links with childhood. These children reminded me what it is to be human: to never lose touch with what is important.

Perhaps next time you are feeling stressed you should think of the little children at Great Ormond Street, smiling though their sickness. They don't know the meaning of stress, just a daily fight with pain. Their battle is nothing short of courageous.

Charles Dickens summed it up well when he wrote, 'A sick child is like a cold summer. But to quench the summer in a child's heart is, thank God, not easy.'

And you couldn't quench the sense of mischief in some of the children either . . .

Great Ormond Street, like the Norland, was a great believer in the restorative power of fresh air, and patients were wheeled out every day to get their dose.

The year before I had started, the new Southwood Building, complete with balconies, had just opened. Children who were in the recovery stage were wheeled out in their wrought-iron cots onto their balcony. Can you imagine the sight of all these rows of children in their cots staring down from on high?

Apparently, neighbours complained bitterly about the noise but the fresh air breaks was deemed too important to be sacrificed. They also gave children who hated their uninspired lunch of watery mince and tapioca the chance to sneak it outside under their sheets and hurl it off the side of the balcony. There were great shrieks of laughter when some tapioca landed with a splat on the glass roof of a balcony below.

The children's laughter was always music to my ears, and some of the happiest times came from seeing the delight on their little faces when we served up jam sandwiches for tea.

There wasn't much room for sentimentality, or fun for that matter, at Great Ormond Street, mind you. There simply wasn't time. As well as the daily cleaning of the wards, bed making, bedpan clearing and hundreds of other tasks, my job was to look after the babies with cleft palates. There were four of the poor little mites, all under the age of three months and all at various stages of surgery.

Their surgery was in the hands of an extraordinary man by the name of Sir Denis Browne.

Towering over everyone at 6ft 5in, he cut an imposing figure as strode through the wards, his underlings frantically trying to keep up. One always knew he was coming; it was like the parting of the Red Sea. Junior staff were simply swept aside whenever he made his rounds. All consultants received this treatment to some extent, mind you: they were treated like gods.

Legend had it that Sir Denis, a proficient tennis player in his youth, would clear seats from the outpatients' hall and practise his shots after hours, while his maid was constantly restoring his furniture to its proper place so that he could not do the same thing at home. Apparently he was so infuriated by this that he nailed his chair to the floor.

He was better known, though, for being the founder of modern paediatric surgery and he made advances in many fields of surgery, particularly club feet, hypospadias and cleft palate in newborns.

But while the surgery of the babies' cleft palates was in Sir Denis's skilled hands, their feeding was left to the less auspicious and experienced hands of one Brenda Ashford.

When I was first allocated the task I wasn't too daunted. I had fed my brother his bottle all the time when he was just a babe in arms. Surely it couldn't be that difficult, right? Wrong.

I spent hours trying to feed those poor little babies. I was never taught or shown how to, just left to get on with it. The milk would bubble out their noses or come gushing out the sides of their mouths.

All the while their little faces would grow red with frustration and hunger as they roared for food. It was so distressing and heartbreaking. At night their cries echoed in my ears.

I didn't dare tell ward sister I felt uncomfortable doing it. I would doubtless have been sent off with a flea in my ear.

Once it was assigned to a junior nurse but I heard her mutter to her colleague, 'Let the Norlanders do it.' After that I knew my place.

Today the job of caring for a newborn with a cleft palate is considered tricky and given to a specialist in the field with appropriate training, but back in 1939 it was left to girls with very little experience.

As far as I was concerned it all just compounded my sense of failure at the hospital.

It probably didn't help that I also seemed to be continually ill.

If I wasn't struck down with a vicious strep throat and confined to quarantine in my room, I was sporting some impressive warts.

Soon after a particularly nasty one had sprouted on my hand, ward sister informed us we were to be ready to receive a very important visitor. Princess Marina, the wife of the Duke of Kent, was to pay a visit to our ward. Great Ormond Street has always had close links with the Royal Family, ever since Queen Victoria became a patron.

'Keep your cuffs on and don't speak unless spoken to,' ward sister told us when she assembled us all together in the ward.

Apparently Princess Marina was very interested to meet Norland nurses training on the wards. She herself had been cared for by a Norland Nurse, one Kate Fox. Nurse Fox looked after her in the royal palace in Athens and taught Princess Marina her prayers in English, even before she learnt them in her native Greek. It was said that as a six-year-old she had aspired to a career as a Norland Nurse, even making herself a uniform and organising her dolls into a Norland nursery.

I'm sure it would have been lovely to hear of these reminisces from Princess Marina but by that point my confidence was badly dented. So terrified was I of doing or saying the wrong thing to the visiting Princess, that I'm ashamed to say I hid in the milk room when she arrived at my ward. Mercifully for Princess Marina, she was spared from shaking my wart-covered hand.

Shortly after the Princess's visit I was scurrying up the stairs to the wards one morning, silently cursing my leather shoes for squeaking so loudly on the highly polished steps, when I clean forgot not to overtake someone on the stairs. I was lost in my own thoughts.

Must not be late Brenda. Must not be late.

I had at least twenty bedpans to clean before lunch and my cleft palate babies to feed, milk to prepare, beds to strip . . .

Suddenly a voice carried up the stairs behind me.

'Excuse me, wait a moment.'

My heart practically stopped. Oh no. What on earth had I done now? Whirling round, despair hit me between the eyes.

The voice belonged to a nurse more senior than me. I'd walked up the stairs in front of her. Why did I keep on making mistakes? Why? I was like a round peg in a square hole.

'I'm sorry,' I said miserably, quite unable to meet her gaze.

The voice when it came was not at all what I expected.

'It's fine,' said the small, soft voice.

I looked up hesitantly. The voice belonged to the most unusual person I'd ever seen.

I'd not seen many black people. There were hardly any where I came from.

This lady was quite exquisite. She reminded me of a little bird. Her features were so tiny and delicate she looked like she'd been carved from marble. Enormous eyes the colour of milk chocolate gazed out from a petite face. I felt like a gallumping great carthorse in comparison.

Then she smiled and placed a delicate hand on mine. Her slender fingers were cool and strangely comforting.

'You wouldn't do me an enormous favour, would you?' she said, smiling sweetly. 'I've laddered my stockings. I have to see matron this morning and I urgently need a new pair. There's a shop round the corner that sells them.'

She was fragrant charm itself. The bedpans could wait. I'd walk to the ends of the earth for this lady.

'Of course,' I gushed. 'Right away.'

Instinctively, I liked her. She spoke with a gentleness that reminded me of my mother. She wasn't efficient and brusque like all the other staff here.

Black stockings duly purchased, I rushed back to find the mystery lady. I was so gratified at being given a task I knew would earn me praise that I didn't even mind the prospect of a dressing down from the ward sister.

My mystery lady was so grateful she even invited me for a cup of tea in her room later. It was here that I found out more about her. Instinct told me she had a fascinating story and I was not wrong.

Her name was Princess Tsahai and she was the third daughter of Emperor Haile Selassie of Abyssinia (modern-day Ethiopia).

'I was forced to flee in 1936 after Germany's ally Italy, under the leadership of Mussolini, invaded my country.'

Her soft voice was tinged with sadness as she played with the hem of her skirt.

I was mesmerised by the sight of her tiny, delicate hands gently stroking the cotton hem.

'My beautiful country is being devastated and our people slaughtered,' she sighed.

'You must miss your family and homeland very much,' I said, feeling suddenly very homesick myself.

She fixed me with a dazzling smile. 'I do, Brenda, but I am very lucky to be able to use this time in exile by training here as a nurse. I love children so much,' she went on.

'Oh me too,' I agreed.

'I'd like to take what I learn here and set up a hospital in Abyssinia when I return, so women can have access to trained midwives and our children can have the same health services they have here in the UK.'

'Do children suffer in your country?' I asked, all naivety.

'There is much poverty and many women and children die young. We have to change this.'

Her soft voice was suddenly stirred with passion and conviction and I saw fire in those big brown eyes. Her body may have been tiny but a lion's heart beat within it. There was no doubt in my mind she would achieve her goal.

I was in total awe of this lady and suddenly I felt quite unworthy. All this time I'd been feeling sorry for myself for being a fish out of water. How could I feel homesick and self-pitying when she'd been forced to flee her country? Her story touched my heart.

After that I found an ally in the Princess. I was just a lowly student nanny and she was royalty from an incredible dynasty. Her family ancestry could be traced all the way back to the exotic and mysterious Queen of Sheba.

Yet there were no airs and graces with the Princess. On the wards she always greeted me with a ravishing smile and made time to enquire how I was. Every time I committed another etiquette faux pas the Princess would seek me out. One gentle smile of understanding from her and my worries would melt away.

I watched her with the children and her love and gentleness with these little folk was quite instinctive. Many of them were the poorest of the poor from local districts and I doubted they had the faintest clue the little lady with the big brown eyes who tended to them so gently was a real life princess.

My friendship with her was a truly humbling experience. It may have started with stockings but I like to think it blossomed into a mutual respect based on a love of children.

Life has many twists and turns, and tragically, fate had other plans for the Princess.

She did indeed return home to newly liberated and renamed Ethiopia in June 1941, her heart stirred by all she had learnt and with a clutch of diplomas from Great Ormond Street Hospital and Guy's Hospital under her nurse's belt. She immediately set about her plans to use her newly acquired skills to help the sick children of her country. The Princess also found love with a General and fell pregnant.

Within a year of her return she died from complications during childbirth. Her child also died. She was just 24.

Princess Tsahai had survived Mussolini's invasion and Hitler's bombs only be to killed by the failings in medical expertise she was so desperate to eradicate.

A memorial hospital bearing her name was later established in Addis Ababa, in the shadow of a holy volcanic mountain. Her diplomas hang proudly on the walls and an elegant statue carved from marble with a small child at its feet graces the main hallway. I shall never forget her quiet strength and kindness.

When you are bogged down in the everyday details and

routine of a big institution like Great Ormond Street it's easy to forget that there is life outside. As at the Norland itself, we didn't get much time off, and the wider world didn't permeate the intense order of the hospital wards.

In any case, student nurses didn't want to socialise with us 'untrained' Norlanders so most evenings I sat in my room reading, or simply fell asleep exhausted. I was so focussed on my children and trying not to get into trouble that I quite forgot we were slap bang in the middle of a seething metropolis.

A city that was about to undergo one of the most devastating events in its history.

I was cleaning out a bedpan and thinking about the following day. I was due to get my warts zapped with a new treatment at the hospital called electro-cautery.

I was just thinking what a blessed relief it would be to get rid of the unsightly things when the ward sister approached me.

'You and the rest of the Norlanders are to report to matron's office immediately,' she said.

I hurried down the corridor after her and waited to be announced to the matron. Once we were all ushered inside, the matron opened her mouth to speak and seconds later, all worries of my wart suddenly paled into insignificance.

Matron's usually composed features were ashen. Her voice when it came was strangely stilted.

'At 11.15 this morning Prime Minister Neville Chamberlain speaking on BBC radio announced the news that we are at war with Germany. The hospital is being evacuated. You are to go home immediately and await further instruction from the Norland.'

We sat in deafening silence before getting to our feet and thanking matron.

The unthinkable had happened.

As I exited the hospital, blinking in the sunlight, I took great gulps of fresh air. I felt waves of relief wash over me: I was out of that place. No more dressing downs from ward sister, no more invisible codes of conduct or rules to unwittingly break. I was free.

Just as quickly as it had arrived, the relief was replaced with guilt. How could I count my blessings when war had just broken out?

For a good few minutes I stood stock still on the pavement, my head spinning. Everything had happened so fast, I felt as if I'd been dumped here by a whirlwind. I hadn't even had a chance to say goodbye to my cleft palate babies or Princess Tsahai.

I must have been the only person in London standing still. The streets were a teeming mass of bewildered people, all scurrying around like worker ants. It was truly a strange sight to behold.

There was an urgent pace to people's movements. A breathless stillness hung over the buildings. People stopped, looked to the skies as if they half expected a German bomber to fly overhead there and then, before briskly walking on, lost in their own thoughts.

The sense of urgency lay over everything like a black cloud.

Plans were aborted, meals hurriedly finished and offices closed for the day.

Catching the tube and then the train on my own would usually have been a thing of great fear and uncertainty, but I took this journey in a total daze. Even my feet seemed to move with a life of their own.

It was gone 10.00 p.m. by the time I alighted at Leatherhead station but despite the dark, the streets here were teeming with life and activity, too.

Brick dust and mortar hung in the air from where people had started adapting old outhouses into rest centres. In my absence many people, predicting the outbreak of war, had already erected Anderson shelters in their back gardens. Trucks trundled past loaded with green stretchers and blankets. First aid posts and air raid shelters were springing up all over the place.

Civil defence plans were already bursting into life. Everyone had been expecting it, had seen it coming. Suddenly I felt a little foolish. With all the arrogance of youth I had been so immersed in my life that I had failed to see what was going on in the wider world.

Wearily I let myself into the kitchen, much to the surprise of my mother and father.

'We'd have collected you if we'd known you were coming back so soon,' gasped mother.

All the boys were still on the Isle of Wight and Kathleen in London so I sat at the table with Mother and Father drinking cups of hot sweet tea. We didn't want to go to bed; I doubt anyone did that night.

Instead we listened to the wireless and a repeat of the King's Speech. I think I was too young to appreciate the gravity of his words but I fell silent out of respect as the King's hesitant voice crackled out of the wireless to all the people of his empire.

In this grave hour, perhaps the most fateful in our history, I send to every household of my peoples, both at home and overseas, this message, spoken with the same depth of feeling for each one of you as if I were able to cross your threshold and speak to you myself. For the second time in the lives of most of us, we are at war. Over and over again, we have tried to find a peaceful way out of the differences between ourselves and those who are now our enemies; but it has been in vain. We have been forced into a conflict, for we are called, with our allies, to meet the challenge of a principle which, if it were to prevail, would be fatal to any civilised order in the world. It is a principle which permits a state, in the selfish pursuit of power, to disregard its treaties and its solemn pledges, which sanctions the use of force or threat of force against the sovereignty and independence of other states. Such a principle, stripped of all disguise, is surely the mere primitive doctrine that might is right, and if this principle were established through the world, the freedom of our own country and of the whole British Commonwealth of nations would be in danger. But far more than this, the peoples of the world would be kept in bondage of fear, and all hopes of settled peace and of security, of justice and liberty, among nations, would be ended. This is the ultimate issue which confronts us. For the sake of all that we ourselves hold dear, and of the world order and peace, it is unthinkable that we should refuse to meet the challenge. It is to this high purpose that I now call my people at home, and my peoples across the seas, who will make our cause their own. I ask them to stand calm and firm and united in this time of trial. The task will be hard. There may be dark days ahead, and war can no longer be confined to the battlefield, but we can only do the right as we see the right, and reverently commit our cause to God. If one and all we keep resolutely faithful to it, ready for whatever service or sacrifice it may demand, then with God's help, we shall prevail. May he bless and keep us all.

When the King's voice fell silent, Father looked emotionally wrung out. He squeezed his eyes shut and leant back heavily in his chair. And so it was. World War Two had begun.

Having fought on the front line in World War One and witnessed unimaginable loss of life, he knew what I could never even begin to fathom. There are no winners in war.

'Will you go to war, Father?' I asked eventually.

His proud face stiffened.

'No,' he snapped, suddenly full of indignant rage. 'They say I'm too old. What rubbish. I am only fifty. I could teach those young men a thing or two.'

I thought of the Military Cross medal he'd been awarded for his bravery during the conflict, hidden away in a drawer upstairs. I didn't doubt it for a second.

Two days later an air-raid siren was installed in the centre of our community and it was quickly agreed that a trial run was necessary.

Nothing could have prepared me for the noise. I was helping mother peel potatoes when it sounded. My knife dropped into the sink with a clatter.

The siren's haunting wail left us speechless. I could feel its sickening drone right down in the pit of my tummy. Paralysed with fear I stayed rooted to the spot.

Mother put her arm round me to comfort me but this was one fear she couldn't banish with a cuddle.

Stray ships moved on a dark sea, people huddled down in shelters. The world watched . . . and waited.

5

East End Evacuees

Twinkle twinkle little star, how I wonder what you are.
Up above the world so high, like a diamond in the sky.
English nineteenth-century lullaby

WITH THE sound of the siren still ringing in my ears I boarded a train bound for Ashford in Kent. I had received word that I was to join the Norland to continue my third and final term of training at Hothfield Place in the village of Hothfield.

As the train clattered out of London and the densely packed streets gave way to wide open spaces and green fields, I felt my spirits lift. The sickening feeling of terror that had clawed at my heart ever since hearing that infernal siren seemed to loosen with every mile.

Bathed in late summer sunshine Kent looked absolutely glorious. The skies were dappled with cloud and the apple orchards took on a pinkish hue.

'I think I'm going to like it here,' I thought as I settled back in my seat and let the rocking of the train lull me into a warm, safe dream.

The loud shriek of the train's whistle pulled me from my slumber and announced my arrival.

Lugging my huge trunk onto the station platform I tried to get my bearings. The babble of travellers' voices and the heat from the steam made me feel suddenly weary.

Just then the steam cleared and a familiar figure emerged.

It was none other than tall, athletic and highly efficient Mary Rutherford, our head girl. With her Norland cape flapping behind her as she bounded along the steamy train platform, she looked like a super-nanny!

'Brenda,' boomed Mary, enveloping me in an enthusiastic hug. 'Marvellous to see you again old thing.'

Ever punctual, Mary had taken an earlier train, but it looked as if the rest of our set would be arriving later, so Mary and I settled down in the station café over a pot of tea to chat while we waited. There was a lot to talk about: the world had changed a great deal since the last time we were together.

Soon we were joined by the rest of the gang, shy country girl Joan, exotic French aristo Yvonne and lovely Scottish Margaret.

The babble of excited teenage voices filled the air.

'Where are we going?' piped up Margaret, her once broad Scottish accent now softened by months of Norland's elocution lessons.

'I hear it's a stately home, no less,' said Joan. 'Wonder if it still has servants.'

'Shouldn't think so,' sniffed Yvonne. 'Daddy had to get rid of most of his after the First War.'

Joan and I exchanged a secret smile. Aristo Yvonne still hadn't quite lived down the humiliation of having to learn to make her own bed at Pembridge Square.

Norland sent a car to collect us and soon we were whizzing through the stunning Kent countryside.

I thought where we lived in Surrey was picturesque but the landscape of the garden of England was simply beautiful. Hop farms and orchards, still groaning with late summer fruit, stretched out as far as the eye could see. A light dreamy mist swirled over the fields, only punctuated by the tips of the roofs of curious looking oast houses.

As we got closer to Hothfield the landscape changed.

Hothfield Place was located in the ancient village of the same name. Wide flat boggy heath led into the village centre, with a beautiful common and a thirteenth-century church at its heart.

Livestock grazed on the common and a sense of idle tranquillity abounded. People round these parts lived off the fat of the land and village life had remained unchanged for centuries.

It was a peaceful idyll. The only sounds were the gentle warbling salute of a blackbird from the eaves of a stone cottage and the far off rumble of a tractor.

As the late afternoon shadows lengthened and the sun dipped over the church spire I could make out blackberries glistening invitingly from the hedgerows, just begging to be picked.

Smoke curled from the chimney pots of warmly lit cottages as young boys playing football on the common packed up and headed for home, summoned by the thought of dripping-covered toast in front of a parlour fire.

'Hard to believe we're at war,' murmured Joan, gazing out the window.

I nodded. Where were the German bombers and constant air raid sirens we'd all been prepared for?

That blissful six-month period came to be known as the phoney war, a slow start to hostilities that would soon enough become horrific beyond our comprehension, but back then it was all too easy to fool oneself into thinking that Neville Chamberlain's announcement had all been just a nasty dream.

I had heard that Hothfield Place was a stately home but nothing could have prepared me for its dramatic beauty.

As the car turned a corner onto a long drive, us five girls all gasped simultaneously.

A beautiful big Adams mansion set in 350 acres of rolling parkland stood before us. The gathering dusk only served to make its facade more dramatic.

'Wow,' whistled Joan.

'So beautiful,' sighed Margaret.

'I can't believe this is to be our home girls,' I said, grinning excitedly.

By the time our car slid to a halt, it was obvious that the old home was in fact a hive of bustling activity. As well as the nursery staff and the rest of the students, the entire Bethnal Green day nursery were here too, having been evacuated lock, stock and barrel a couple of weeks before. We numbered forty-four children and seventy-five adults in all!

Heavy furniture was being lifted in and out of the magnificent stone arched doorway, coach prams were lined up like soldiers on parade in the driveway and excited little children tore round the grounds like mini tornados.

Where once, horse-drawn carriages would have slowed to a halt and aristocratic ladies and gentleman graciously alighted, now little East End evacuees chased each other in a riot of noise. The babble of their excited voices merged into one big humming sound. Doleful-looking cows in neighbouring fields stared curiously over the fences at the commotion.

Presiding over the lot, like an oasis of calm was Miss White-head, still managing to look immaculate and unflustered in her blue uniform and scarlet-lined cape.

One little girl nearly knocked Miss Whitehead clean off her feet as she chased a little boy hollering up the drive, her blonde curls bobbing furiously.

I smiled as I remembered the games of cowboys and Indians that my brothers and I had played growing up at Hallcroft.

Children's games don't seem to change that much, wherever you're from.

'Slow down Elsie,' barked Miss Whitehead. 'You'll do someone an injury.'

But instead of cowering under the principal's steely gaze the little girl grinned cheekily up at her, her blue eyes flashing with an irrepressible spirit.

She may have had the face of an angel but her voice when she spoke was like nothing I'd heard before.

'Gor blimey, it aint arf perishing ere Miss White'ead. I goddi go in the cat and mouse and get me weasel and stoat so as I ave,' she jabbered. 'If you sees that Pete Brown tell 'im 'e better watch it an all, reckons I pen and ink like a bleedin pig 'e does, 'e can stick that right up 'is Kyber I'm tellin 'yer.'

I didn't have a clue what it was she had said but it was all rattled off like machine gun fire. Pen and ink . . . weasel and stoat? Elsie may as well have been speaking in Spanish.

Born and bred in the back streets of the East End, this girl had been brought up around the rich and colourful dialect that is cockney rhyming slang.

I only really understood snippets of what she said but I liked her instinctively. She was bursting with exuberant joy.

I winked at Elsie and she winked back.

The Bethnal Green evacuees or Bethnal Greenies as they came to be known were like no children I'd ever met before. They were tough little kids that walked with a swagger and talked in a language of their own. They may have been uprooted from their homes and separated from their families but nothing could crush their spirits, nor dampen their excitement at being in Hothfield. Most of them had never left Bethnal Green, much less been to the countryside. A few may have been to Kent before with their families for the annual hop-picking harvest, where whole East End families worked by day in the fields collecting the hops and slept in barns at night, and treated it as a holiday. But for most, the fresh air, fields and wildlife of the countryside were completely alien.

Imagine never having seen a pig, sheep or cow in your life, then suddenly being exposed to them all, aged five. All this, not to mention that the sight of the enormous house had them in raptures.

'Are you having a lovely time?' I asked Elsie as Miss Whitehead retreated back into the safety of the house.

'Not arf,' she said, wiping her runny nose on her sleeve. 'We saw a cow being milked afore. Knows where the milk comes from?'

Her blue eyes grew as wide as dinner plates.

'Only from a 'ole in it's bum.'

I snorted with laughter.

Seconds later she was gone, sprinting towards the house and bounding up the stairs two at a time.

'I think I'm going to like it here very much,' I said to Joan, linking arms with her and walking into my new home.

Joan and I paused inside the black and white marble hall and stopped to take in our surroundings.

'Wow,' I whistled. 'This hall is bigger than my whole house.'

Heading up a sweeping marble staircase and onto the first floor, we found the sense of excitement and confusion was only slightly reined in.

Norland's registrar, Miss Hewer, a usually unflappable woman in her fifties who always wore her grey hair scraped back in a rather severe bun, was looking decidedly flustered as she stood in what was once the drawing room. Priceless furniture and valuable heirlooms were stacked up in the middle of the room looking for all the world like an antiques bonfire.

'One knows not where to start,' she muttered, staring at a sea of boxes.

All the babies were in two nurseries called Daisy and Spring, older children in night nurseries around the Gallery that looked down on the main hall. The Bethnal Greenies were in a big nursery in what was once the billiard room. Miss Whitehead's office was in a small drawing room. The library was turned over to a communal day nursery for meals, play and lectures. Our kitchen was an old stillroom and a laundry was made of a brushing room. Dozens of bicycles for our use were lined up in the stables.

Centuries of unchanged tradition had all been turned on its head in the space of weeks.

Best of all, all the children's rooms had the most wonderful views over lush green fields. Painted in sunshine yellow they contrasted beautifully with the wooden nursery furniture.

A nursery today might contain any number of things, from musical mobiles, digital video baby monitors and bottle warmers to nappy bins and fleece-topped baby changing tables.

Back then all they contained was a plain wooden cot with cotton sheets and an eiderdown, pink for the girls, blue for the boys and a few simple toys donated by generous locals from the village, alongside a plain wardrobe.

We didn't rely on monitors, a baby's cry was usually sufficient to wake us and we had no need of nappy bins. All the dirty nappies were dumped in a bucket of warm water to soak before being scrubbed clean.

As we wandered round the huge house I couldn't help but speculate about the previous occupants of Hothfield Place. Just where were the owners of this treasure trove of a house? Had they offered it to the Norland, had the house been requisitioned for our use or had they simply left at the outbreak of war? It was so strange and baffling.

One thing was for sure, the house fair hummed with the spirit of its ancestors. All along the walls, ancient paintings of past generations of Hothfield's resident family, the Tuftons, gazed down on us with a look of mild surprise. How shocked they would have been to see the Bethnal Greenies tearing around the grounds.

Suddenly we became aware of Miss Whitehead clapping her hands and summoning everyone into the library. We hurried in and took our places.

'Your attention, ladies, please,' she called.

A hush descended over the library.

Staring at the cool and unruffled Miss Whitehead I marvelled at her stamina.

Over the past two weeks she had overseen the entire evacuation, including every last item of furniture and every small person, from London to Kent. I don't think I fully appreciated at the time what an organisational undertaking that was. Not only that but she had lost numerous members of staff who had left to offer their services to the war effort. Our principal was keeping the Institute going on a skeleton staff.

But if anyone could do it then the formidable Miss Whitehead could. Heroes and heroines are born in times of crisis and I had every faith our principal would guide us through this war.

Conflict was nothing new to the Norland, mind you. During World War One the Institute took in refugees, and the children in the nursery school did their bit by fraying scraps of material with which cushions for wounded limbs were stuffed.

We would rise to the challenge once again.

Miss Whitehead cleared her throat.

'Lord Hothfield, by whose generosity we are here, is letting us have practically the whole house, which has not been used for some time. He and his family live in only a small part of it but you must show them the utmost consideration and courtesy should your paths cross.'

Heads nodded eagerly.

Ahh, the mystery was solved. How generous this gentleman was to hand his magnificent house over to the Institute. Mind you, I suspect he found it hard to say no to a request from Miss Whitehead.

'What a hideous change has taken place in the world since we last met,' she continued. 'The dreaded war has now come. The only person left in Pembridge Square is Miss Bidden who valiantly remains to carry on with the uniform department. The rooms are stacked with what furniture couldn't be brought and the empty nurseries echo at night.'

I shuddered to think of the solitary lecturer sitting behind her vast sewing machine. Hitler may have had London in his sights but that wasn't enough to tear that brave lady away from her sewing duties.

A look of quiet satisfaction flashed over Miss Whitehead's face as she imparted her next piece of news.

'I met recently with the Archbishop of Canterbury.'

She paused to allow the revelation of her impressive connections to sink in.

'He would like you all to know that he has high regard for the nature of your work. The Archbishop told us we must continue to lead normal lives and be "steadfast, courageous and full of good cheer."'

A wave of applause went up round the room. A tingle of excitement prickled up my spine. By Golly we'd show the Jerries.

'Our part, ladies, is to keep war from the children, to give the evacuees' parents the comfort and security of knowing they are happy and safe, and to carry on as normally as we can. If we can enjoy a realisation that what we are doing is useful, then some personal discomfort should be of minor importance. To these small folk, the war with all its suffering and anxieties must be a sealed book.'

I thought of little Elsie's parents, still living and working in Bethnal Green, facing God knows what dangers. What they wouldn't do to be in this haven of tranquillity with their beloved little girl. I owed it to them to care for Elsie as if she were my own blood.

'These days of war are anxious days for everyone,' Miss Whitehead continued. 'The future seems to hold so much to dread and so little to hope for, but we must have hope. It is out highest duty.'

With that she nodded, then swept from the room leaving us students gazing after her in awe. She could give Churchill a run for his money!

Night-time falls quickly in the countryside and after a delicious supper of cold meat and potatoes, followed by blackberry and apple pie drowned under a blanket of thick double cream, it was time to retire to our beds.

By 8.00 p.m. the whole house lay under a heavy blanket of velvety dark, with just a dusting of stars. I had never known a night like it. With no street lights and not even a solitary lamp from the village twinkling over the fields, we were engulfed in the black of the night.

It was not helped by the blackout. Every window in the house was covered with regulation thick blackout material. Finding our way round this pitch-black stately home at night was going to be no mean feat.

The girls and I giggled as we fumbled our way up the three flights of stairs to our bedroom. Because of a shortage of batteries we had just one torch between us. The tiredness and excitement of the day had whipped us into a fever pitch of nervous hysteria and every time the torch fell on the face of an ancient Tufton gazing down solemnly from a picture, we'd scream and clutch one another.

Our shins were bashed black and blue on random pieces of furniture as we yelped and giggled our way through the darkness of the old house.

By the time we reached our rooms in the former servants' quarters up in the attic, we were beyond help.

The old door looked forbidding.

'You go first,' I hissed to Yvonne.

'No, you,' she said with a shiver.

'Oh stand aside,' Mary said. 'I'll go.'

As Mary pushed open the door to the dark room I felt a cold chill wrap around my spine. It was so spooky.

Our torch threw long shadows, which flickered over the stone walls. The old servants' quarters were icy cold, situated as they were in the roof with no means of heating except tiny grates for coal fires. They hadn't been used for generations and the cold seemed to creep right through to my bones. I shivered and pulled my coat tightly around me as I sank exhausted onto a hard single bed.

The rooms had recently been decorated with a glue-based distemper and the foul smell of old chalk, glue, disinfectant and damp crept up my nostrils and turned my stomach.

Everywhere whispered with the ghosts of servants past. If I closed my eyes I could almost see the faint outline of a chambermaid scurrying to bed.

'Wonder if these rooms are haunted?' whispered Yvonne.

'Aye,' said Margaret with a naughty grin. 'Bet they are. I heard the butler had an affair with a young maid and not wanting his wife to discover, he murdered her. Her headless body still roams these rooms seeking revenge on her former lover.'

She paused for dramatic effect.

'She slept in that bed right where you are sitting now, Brenda.'

I froze.

'Booh,' yelled Mary. I jumped so violently my torch clattered to the stone floor.

'Quiet up there, girls,' hissed a voice from down below.

Of course, Margaret's story was just that, a silly story, but as we huddled under our blankets I couldn't help but wonder who had slept here all those years before. This grand old house must have seen some sights in its day and if its walls could talk you could be sure they'd have some tales to tell.

Back in the sixteenth century, Hothfield Place belonged to the Archbishop of Canterbury before he gave it to a man by the name of John Tufton for unknown services rendered, for which the King also awarded him the title First Baron of Hothfield in 1542.

Henry James Tufton was the first to be created Lord Hothfield in the late nineteenth century, by which time the estate, comprising 1,815 acres, ranked as one of the most affluent of its time.

Lord Hothfield and his wife, Alice, had three sons, Johnnie, Sackville and Charlie and one daughter, Rosamund.

The property boasted a dairy herd of Guernsey cows, stables, dovecotes, a waterfall, a laundry, a brew house, a dairy, a churning house, fruit, corn and wool rooms. The family were entirely self-sufficient and even had their own gas works for lighting, an icehouse and a timber yard, oh and a fire station! There simply was no need ever to leave Hothfield.

If they did wish to, they could always use the railway station Lord Hothfield had built, which he called Hothfield Halt. The train transported produce from his walled garden at Hothfield to his London house, via the Ashford to London line.

To keep this estate serviced the Tuftons employed a small army of domestic servants.

On the ground floor there was a butler's flat, a bath, a vast kitchen area, servants' hall, lifts and five toilets.

Servants were a vital indicator of status and Lord Hothfield had forty at the mansion alone, including first and second coachmen, seven strappers to look after the horses, serving maids and scullery maids. That figure doesn't include all the farmhands, gardeners, carpenters, gamekeepers, gas engineers, ice workers and milk maids, right down to the lowly laundry maids, most of whom lived in the village, which was largely owned by Lord Hothfield.

He also had a home in Chesterfield Gardens in London and large estates at Appleby Castle in Cumbria and Skipton Castle in Yorkshire. He usually only visited Hothfield with his family at Christmas, when Lady Hothfield arranged a party and concert at the mansion, and for two months in the summer for the Hothfield Park Cricket Club matches.

Lady Hothfield was a legendary socialite and had a great reputation for running her houses. Houseguests would stay for weeks at a time and their every need and whim was catered for.

The divisions between Lord Hothfield and his staff, and between staff themselves were carefully maintained. There was strict protocol dictating into which parts of the house servants might venture, which corridors, stairs and doors they could use, depending on whether they were an upper house or lower house servant. A whole army of servants beavered away, behind the scenes and out of sight of the Tuftons.

It was a hard life. I thought of the young chambermaids who would have lain down exhausted, where I was right now, after working a sixteen-hour day.

They rose at 6.00 a.m. and before the wealthier members of the house stirred had lit fires, swept and dusted the rooms.

Then their days would have been filled with tasks such as scrubbing floors, cleaning toilets, fetching and carrying pails of hot water, cleaning out oven ranges and coal fires, polishing furniture, mirrors, windows and countless other tasks before falling into bed at 10.00 p.m.

I wondered what the efficient hostess, Lady Hothfield, was like to work for. I could only be grateful I hadn't been around to find out because you could be sure if there was a servant who would venture accidentally into the wrong corridor or open the wrong door it would be me! My brief spell doing the back-breaking washing and flat-ironing at Pembridge Square was enough to make me thank my lucky stars I wasn't born to a life of doing Hothfield's extensive laundry.

After the turmoil of the First World War country house life was never the same again. Young girls became reluctant to go into service when they could work in shops, factories and offices, while the men who had gone to war ended up 'spoiled for service' after the novelty of generous military pay. Add to that the costs of rebuilding the nation after the horrific conflict and the global economic crisis of the 1930s, and many families found they simply could not afford to live as they once had. A way of life was gone for good. From 1930 the influence of the Tuftons declined.

And so it was that we Norlanders found ourselves living in this vast house, albeit not in the grand style of Lady Hothfield's houseguests. It was ironic, I thought to myself, that Emily Ward fought so hard not to have Norland nannies treated like servants yet here we all were, confined to the servants' quarters. But then I suppose war does strange things.

For the rest of the night not a living soul stirred.

I slept fitfully and the next morning felt quite exhausted and bleary-eyed. Not for long.

Us girls were required to wash in the ground floor

washroom where the servants once bathed. Three enamel baths were sunk into the floor, surrounded by vast flagstone tiles. It was so cold that ice formed on the inside of the small windows. The water, warm when it was poured in, became icy cold in minutes.

There was no privacy and we all had to get undressed in front of one another and jump in. Not that anyone minded getting naked in front of their fellow students. There was no time to worry about whether our bottoms looked big. We were too busy concentrating on how quickly we could get in, scrub ourselves with soap then hop out again. At least our bleary heads were quickly cleared with an icy rub down.

Seconds later the basement was filled with the sound of chattering teeth as we hopped about, drying off our goose bumps and changing into our uniforms.

Fortunately we were only required to bathe twice a week. Just as well as we'd surely have contracted pneumonia bathing in the basement every day!

On that first day, after a warming breakfast of porridge we had a walk around and bumped into Miss Edith Taylor, who ran the Bethnal Green nurseries and was in overall charge of the evacuees. She was coming back from a walk with some of her charges.

Her merry laugh and open features always inspired trust and confidence.

'Everyone has been so kind and we are so indebted to Miss Whitehead for bringing us here,' she said. 'Well-wishers have sent our little children glucose sweets and tins of biscuits. I think it's safe to say they are having the time of their lives.'

Right on cue, a curious noise rang out from a neighbouring field.

'Weee . . . weeeeee . . . weeeeee.'

The pitch grew higher and higher.

Suddenly a squealing little pink piglet burst out of a hedge-row and galloped full tilt the length of the field, with a crowd of Bethnal Greenies in hot pursuit on the other side of the fence.

'Children, calm down,' hollered Miss Taylor as they disappeared behind an ancient beech tree.

'Forgive them,' she said, with an apologetic smile. 'It's a new experience and the fresh air has quite gone to their heads.'

'Nothing to forgive,' I said. 'I love to see them playing so carefree.'

Miss Taylor nodded her agreement.

'True, Nurse Brenda. They are well, sturdy and happy and that is the most we can hope for. Their little souls are being filled with the beauty of nature.'

Suddenly I felt ashamed. I had grown up surrounded by green fields and places to roam. For these little children the streets were their playground. They had no mother to tempt them home with wafts of baking . . . their mothers were out working all the hours sent, cleaning offices. Guilt settled over my heart and I vowed never to take my good fortune for granted.

Over the coming days, as the Bethnal Greenies grew accustomed to their new home, I lived to see their little faces light up when they made some magical new countryside discovery.

The gentle slopes on the far side of the parkland made a perfect spot for roly-polies and you could bet little Elsie would be first to hurl herself down with a whoop, skirts tucked into her knickers.

Her joy and love of our new home was infectious.

''Ere, Brenda,' she called to me one morning. 'Cook said I could 'elp collects the eggs for breakfast. I was looking in the trees so I was . . . they only come from an 'en's arse.'

Later, at playtime, I saw her poking around in the

ornamental pond in the garden with a stick, her skirts spattered with mud.

I chuckled then thought nervously of other stories I had heard of evacuee children frying goldfish they had found to eat.

When they weren't climbing trees, wading in streams and collecting feathers, they'd come in from their walks their mouths stained bright purple from eating blackberries straight from the hedgerows.

'There's a lot of room in the countryside aint there,' Elsie remarked one day.

I couldn't have put it better myself.

Over the weeks the children grew to love and respect the countryside and it's furry occupants. Particularly young Elsie. She befriended every horse, pig and cow within a twenty-mile radius.

But one crisp morning Elsie and her gang saw something that I am sure, if they are still alive today, they will remember as if it were yesterday.

We were coming back from a stroll when a shrill and rapid noise screamed across the fields.

Every animal and small child in the vicinity paused, their nostrils quivering.

Seconds later a fox leapt from its hiding place and tore across the fields towards us . . . shortly followed by a pack of slavering beagles, in hot pursuit.

The children didn't know it but they were witnessing the local Ashford Valley Hunt and a countryside tradition.

Suddenly the ground seemed to shake beneath our very feet as over the brow of a hill a dozen or so magnificent horses galloped towards us, their tails streaming behind them.

The master, resplendent in his scarlet jacket, had the fox in his sights and the hunt was on.

The dogs, scenting a kill, upped their pace.

The terrified fox bobbed this way and that but he was no match for the dogs and he seemed certain to meet a grisly and bloody end in the jaws of one of those beasts.

Suddenly, little Elsie drew herself up, her face red with rage.

'Flamin' cheek,' she huffed. 'Who they fink they are chasing an 'armless fox? RUN,' she hollered.

She was joined by the rest of the Bethnal Greenies.

'LEG IT, RUN,' they whooped and yelled, stamping their feet and bellowing like a pack of angry fishwives.

Perhaps his own personal East End cheerleading team spurred the fox on because he ducked into thick brambles and outwitted the dogs, much to the relief of Elsie and her gang.

'Aah,' sighed Miss Whitehead behind us. 'The agonies of anxiety.'

I'd have loved to spend more time with the Bethnal Greenies but my attentions had to be elsewhere. Knowing how we loved the babies, Miss Whitehead had put Joan and me in charge of the baby nursery. Every student had to have a go and presently it was our turn.

We had five babies in all and when we were on night duty we would both sleep in the large double bed in the nursery that served as the perfect place to change a baby's nappy during the day.

When one sense is blocked out the others quickly become more acute. The darker the nights got as the year turned to autumn and the less we could see, the more sensitive my hearing became.

The old house was forever creaking and groaning, the ancient plumbing put under extra strain by its new occupants. Burst pipes were often followed by sudden deluges through the roof.

The hooting of owls drifted through the night sky and occasionally the soft cry of a little Bethnal Greenie, suddenly missing his or her mum, would reach the baby nursery.

Upon hearing those pitiful little cries my mind always returned to my own family. At night I missed Mother, Father and little David. I thought of them all sharing cocoa and listening to Father reading Rupert the Bear and my heart ached just a little.

Christopher, Michael and Basil all had each other for comfort on the Isle of Wight and Kathleen was busy with her training in London but little David was at home with Mother and Father.

How I longed to have a cuddle with them all.

Thankfully during the day there were plenty of chubby little souls that needed my cuddles and love and I was in my element caring for these new-born babies.

They were illegitimate babies, born as a result of a no doubt scandalous liaison. It is impossible to overstate the stigma then attached to childbirth out of wedlock. To find yourself unmarried and pregnant in the 1930s was a quite intolerable position in those harsher, more judgmental times.

Child adoption only became legal in 1926 so the fate for babies born out of wedlock was often uncertain. This was where the Norland stepped in. They gave a home for young mothers and their children until more permanent arrangements could be made.

In return for cooking, cleaning and general domestic duties young mothers could lodge at Hothfield, and us students would care for their babies and gain valuable experience in childcare. The mothers would come and breastfeed their children before returning them to us for their day-to-day care.

We weren't allowed to form friendships with them or even eat with them.

This may all sound strange to you but in many ways it was a godsend for the mothers. They had a roof over their heads, regular meals and the knowledge their babies were being cared for, all away from society's prying and judgmental eyes.

These ladies turned up at all hours with tiny babies in tow and we never knew who they were. I knew better than to ask where they had come from or what their stories were. But it didn't stop us wondering. Were they illicit liaisons between workhouse masters and young inmates, perhaps a chamber-maid at a London hotel and a wealthy married businessman? One thing was for sure, these women were nearly always young, pretty and vulnerable.

One morning I was summoned to the nursery to meet a new resident who would be under my care. The baby allo-cated to me was about ten days old and screaming at the top of her lungs, and her mother, Rose, a pretty, timid little thing about the same age as me, looked utterly distraught.

'M . . . my milk hasn't come in,' she managed between sobs. 'My baby Lilly. She won't feed.'

Breastfeeding had always been championed by the Institute and it was drummed into us that only three things are needed to establish successful breastfeeding: a healthy mother, a good sucking baby, and a stable nervous system.

Miss Liddiard of the Mothercraft Training Society asserted that, 'the mother should have good food, not too much, fresh air and healthy occupation. The only excuse for failure would be a very poor mother living on the dole.'

Well, this girl, slim as she was, didn't look as if she were starving.

'A good sucky baby. Some babies are rather sleepy and require concentration.'

It couldn't be that, this little one was raising Hothfield's rafters.

A stable nervous system. 'The nervous mother, unsure of herself, frightened that the baby is not progressing, imagines all sorts of non-existent complications, which reacts on the baby.'

I suspected this was the problem. Poor Rose looked scared stiff and who could blame her? She was such a pretty little thing, big brown eyes and soft brown curls. I wondered, as I always did, what on earth had led her here.

One thing was for certain. Whoever the father was he didn't want to know, otherwise she wouldn't have been here, but he was obviously wealthy. This baby wanted for nothing but stability. She had the best of the best, a shiny new Burlington carriage pram no doubt purchased from that emporium of fine goods, Gamages in Holborn, and the finest soft smock dresses. But her poor mother looked like she would have traded it all in a heartbeat for some love and a kind word. She was so shy she could barely meet my eye.

I thought of my first trembling days at the Institute.

'Come here,' I said, smiling and laying my hand on her shoulder. I felt her relax to my touch. 'Let's see if we can't get that milk to come. Your little girl is hungry.'

Together we gently applied the breast massage I'd been taught at Pembridge Square and when the first trickle of milk came in, her eyes shone and she gasped. 'Oh thank you,' she cried.

Picking up her baby, I handed her to Rose and the little one instantly latched on, gently suckling milk.

The screaming stopped and peace descended on the nursery.

'You're doing marvellously,' I reassured her, fetching her a glass of water.

I wondered at the bond between mother and baby as I watched this most magic and bonding of rituals.

When the baby finally fell contentedly asleep, little pools of milk gathered at the corners of her mouth, rosy cheeks gorged with her mother's milk, I felt a warm glow of satisfaction. The mother smiled at me and I knew in an instant that life didn't feel quite so bad for her.

'I have to go and report to Miss Whitehead for my duties now but thank you, Miss,' she said, looking me in the eye. She handed me her sleeping babe and scurried off.

We didn't speak much after that and I didn't dare risk a telling off by inviting friendship but an unspoken bond existed between us. She entrusted me with her baby day after day.

I often wonder what became of Rose and baby Lilly after I left Hothfield. I have no idea, but I hope she found the peace and security she and her little girl needed.

With each passing season the bonds between us girls strengthened and the camaraderie deepened. The misery of Great Ormond Street was long forgotten and even Amberley and my beloved baby brother didn't crowd my thoughts as they once had.

Autumn blew in and Hothfield became a kaleidoscope of red and gold. The damp smell of fallen leaves carried in the breeze.

The annual burning of winter bracken took place on the common nearby and its rich smell revived the senses. Windblown conkers were eagerly scooped up by the Bethnal Greenies, who challenged each other to conker fights.

But the lovely autumn quickly gave way to freezing cold snow.

We awoke one morning and pulled aside the blackout curtains to see a blanket of powdery snow had arrived overnight, covering everything as far as the eye could see. It was utterly magical.

Muffled squeals of delight rang out over the house when the Bethnal Greenies realised their playground had been transformed to a winter wonderland.

Wellies and mittens were hurriedly pulled on as the children charged outside between lessons. It was so deep it went right over the tops of their boots and Elsie and her gang let out great excited yelps as the snow melted and trickled between their toes. It would take more than soggy socks to stop these intrepid children and soon the gardens glittered like a snow storm as snowballs were hurled back and forth.

The winter of 1940 was the coldest winter recorded for forty-five years and the snows lasted for weeks. I can't remember anything like that winter in all my life. Milk, butter and other supplies were brought in from the village by sledge and the pipes constantly freezing were enough to try Miss Whitehead's legendary calm to the limit. The building looked like a giant white wedding cake with huge drifts of snow piled on the roof and fringes of icicles hanging off the edge of the porch.

But even the sub-zero temperatures weren't enough to stop Miss Whitehead from insisting that all the babies receive their daily dose of fresh air. We couldn't wheel the prams outside in such thick snow so instead we moved all the cots out there. Nothing but nothing would come between those babies and their fresh air!

What a sight! Rows of cots were lined up in the snow. Inside, chubby, rosy little faces peeked out from a warm nest of blankets.

They looked so cosy nestled up that I half-longed to join them, but there was far too much fun to be had at break times joining the Bethnal Greenies.

'Gotcha,' yelled Elsie as an expertly rolled snowball caught me right round the side of the face.

'That does it,' I yelled, charging after her.

Joan, Margaret, Yvonne, Mary and I couldn't resist joining the children. The tough little East Enders were expert at dodging this way and that and their snowballs were delivered with stinging precision. Suffice to say we students came off a lot worse than them!

The same slopes that had made such a perfect place for roly-polies in the late autumn sunshine now made ideal sledging ground.

Many an exciting hour was spent clinging to the edge of a toboggan as Elsie and her gang launched you off down the icy slopes. With the cries of 'ang on Brenda,' still ringing in my ears, my nerves tingled all over as I hit a tree stump and found myself suddenly airborne.

Later, as a clear moon rose over the house and the temperatures suddenly plunged, we all trooped inside for a warming mug of cocoa.

Having so much fun and banter on a daily basis it was so easy to forget we were in the middle of a war. In all the weeks we'd been here there hadn't been so much as a whiff of Hitler's forces or the threat of imminent invasion that had driven us all to this beautiful corner of Kent.

'What a funny collection of people we are, gathered under this roof,' I mused to myself one evening. Norland matrons, young students, Bethnal Green evacuees, illegitimate children and the ghosts of a bygone family. All blissfully coexisting, all helping one another through these uncertain, troubled times. I had grown most fond of our little community and the safety and warmth it represented. In fact I thought it couldn't get any better. Until Christmas and all its seasonal magic arrived.

What a joyous occasion. We had a 'never to be forgotten festival' and each child was sent presents and photos from home.

There were tears as little children suddenly remembered their mamas and papas left behind in London. But tears were quickly replaced with gasps of delight when after a dinner of turkey with all the trimmings, kindly donated by local farmers, each child opened a home-made and well filled Christmas stocking made by us nurses.

Then we all trooped upstairs to the spacious hall where Miss Whitehead had prepared an enormous tree. A toy babe snuggled underneath in a manger. The lights twinkled on the tree and then . . . the most magical thing of all happened.

The door swung open and a jolly fellow in a red suit appeared.

'It's Father Christmas,' screamed little Elsie.

Forty-four little jaws hit the floor.

Chaos broke out as Father Christmas walked in ringing a large bell and, joy of joy, pulling a sleigh groaning with presents.

'Me . . . me . . . me,' clamoured the excited evacuees. The joy was written all over their happy little faces.

Wrapping paper was eagerly torn off and discarded and murmurs and whoops of delight filled the room.

I looked over at Miss Whitehead. She was standing back, watching with a tired but happy little smile on her face. Only a woman such as her could have pulled all this out the bag in the middle of wartime!

Next we sat down to a tea of ham sandwiches and fairy cakes followed by party games.

As I watched the evacuees and the nurses I realised we were in a haven of security and joy. We may not have had our loved ones around us, we knew not what the future held, but we were all making the most of it. Even shy Rose was joining in with the games, laughing and clapping, her pretty brown eyes shining with delight.

That night the great house was comfortably silent as every occupant fell into a deep, exhausted and contented sleep.

Out in the wider world the phoney war was beginning to grate as people everywhere wondered what was going on and a sense of anti-climax settled in.

Mollie Panter-Downes, the *New Yorker*'s London correspondent described the public as 'feeling like a little boy who stuffs his fingers in his ears on the fourth of July, only to discover that the cannon cracker has not gone off after all.' Another journalist noted 'there was a greater danger of being hit by a vegetable marrow falling off the roof of an air raid shelter than of being struck by a bomb.'

Even the King in his Christmas broadcast said, 'We cannot tell what the New Year will bring. If it brings peace, how happy we shall all be.'

Eventually the freezing snows of winter thawed and revealed a countryside beautiful almost beyond recognition. Lambs frolicked round the fields, giving endless joy to Elsie and her crew of Bethnal Greenies, wild flowers burst from the hedgerows, and a mist of blossom spread over the orchards. The woodland around the common was blanketed in bluebells.

Again I marvelled at the fact that we were in the middle of a war. Rationing didn't much affect us, thanks to the abundant food supplies in the countryside and the kindness of the locals. The skies were endless and blue, without an enemy plane in sight. No one knew what the future held, so all we could do was live in the present.

And then, suddenly, I had more pressing problems than worrying about the German army. I was fighting a war of my own . . . against jaundice.

It had been going round the children and nurses like wildfire so I suppose it should have come as no surprise when I woke one morning to find every limb in my body aching. When I looked in the mirror, my hands flew to my face in horror.

'I'm yellow,' I screamed to a senior nurse. She took one look at me. 'Jaundice,' she said.

Within half an hour I was in quarantine in an upstairs bedroom and there I remained for the next fortnight, alone with only my thoughts for comfort. Dinner was left outside on a tray and I wallowed inside in utter misery.

I knew jaundice left you feeling yellow but I didn't realise it left you blue too! My emotions were all over the place and I cried at the drop of a hat. Suddenly I missed Mother, my babies in the nursery and my beloved David. And worst of all I had to take my final written examination.

'How will I do it feeling like this?' I cried.

There was no choice but to take the exam in my sickened state.

Mother had written to inform me she had a job with a family friend lined up for me the moment I passed, plus if I missed the exam, I might not get the funding for another term as my bursary would run out.

And so I found myself one spring morning in an upstairs bedroom, come examination room, sitting in a dressing gown staring balefully at an exam paper.

'Your time starts now,' said Miss Whitehead, leaving me alone.

I stared out across the green fields and enviously watched the lambs playing and greedily sucking at their mothers' milk.

My eyes came to rest on a little lamb lying in the far corner of the field. How strange. The lamb hadn't moved for minutes. Then it dawned on me. The poor thing was dead.

My emotions got the better of me and suddenly, fat, salty tears rolled down my cheeks. I was just so ill and so emotional, my poor old mind began to spin out of control. Images came to me like snapshots, whirling through my brain at breakneck speed. Dead lambs . . . yellow skin . . . decay . . . dark skies and invisible enemy bombers . . .

It was all too much.

A huge tear trickled down my cheek and landed with a plop on the exam paper.

'Question 1: What do you consider Froebel's most notable characteristics as an educator?' became blotted and blurred.

The first teardrop was quickly joined by another.

'Question 2: Define the following methods of cooking: baking, stewing, roasting and steaming,' soon became an inky jumbled blur.

'Question 3: Why is air the greatest necessity of animal life and how do we ensure that children get a constant supply of it night and day?' washed away under the deluge of tears.

Soon my eyes were a puffy mess as I broke down, my whole body juddering as I sobbed. My head pounded and everything ached, even my eyeballs throbbed.

Finally I cast one bleary eye at the clock. Oh crumbs. I'd been sobbing for nearly an hour, I had just half an hour to finish the paper.

Suddenly I realised this was my only chance. If I failed this I doubted I'd ever receive another bursary, I'd be letting Norland down, letting my family down, letting myself down.

And then what? Back to Amberley and an uncertain future. I'd wasted so much precious time already. 'Pull yourself together Brenda Ashford, you can do this.'

After that my pen became a blur as it whizzed over the page at breakneck speed.

Forcing myself not to sneak another peek at the dead lamb, I pointed out the differences between an Irish stew and a leg of mutton, showed I knew the correct way to wash flannels,

Here I am with my siblings, left to right: Michael, Kathleen, Christopher, David, me, Basil. There was never a dull moment, and nor was I short of a playmate or two.

Hallcroft, the house my father built in 1929. Here we enjoyed an idyllic childhood, the garden and surrounding fields were a perfect playground.

Mrs Emily Ward, who founded Norland in 1892.
This indomitable and visionary woman revolutionised
childcare and banished fear from the nursery.

My precious leather-bound Norland
Testimonial Handbook, given to me on my
first day of training, 23rd March 1939, aged 18.

The Norland 'charge' dress
worn for special occasions.

The drafty lecture
hall – note the ever
open window.

The dreaded laundry. We spent many hours toiling in here.

An immaculate student dormitory.

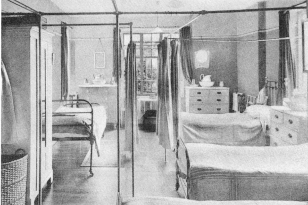

Nurses on pram parade ready for the afternoon inspection.

Hothfield Place in Kent, in 1939. Miss Whitehead in a dark dress. The Norland Institute evacuated here when the Second World War broke out.

Our 'set' at Hothfield, September 1939. I'm kneeling, second from left.

Out for our daily constitutional. Most of the evacuees were seeing the countryside for the first time.

The winter of 1940 was the coldest on record. Sledging and snowball fights with the Bethnal Greenies.

Princess Tsahai. Her gentle manner touched so many hearts, which made the later tragedy all the more heartbreaking.

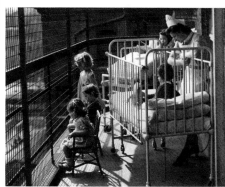

Out on the balcony at Great Ormond Street Hospital, for some fresh air on doctor's orders.

Jam sandwiches for tea always guaranteed plenty of smiles.

At last! A fully-fledged nurse with my young charges.

Nurse Sybil Trudgett. Midwife, MBE and in my eyes, miracle worker. This indomitable woman delivered 2,500 babies and taught me to be a nanny without prejudice.

In safe hands. While women were doing their bit for the war effort in factories we at the Redbourn War Nursery were doing our bit by caring for their babies.

The Hildenborough Hall Methodist Conference 1948.
Religious rallies such as this offered hope and direction after the devastation and loss of life experienced during the war.

Smiles, cuddles and love. I feel honoured and privileged to have shared my life with so many children, every one as precious as the last.

silks and fine whites and proved I knew precisely how to feed an infant from nine to eighteen months.

By the time I put my pen down I was spent.

It was a miracle I passed. Seventy-six out of 100 meant I was in line to receive the preliminary certificate of training from the Institute. It would be another year of successful work in a private post before I could receive the full certificate, but I had done it. Along with the rest of my set, my time at Hothfield had sadly come to an end.

I held back tears as I kissed my beloved Bethnal Greenies goodbye, my beautiful little illegitimate baby Lilly, and her shy mother, Rose, not to mention my loyal friends.

Everyone knew this was the end of an era. Not a single person's future was secure.

'I don't know when I'll see you again,' said Margaret, hugging me tight. 'But thanks for your kindness. I'll never forget it.'

I smiled wryly. The world was already such a changed place since Margaret was asked to take elocution lessons thirteen months previously. Now, in the grand scheme of things, the way she spoke barely mattered.

The grand stone porch was filled with leather trunks, bags and sobbed farewells. Promises to stay in touch however or wherever we could echoed round the steps.

Even Miss Whitehead looked moved.

My funny little family was to be scattered to all parts of the country.

Sad times, but with all the arrogance of a nineteen-year-old, I didn't even look back. I picked up my case, and as a newly qualified Norlander, marched onto my first post with a spring in my step and a song in my heart. War . . . pah, what war? I saw no evidence of it, how bad could it really be?

But as I travelled north by train, huge changes were already taking place. And these changes when they arrived came thick, fast and full of terrifying surprises.

Four weeks after I left, in May 1940, parts of France were in enemy hands and Kent was designated a military area. Hothfield was directly in the path of enemy bombers.

Miss Whitehead hurriedly organised yet another evacuation and the Institute was moved to Belvoir House in Bideford, Devon. Large stately homes in Devon were much in demand as safe havens for evacuating institutions, so Miss Whitehead must have used every ounce of her persuasive if slightly forceful charm.

Once there she had to add extra baths, contrive extra gas stoves, refrigerators, hot water, take extra rooms, transport furniture and make two cabbages grow where one stick of asparagus grew before.

And as for the Bethnal Greenies, the nursery was to be taken over by the Local Health Authority and moved to Hildenborough in Kent.

Although I didn't know it at the time, as the Norland staff were packing up to leave Hothfield, the British army marched in and requisitioned the house and grounds for Battalion HQ. Miss Whitehead was carrying boxes down the sweeping marble staircase as the soldiers in their heavy hobnail boots were clattering up it. The Home Guard mounted a parachute watch on the roof, armed with Sten guns and ball ammunition. Heavy tanks rolled over the glorious parkland and crushed the spring flowers. Before long, the sounds of happy evacuee laughter had been replaced by the ferocious crack of gunfire and the ceaseless thud of incendiary bombs. The phoney war was well and truly over.

6

Battle of Britain

The best way to make children good is to make them happy.
                                                    Oscar Wilde

I FELL in love with twelve-week-old Benjy Beaumont the moment he fixed his big, melting, chocolate-brown eyes on me.

Benjy's mother or father must have been of Eurasian origin as he had the softest, dusky skin and a thick head of jet-black hair. There was no doubt this little chap was going to grow up to be heartbreakingly handsome.

'Well, aren't you a dear little fellow?' I said, beaming, as I tickled his chin.

A big gummy smile spread over his face and it was like the sun coming out from behind a cloud. His dimpled cheeks creased in delight as he pumped his chubby little legs and arms in frantic excitement.

What a perfectly adorable little man.

'I think you and I are going to get along just fine,' I laughed, scooping him into my arms.

As I breathed in his sweet milky smell the years rolled away and I found myself smiling as I remembered the first magical time I held my baby brother.

Why would anyone want to give this little angel away?

Benjy was adopted, you see, as was his new brother,

two-year-old Peter, and along with his adopted parents, Iris and Frank Beaumont, they were to be my new family.

My first charges in my first proper job!

Iris and Frank Beaumont were wealthy and well-respected members of the local community in their home of Appleton, and good friends of my parents.

Frank's father was the minister of the local church, where his rousing sermons and strong morals made him a popular figure. Frank shared his father's religious ideals but had made his money in the textiles industry and obviously was not short of a bob or two.

When Iris told my mother they were planning on adopting Benjy and Peter she instantly suggested me as the boys' new nanny.

I think Mother was keen to help Iris in any way she could. Iris and Frank had been good to my parents after Father had lost all his money, lending us bell tents and a caravan to take cheap holidays in. I was very grateful to Iris, if perhaps a touch intimidated by her.

She was exquisitely beautiful with high cheekbones and a cut-glass accent to match. She had a complexion like double cream and intense cornflower-blue eyes that narrowed like a cat's when she looked at you.

Her chauffeur-driven navy-blue Rolls Royce was a familiar sight about the village of Appleton as she nipped from the golf course to the various parish lunches she hosted.

Iris had been caring for the boys on her own these past few weeks while she waited for me to complete my studies, and seemed awfully relieved that I was finally here.

'I'm exhausted,' she cried, fanning her beautiful face as she placed Peter into the crook of my other arm. 'Thank goodness you're here, Brenda, or Nurse Brenda as I shall call you from now on.'

I nodded eagerly.

'I should warn you,' she added. 'I like things to be done in the traditional way. You are to wear your uniform at all times and I expect the boys to be well turned out. Cook will bring you tea in the nursery at 4.00 p.m. prompt every day, when I shall also visit. There may be a war on but there is no need to let standards slip, wouldn't you agree, Nurse Brenda?'

I nodded even more furiously. 'Absolutely, Mrs Beaumont. You know, they're gorgeous boys,' I smiled. 'You must be so proud.'

'Well, yes,' she muttered. 'We got them from orphanage in London.'

I quickly came to see that Iris, for all her beauty, was not a particularly loving woman and was not prone to shows of affection. Nor did she ever seem entirely at ease with the boys.

But I couldn't judge her for that. She had demonstrated the ultimate act of love after all. She had plucked these two boys from an orphanage that still operated according to Victorian notions of discipline, and now they had a beautiful, rambling farmhouse to call their home.

Their world had been transformed. Stark dormitories had been replaced with day and night nurseries, painted in a soft powder blue. The spacious sunlit rooms were stocked full of fine clothes and the best toys, including an electric Hornby railway set, which can't have been easy to find. Supplies of toys had fallen by 75 per cent since the outbreak of war so most people improvised, making cars out of tin cans and sewing their own teddies. Not so for the Beaumont boys. In fact, the whole house oozed comfort.

As well as the chauffeur, a good-looking young man by the name of Bill, Frank and Iris employed their own cook, and not only that: Cook had a fridge. She was a short, dumpy, no-nonsense woman who came in daily from the village, and she was extremely proud of her fridge. Only she was allowed access to it and she guarded it as if it contained the crown jewels.

I suppose that's not so surprising when you consider that only 25 per cent of people had a fridge in those days. As with most kitchen appliances, mass production of fridges didn't really begin until after the war. The price of such luxuries simply put them beyond the means of most families, so food was kept cold on a marble slab at the back of the larder, or outdoors. Fridge adverts at the time boasted 'how big is yours?' Well, the Beaumonts' was huge.

For all her bristly ferocity Cook was truly excellent at her job and could seemingly make a feast out of nothing. Food rationing had stepped up since the Hothfield days when only sugar, butter and bacon were rationed. For the last four months more or less everything had been rationed, but thanks to vegetables in the garden and the odd rabbit or chicken given to Frank by local farmers, the boys and I were to eat like royalty.

Cook's omelettes, made up of Mullins powdered egg and bulked out with stale breadcrumbs, tasted as good as the real thing, and she had an excellent trick of dipping stale bread in milk and then heating it in the oven with cinnamon to make a delicious afternoon tea for the boys.

I had a day and night nursery to work in, which were to be totally my domain, a comfortable salary of £15 a week and half a day off a week.

These little chaps were to want for nothing, except maybe a cuddle from their new mother.

Mother had told me that Iris and Frank couldn't have their own children; they had been trying without luck for four years. To go from living a life unencumbered by children to suddenly having two under the age of two in your late thirties cannot have been easy.

I had to remind myself that not every parent was as tactile

or loving as my mother and father, and for the hundredth time since leaving home I blessed my lucky stars for having such wonderful parents.

Besides, it didn't matter that Benjy and Peter only received a cool little kiss on the head from their new mother as she breezed out the nursery to play golf; they had me to shower them with love and kisses now. I was determined they would have the same happy childhood I had enjoyed.

Benjy and Peter stared sadly after their mother as the door swung shut, leaving us in a cloud of Chanel N°5.

I looked out the window as Iris's chauffeur-driven Rolls slid away from the house, then turned back to my new charges.

'Right boys,' I cried. 'Who would like to go for a walk and feed the ducks?'

There may have been a war on but we still had to get outside for our daily blast of fresh air. To stay in was considered positively degenerate.

'Quack, quack,' said Peter, bouncing about on the spot. Benjy gazed adoringly up at his new big brother as if he couldn't quite believe his good fortune.

Peter's skin was as milky white as his new brother's was dark but it gave me such a glow to see the way they looked at each other. They didn't see each other's skin colour, just a fun new playmate.

Having tucked them both up in their beautiful new coach pram, we set out to walk the village streets. Perhaps I'd even have time to pop in and show off my new charges to Mother. Amberley wasn't far away.

Walking out down the drive, my palms felt suddenly clammy on the pram handles. Fear nagged. Two young lives were entirely in my hands . . . in the middle of war. All the training of the previous year buzzed around my head. Did I have spare clothes and cloth nappies, a drink of water? Were the boys' clothes immaculate and their faces squeaky clean? These were the minister's grandsons after all, and it wouldn't do for them to be seen around town with grubby faces and hands.

No, a thorough inspection revealed them to be the picture of angelic respectability propped up in their pram in their new sailor suits.

My freshly ironed and starched Norland uniform was immaculate, my leather shoes gleamed and my Norland cape swung merrily behind me as I marched up the drive.

Suddenly I screeched to a halt, sending poor Benjy and Peter flying forward in their pram.

'Brenda you fool,' I muttered. 'You forgot their gas masks.'

What a silly mistake, well, more than a silly mistake. It had been drummed into us time and time again that no child should ever leave home without theirs. The bombs hadn't arrived in our part of England yet but it was widely believed that Hitler would drop some form of poison gas on civilians so the government had issued 38 million gas masks.

I only had three of the tiresome things in my possession and I couldn't even remember those.

'Come on Brenda, pull yourself together,' I scolded myself.

I rushed back to the house and grabbed the three grey cardboard boxes from the hall table. Mine was standard black, Peter, like a lot of children, had a Mickey Mouse one with red rubber pieces and bright eye rims, but it was Benjy's mask that really broke my heart. His was a gas helmet, not a mask, which in the event of poison gas being dropped, his whole body would have to be placed into. It came with a pair of bellows, which would enable me to pump air into it. When we'd had our trial run with it he looked a pitiful sight, his big brown eyes staring dolefully out, little legs kicking the inside of the helmet.

He and Peter had both looked terrified bless their hearts.

'Look at Nanny's funny face,' I'd said, putting my mask on to try and lighten the mood.

It hadn't really worked, mind you, and shuddering, I took the three masks and placed them carefully in the bottom of the pram. How I hoped we would never have occasion to use them.

Feeling better, I set out again and strolled into the centre of the village. Hadn't Surrey changed since I left for Hothfield nine months previously, at the outbreak of war? Now it was the end of May 1940. The phoney war was firmly at an end and the war proper had begun. Winston Churchill was our new Prime Minister.

Hitler had invaded the Low Countries and the evacuation of thousands of Allied soldiers from the beaches of Dunkirk was taking place. Events were escalating rapidly but Churchill was putting fire in our bellies.

'We shall never surrender,' he said in a speech in June 1940 that united every British man and woman.

Father had always been a staunch liberal but when Churchill came to power he suddenly became a Tory. He was the man to save us from tyranny, of that Father was certain.

They say that behind every great man there is a great woman.

Well, Churchill was raised by one of the very best – a lovely English nanny by the name of Mrs Everest, whom he adored.

Whatever she had taught him in childhood it was now clearly paying off. The peril facing Britain was now widely realised and Churchill was recognised as the best person to lead our country.

'The battle of France is over,' our leader had said gravely. 'The battle of Britain is about to begin.'

The once sleepy village streets were filled with an air of excitement and purpose, their inhabitants were damned if they were going to let the Jerries take over their high street.

Life in Britain was never to be the same again.

The first wave of evacuations had already taken place and it was an exodus bigger than Moses'. Just like the Bethnal Greenies, 827,000 schoolchildren, along with 103,000 teachers, had left the cities for new lives in the countryside. A total of 524,000 children under school age and their mothers had also gone out into the unknown, not to mention 12,000 pregnant women.

Now, thanks to Dunkirk and the threat of German invasion, the second wave was taking place.

Can you imagine the undertaking of such evacuations? Think of the committees and sub-committees that would need to be formed if the government today had to evacuate that many children. Could it be done, I wonder?

The call up had left the streets of Appleton devoid of young men but filled with the new faces of children I didn't know. Many of the villagers now had at least one, if not more, evacuees billeted with them.

But then I spotted a face I did recognise.

Iris and Frank had a garage nearby that had been converted to an Air Raid Protection (ARP) headquarters. It was smack bang next door to the church hall, which was now the headquarters of the Red Cross. Wardens and Red Cross workers milled about drinking tea and playing cards. The 'post' as it was known, was the hub of the local community and for many people it was a second home as they put in shift work before and after their day jobs.

The village air-raid siren was fixed up near the post so when the alert came through it was the job of the duty warden to switch on that sickening wail.

But despite its chilling purpose, happiness and life flowed

from that shelter, with music and excited chatter spilling out onto the street. The kettle was barely off. In spite of the hard work there was a lot of laughter and camaraderie.

Now I could hear voices drifting out from the post.

'Morning Mr Ashford, Sir, number one reporting for duty . . . yes I can work weekends and evenings . . . I don't mind a bit of blood or scrubbing up, I've seen it all afore.'

There in the middle of it all, with a tin hat marked with a capital W perched on his head and navy-blue overalls, was my father.

Father was the very proud new Home Guard manager for Appleton, or as he and his colleagues described themselves: 'the eyes and ears of civil defence'. With his military training and the Military Cross he had won for his bravery as a lieutenant on the front line during the First War, he'd been itching to get back into action and do his bit. Being told he was too old to sign up had been a blow to my father.

But now his eyes were shining and there was a look of determination on his face I hadn't seen in a good few years.

When he spotted me his face creased into an enormous smile. When Father smiled it reached right to the edges of his crinkly blue eyes.

'Hello, love,' he said warmly, giving me a kiss. 'D . . . d . . . don't you look smart.'

'What are you looking so pleased with yourself for?' I asked, with a smile.

'I've been organising my troops,' he said, grinning at me as he thrust his hands in his pockets and leant back smugly.

'Where are they?' I asked.

He tapped the side of his nose and winked.

'I've hidden half my men in a training exercise and the other half are out looking for them. I've hidden them so well

they can't find them. They've been out there hunting for
hours.'

Bless him. He was clearly having the time of his life!

After the devastation of being tricked out of his business
and the shame of bankruptcy, this war was giving him a
renewed purpose and a sense of honour. This was something
he did know how to do well!

Perhaps that was one thing the Nazis hadn't counted on.
There were thousands of men like my father the length and
breadth of Britain. Honest, hard-working men who'd already
lived through the horror of one war, lost loved ones and seen
hardship and tragedy, and they were damned if they were
going to let Hitler invade our shores.

Father had never breathed a word of what he'd witnessed
during the notoriously brutal battles at Hill 60, during the
Great War. When I read survivors' accounts in later life, they
virtually turned the blood in my veins to ice.

'At times, the slopes were littered with corpses and it
was a nightmarish place of smoke, noise and the horror of
hand-to-hand fighting,' wrote one soldier. 'Attack followed
counter-attack as the armies struggled to gain or maintain
supremacy, and with men caught out in the open during these
actions, every square metre of Hill 60 became the scene of
somebody's private battle and of someone's unknown grave,'
wrote another.

The ground beyond the trenches was a morass of thick
mud filled with partially buried bodies and swirling with
dense mist. Rats the size of rabbits scuttered along the dug
outs at night.

Can you even begin to imagine the horror of living day
and night in those trenches? Hundreds of men were packed
cheek by jowl in cold waterlogged conditions. Trench foot, a
rotting of the skin caused by fungal infection, was common,

as too were the lice, which sucked off the rotting flesh of soldiers. There was little by way of sanitation, running water or hot food.

But the real horrors lay over the top. When men were ordered over and into the line of fire, for the majority it was to a certain death, with many men being instantly blown to smithereens. If gunfire didn't get them then the exploding mines seemed certain to.

One soldier, Philip Gibbs, recalled the terrible sight of an exploding mine at Hill 60. 'The most diabolic splendour I have ever seen. Out of the dark ridges of that ill-famed Hill 60 there gushed out and up enormous volumes of scarlet flame from exploding mines, and earth and smoke all lighted so that the countryside was illuminated by red light.'

After surviving Hill 60, it would take more than the Nazis to intimidate Father, and the same went for all the older generation of the village.

Bidding my father farewell I set off in the direction of my parents' house.

'Watch out when you get home,' he called after me. 'You might end up with a couple more in that pram.'

Baffled, I went on my way.

Nearby the Women's Voluntary Service was running a canteen for the ARP and Home Guard volunteers. They dished out tomato and tinned salmon sandwiches or sausage, chips and fried bread, all with a cheery smile. 'Get that down ya,' they said. 'Can't beat Jerry on an empty stomach, can we.' Working late into the night and then stumbling home in the dark without torches took guts.

Local girls cycled round delivering *Land Girl* magazines with a cheery wave and greeting. Even the local Women's Institute was doing their bit by donating bottles of jam and fruit to the canteen.

The village had come alive in a way I least expected. The community was thriving and people were determined to look after one another, come what may.

Our country, to quote Churchill, had found its soul.

By the time I reached Mother's I must have passed a dozen houses with their windows criss-crossed with sticky tape to stop them shattering. Every window had blackout curtains ready to be drawn at dusk and heavy sandbags on their door-steps to put out fires.

Most back gardens had also been transformed, with everyone digging up what spare land they had to form vegetable patches.

The villagers of Appleton and Bookham, like most people, were frantically 'digging for victory'. Carrots, widely believed to help you see in the darkness of the blackout, potatoes and leeks were big favourites and were often thrown together to form cheap and nutritious stews. Potato consumption rose by 60 per cent during the war and we had them with everything! Some people even ate 'Inspiration pie' in which the inspiration lay in using potato for both crust and filling.

'Better pot luck today with Churchill than humble pie with Hitler tomorrow,' as the government propaganda posters told us.

This country was ready for whatever Hitler was about to throw our way.

If I thought Father was happy it wasn't a patch on Mother.

Mother loved babies almost as much as me and when I proudly pushed Benjy and Peter's pram over the threshold of their small cottage, a babble of voices hit me.

There were small people everywhere. I spotted twins, a little girl of about three with red hair and another girl of two with huge violet eyes and poker straight dark hair.

Sat in the middle of them all with her knitting and a look of quiet satisfaction was Mother.

Something was bubbling on the stove for tea, giving off the most mouth-watering smell and a fire flickered in the hearth, a hod of coal placed beside it. The children were all happily playing with our old toys and were dressed in clothes that quite frankly had seen better days.

I thought of Benjy and Peter's well-stocked nursery and realised how cold it felt in comparison to my parents' house.

'Hello, darling,' Mother exclaimed, leaping to her feet to give me a kiss. 'Meet my evacuees, aren't they all just gorgeous.'

I had to laugh. Mother had never hidden her desire to have twins and thanks to the war, her wish had now been granted.

All the boys, including David, were now at boarding school and had been evacuated to the Lake District. I rather suspect the evacuees were helping my mother with her empty nest syndrome.

'They're not with us for long, sadly,' she said, looking at the twins. 'But this little one is Rita,' she said pointing to the serious looking redhead who was clutching a battered old doll. 'And this is Sally. Your father's grumbling that the house has been taken over but I know he's secretly delighted.'

Rita and Sally's stories were fascinating.

Little Rita was from Croydon. Back then Croydon was home to one of the greatest airports in the world and certainly the largest in London, receiving international airfreight into the capital. This made it a major target so Rita's evacuation had been swift.

'Poor little scrap,' whispered mother. 'She's illegitimate you know. Seems to have a new father each week. When she came here she was to be called Rita Ratcliffe. When her mum turned up to visit from Croydon last week she tells me I now have to call her Rita Fowler.'

'Me no Fowler,' piped up little Rita, shaking her head defiantly. 'Me Ratcliffe.'

'That's all she says. I'm at my wits' end with her mother.'

Seems little Rita's mum had been using the cheap railway fares the government had issued specifically so mothers could visit their evacuated children, to go off for jaunts with her latest fancy man.

'She turned up last weekend and spent an hour with Rita than vanished and was gone for days. Fed me some cock and bull story about getting lost but I'm not daft you know. I know she was getting up to fun and games.'

I could see why Mother was cross. Rita's mother had turned the war to her advantage, now she had free child-care for her child and the means to get up to goodness only knows what.

I stared at little Rita, who had climbed onto my mother's knee and was now happily curled on her lap.

'She calls me her mummy now,' smiled Mother, reaching out to stroke her hair.

Her smile was so tender and her manner with these little evacuees so gentle. It was plain to see she had already formed strong bonds with the girls. I felt alarm bells jangle at the back of my mind. One day these children would have to go home, how would she cope then?

Now her eyes were shining with love as she told me Sally's story.

'She's illegitimate too, her mother had been working in a hotel and having it off with all sorts and didn't have a clue who the father was. Then she was adopted by Lady Lillian. Her Ladyship is single, but I imagine as she is titled she pulled some strings and was able to adopt Sally.'

I had heard of Lady Lillian, she was a well-known member of the aristocracy who lived nearby in a very grand home.

Back then it would have been almost impossible to adopt as a single woman but she'd obviously used her considerable influence.

But there was one thing puzzling me.

'Why has she been evacuated?' I asked Mother. 'She doesn't even live far from here.'

'Lady Lillian has turned her house into a rest home for injured soldiers, says she can't have Sally there during the war. She's been here eight months now but Lady Lillian must be terribly busy as she hasn't visited once.'

I felt rage bubble up inside me. What was wrong with these women? Rita and Sally were beautiful, happy little girls that surely any mother would long to spend time with. Children weren't commodities to be shipped around on a whim.

On the walk back to the Beaumonts' I remembered Norland's motto. 'Love Never Faileth.' It seemed that, thanks to the war, there were more children than ever that needed love and security.

At the time of the evacuations there wasn't a great understanding of children's emotional needs and the impact that loss and separation could have. My Froebel-based Norland training gave me an insight into what it must be like to be a frightened evacuee. All these children were like frail little flowers that had been uprooted. They needed love, security and understanding to flourish and blossom in their new homes.

My resolve to do the best I could by these children stiffened as I let myself back into the Beaumonts' spacious farmhouse.

Suddenly I realised the time. 4.30 p.m.

'Goodness gracious,' I gasped. 'I'd been gone longer than I realised.

There was just enough time to get the children fed their tea and washed and scrubbed up ready to be presented in the drawing room.

In those days it was quite commonplace for children of wealthier families to go to the drawing room for the hour after tea, to spend time in the company of their mother, father and visiting relatives, before being taken back to the nursery. Often it was the only time a parent might spend with their child in the day.

Once their faces were scrubbed clean with a warm flannel and their clothes were neat and tidy, I duly knocked on the door of the drawing room door and presented my charges.

Iris looked like a Hollywood movie star in her stunning satin evening dress. She was sipping a martini. She smiled when she saw the boys but didn't get up.

Frank beamed and leapt to his feet.

'Hello boys, your grandfather is here,' he cried, ushering them in.

There in the corner, nursing a whisky, was Iris's father, the boys' grandfather. A dour Scotsman, I had seen him around in the village before, but I had never warmed to him.

He nodded and issued a gruff welcome. The man positively radiated disapproval.

Then I saw something that made my heart take a nosedive.

He'd looked down at little Benjy and anger and disapproval had flashed in those steely grey eyes.

I'd only seen it fleetingly but it was enough for me to realise. He was not impressed with his new dark-skinned grandchild.

As the drawing room door swung shut behind me I stood stock still on the landing, trembling. I wanted to run back in there and pluck dear sweet little Benjy and take him back to the warmth of the nursery. But I couldn't. I wasn't the boys' mother. I was their nanny.

Later, after I had read them their story and tucked them up in their beds, I spent the evening as I spent every evening, washing nappies, knitting them little woollies or sewing. But the work that usually gave me such comfort couldn't save me from the agony of remembering the look Iris's father had given little Benjy.

Gazing at him sleeping soundly in his cot I planted a gentle kiss on his forehead and said a prayer for his future. In fact I prayed for the good fortunes and secure future of all the children I knew, but especially Benjy, Peter, Rita and Sally.

Unable to settle, I paced the nursery, then sneaked a peek out the window onto the dark, deserted streets. My thoughts were interrupted by a shout from below.

'Deal with your curtains,' yelled a faceless ARP warden.

Letting the curtain drop I looked back round at the nursery.

The winter nights were drawing in so I'd jolly well better get used to this room. I'd be spending a lot of time here.

To distract myself I got out some half-knitted woollies again and flicked on the wireless to hear Churchill making a speech about how we had to achieve victory at all costs.

But the question was, just how hard was the road ahead?

In July 1940, three months after my arrival and exactly as Churchill had predicted, the Battle of Britain began. It was the largest, most sustained aerial bombing campaign our country had ever seen.

Appleton had nearly one hundred air-raid warnings, before, in mid-September, we saw some action.

The siren woke me from my sleep and I sat bolt upright in my bed.

Had I dreamt it? No, there it was. That unmistakable drone that bore right down into the depths of my belly. Sitting in my pitch-black bedroom my brain scrambled to focus.

Come on Brenda, the children, the children.

Leaping out of bed, I threw on my dressing gown and

slippers and tore into the boys' nursery. On the landing, Frank and Iris were emerging sleepily from their room.

'The shelter, Brenda, get down there now,' urged Frank. I hardly had time to question where they were going.

Instead I scooped little Benjy out of his cot and gently woke Peter. Minutes later we were fumbling our way through the dark and out into the garden.

The cold night air stung my cheeks and whipped up and under my dressing gown.

'What's happening?' mumbled Peter, sleepily.

I gripped his hand tighter. 'Nothing darling, we're going to sleep in the shelter tonight, won't that be fun?'

My heart was banging out of my chest by the time we bent down to get into the Anderson shelter at the bottom of the Beaumonts' garden. Once inside, I finally felt I could breathe.

The shelter was small, just 1.4 metres wide and 2 metres long, but there was enough room for two tiny bunks and a box of provisions. Marmite, cocoa, Mullins powdered egg in a tin, KLIM powdered milk and jugs of water and water-purifying tablets. Frank had also left some *Beano* comics there for Peter. Light came from a torch.

But we didn't touch any of the provisions. I drew the boys close to me and we all snuggled together. A nursery rhyme would help fill the time and calm the boys until we got the all clear.

'Twinkle twinkle little star . . . how I wonder what you are,' I sang gently.

Soon the boys' eyelids had grown heavy and they were drifting off.

'Up above the sky so . . .'

BOOM. The sound from up above was so ferocious that my voice trailed off.

BANG. BANG. The bombs were coming thick and fast now.

The noises were like nothing I'd ever heard before. First a low drone, then the scream of the bomb as it hurtled to the ground, then a sickening thud, followed by an explosion. Menacing crunches and whining sounds were heard all over Appleton.

These shelters could withstand most things except a direct hit. I squeezed my eyes shut and issued a silent prayer.

'What that Nanny Brenda?' quivered little Peter, his eyes suddenly wide with terror.

'It's just the bang bang,' I said as I chirpily as I could muster. 'Who wants to hear a story?'

An hour or so later the siren sounded with the all clear and I carried the boys back to their beds. I could barely sleep for the rest of the night. The reverberations of the bombs still seemed to linger.

If we had hoped that the raid was a one-off we were sorely mistaken. Situated as we were eighteen miles from the centre of London, we were the ideal dumping ground for the Luftwaffe's bombs. If the German bombers realised there were barrage balloons ahead that prevented them from reaching London they simply offloaded their lethal cargo on us and quickly headed for home. Likewise if they had some bombs left over after a raid they jettisoned their load on Appleton.

The morning after that first attack, breakfast was a strained and exhausted affair.

Iris came into the day nursery as the boys were tucking into their porridge.

'Everyone OK?' she asked.

'We're all still standing,' I replied.

'Goodo, Nurse Brenda,' she replied. 'Frank and I were at

the post last night helping out. I'm off out to see what needs doing round the village, I'll see you all at tea time.'

It struck me as odd that she wouldn't prefer to stay with her sons in the shelter during a raid, but I bit my lip.

After breakfast we took our morning walk. Talk in the village was of one thing only.

Windows were smashed and lethal-looking shrapnel was embedded in trees and cars. One poor house opposite my parents' had taken a direct hit. Fortunately no one had been killed but what was left was smouldering and the poor inhabitants gazed at the remains of their home, utterly shell shocked.

Despite all this the villagers' spirits remained high. Everyone mucked in and was helping to repair the damage caused by the bombs.

Since the end of World War One, air attack had been seen as the warfare of the future. Predictions about its unstoppable destructive power had been terrifying. There was a real fear that society would quickly collapse under a concerted bombing campaign. But society didn't collapse, far from it. Not in our village and, as I later discovered not in villages, towns and cities all over England.

Father was in the thick of it as usual, helping to coordinate the repair efforts.

'Come on,' he said. 'Let's see what Jerry's left us. Butcher's windows are smashed so we'll need a patch-up over there.'

'The shops are still open, ladies,' shouted one joker. 'More open than usual.'

I laughed along with everyone else. The terror of the previous night was only matched by the sheer pride I felt today.

After lunch I popped in on Mother to check she and her evacuees were all right.

'We're fine, darling, aren't we girls,' she said cheerily.

'Yes, Mother,' said Sally, smiling.

'She's not really your mother, you know,' I said gently to Sally.

The poor little thing looked genuinely bewildered.

My heart ached. This little girl had been shunted from home to home and had now been dumped by her adopted mother. All she wanted was someone to call mummy, a real family to belong to. Not for the first time, I was struck by the thought that these children were war casualties, too.

Sometimes days went by with no bombs, then other times we found ourselves in the shelter twice in one day, all huddled together for warmth and comfort. Occasionally Frank and Iris joined us but more often than not they went to the post when the siren sounded.

Their frequent absence meant that the bond between me and the boys was getting stronger, and my love for Benjy and Peter grew with every hour spent underground.

This love, it seemed, was to be constantly tested. On one occasion I was walking back from Mother's with Benjy and Peter when I heard the wail of the dreaded siren start up.

I stopped dead in my tracks and stared at the skies. Bother. I had at least another fifteen minutes' walk before I would be home, and ten minutes' if I returned to Mother's.

Then my heart sank further when I realised I'd forgotten the gas masks . . . again. Mr Beaumont would kill me.

I felt as if tennis balls were pounding round my chest. The shock must have registered on my face because I noticed that Benjy and Peter were staring at me.

Stay calm, Brenda. Don't let them see your fear.

'We're going to have to run now,' I said, trying to smile and gripping onto the pram handles for dear life. 'Hold on tight, boys.'

With that I set off at a pace, running as fast as I could up the country lanes, the heavy pram bumping over the path. The boys thought it quite hilarious of course and giggled every time the pram hit the curb and flew into the air.

I laughed along too but inside I was screaming; adrenaline pumping through me. Any minute now we'd hear that unmistakable drone as a German bomber hurtled overhead.

Finally, we made it home and I grabbed the boys out the pram and legged it to the safety of the shelter, where finally I could sink, exhausted onto the bunk.

I swear that little incident put years on me.

But, despite all this fear and uncertainty, something extraordinary was happening inside me, too. With every bomb that the Germans dropped on us I found my confidence growing.

The woman that a year ago wouldn't have said boo to a goose, much less dare answer Miss Whitehead back, was now becoming a stronger woman. A woman who could dodge bombs and run through the night with her charges.

Children were more vulnerable than ever and my faith in my childcare calling was growing by the day.

So too was my sense of daring . . .

It began as a raid like any other. The siren had sounded from the post and we had dropped what we were doing and headed to the shelter. This time, though, the bombs sounded perilously close. Our boys up in the skies were clearly having one almighty fight with the Germans, as the rattle of gunfire and bombs testified.

Miss Whitehead's words rang in my ears.

'*Our part, ladies, is to keep war from the children. To these small folk, the war with all its suffering and anxieties must be a sealed book.*'

But our principal clearly hadn't counted on this war being on our doorstep. How could we keep it a sealed book when bombs were exploding all around us?

Sadly, Benjy and Peter were beginning to take it in their stride but this one was louder than all the rest.

An almighty explosion rocked the shelter, sending Peter's eyes out on stalks.

'When will the bang bang stop, Nanny Brenda?' he gasped.

The words of my old lecturers rang in my ears. '*We need absolute truthfulness at all times.*'

What should I say? This wasn't a nursery, it was an air-raid shelter in the middle of a raid.

'I don't know, darling,' I said sadly. 'Soon I hope.'

I'd made a vow never to lie to children and I wasn't about to start now.

Children were encouraged not to lie themselves, but with the country braced for the arrival of the enemy, possibly in plain clothes and masquerading as one of us, it was drummed into everyone, from the oldest to the youngest, that 'careless talk costs lives' and 'loose lips sink ships'. Peter had been told by Frank and Iris that if anyone stopped him and asked him the way, he was to reply, 'I can't say'. That way he didn't let his country down but nor was he telling a lie.

Now, I opted for distraction techniques and sang the boys the hymns and nursery rhymes I'd learnt at Pembridge Square, or told them stories.

'Do you want to hear about the time that Basil, Michael, Christopher and I pretended to be red Indians out on the roughs?' I asked.

All children love to hear what happened to grown ups when they were little.

They nodded, entranced.

As bombs thudded perilously close, I told them tales from my happy childhood. It didn't seem fair that these poor little boys had to hear about my adventures in such cruel circumstances, but I was determined not to give in to fear.

'Another time, Father mowed lines in the grass to look like train tracks.'

Bang. An almighty explosion rocked the shelter and I gasped involuntarily. Composing myself, I took a deep breath and carried on.

'We used to ride our bikes along the tracks and imagined they were trains.'

Eventually, my story worked and they both settled back in their bunks and went to sleep.

I must have been feeling a little too complacent about my ability to face my fears. It was then that curiosity got the better of me.

I couldn't, could I?

One little peek wouldn't hurt, surely. Why should Iris and Frank get all the excitement?

Standing up quietly so as not to wake the boys, I crept to the entrance to the shelter and before I could change my mind, pushed open the door.

Shutting it behind me, I stuck close to the shelter and allowed my gaze to drift up to the grey skies overhead.

Oh my! There, before my very eyes, the Battle of Britain was playing out. Our boys in their Spitfires had intercepted a German fighter plane, probably on his way north to Luton where there was a Vauxhall factory churning out all sorts of war machines. What's more, they were right on the German's tail.

Every nerve ending in my body was on red alert and the hairs on my neck prickled. I had never felt so alive, terrified or excited in all my nineteen years.

Livid flashes leapt across the grey sky as the German and British planes soared right over my head. The noise was ferocious and I felt the crack of gunfire in my belly.

This was marvellous.

Our boys were magnificent and the sight of the red, white and blue circles on the wings of their Spitfires stirred something in my soul.

One soared down so low I swear I could see the outline of the pilot's face, set in grim determination.

The Spitfire pilots of the RAF were fast becoming legends for risking their life daily in dogfight battles with the Luftwaffe. Their bravery would surely save us from tyranny.

The slang language they all talked in only added to the legend. The pilots flew a 'kite', put it away in a 'shed', slept in an 'iron lung' (a Nissan hut), wore 'sleepsuits' for uniforms as they were never out of them and hoped they would not 'go for a Burton' or 'write themselves off'.

Something told me these particular pilots had no intention of going for a Burton.

'Come on boys,' I yelled into the sky. 'Give Jerry something back.'

The pilots swooped round, and in a piece of aerial wizardry, roared up and under the isolated German plane.

Bang . . . bang . . . bang, the rattle of their machine guns was effective and deadly.

Seconds later the German plane took a hit and burst into an orange ball of flames.

My heart was in my throat as I clung to the shelter door.

'They did it,' I cheered.

The German pilot had bailed out! His parachute mushroomed open and his tiny figure drifted down into a nearby field. His plane carried on, pilotless, hurtling through the skies, smoke pouring from its engine.

Just then, near disaster . . .

I felt it before I heard it. A piece of stray shrapnel whistled past my face and landed with a thud in the shelter door, just two inches from my head.

I stood breathless for a second. Was I still alive? The only sound was the pounding of my heart in my ears.

I looked round, then pinched myself. I had been just seconds from death. Of all the stupid . . .

What if little Peter had woken and tottered out the shelter to find his nanny lying slumped at the entrance? What if he had pushed open the door at the moment the shrapnel had landed?

The adrenaline was still pumping through my veins when Frank came storming up the garden. His usually placid face was scarlet with rage. Uh oh. Something told me I was in line for a fearful ticking off.

'Nurse Brenda, what on earth do you think you're doing?'

'S . . . sorry Mr Beaumont,' I stuttered. 'I know I shouldn't have, but everyone else was watching.'

He gave me a roasting, and rightly so.

But I think I was saved from the worst of it when minutes later Iris ran up the garden path, her usually glacially-composed features more animated than I'd ever seen.

'The Jerry's landed in next door's field,' she panted, pulling on her mink coat. 'Bill and I are off to make a citizen's arrest.'

Frank opened his mouth to object but it was too late. She had already leapt into the back of the Rolls and was speeding off to make what must surely have been the most unusual citizen's arrest known to mankind. The German expected Spitfire pilots, surely, but a well-to-do lady in a fur coat and her chauffeur bearing down on him in a Rolls Royce? Probably not.

In the event, he was spared being manhandled by Mrs Beaumont but met an even worse fate. She and Bill the chauffeur were stopped by a local bobby at a hastily erected roadblock. The fighter pilot had fallen in a cesspit and died!

What became of the plane, I don't know, but you could be

sure the local kids would be all over hunting for it. Crashed planes were treated as treasure troves and stripped of precious mementos to be sneaked into school and shown off in the playground.

A nearby school was still recovering after a boy by the name of Wally somehow got hold of an unexploded bomb and smuggled it into school in his satchel. Fortunately his teacher spotted it and a warden managed to dispose of it before any harm was done but this hadn't acted as a deterrent to the boys.

Shrapnel was very much a currency to be exchanged or haggled over. The streets were full of boys pretending to be low-flying aeroplanes, machine-gunning their way up the high street, their pockets stuffed with debris and shrapnel.

I had even heard of some resourceful housewives making frying pans from the remnants of crashed German fighter planes. They'd have needed them, too, as most women had donated their pots and pans to be melted down and made into Spitfires, Hurricanes and Wellingtons.

That night in bed I tingled all over with excitement. Yes, I'd copped a frightful telling off but the incident had fuelled my sense of adventure. I'd seen the war close up.

Soon after, on my half day off and shortly after yet another raid, I decided to wander up to Mother's and give her a hand with her evacuees. I'd only got part of the way there when a commotion in a nearby field caught my attention.

A couple of farmers were furiously shovelling cow dung onto the back of the truck, as if the fate of the world depended on their actions.

I wasn't sure what they were up to but it looked like an adventure. An adventure I wanted to be part of.

'What's going on here?' I asked breathlessly.

'You're Arnold's daughter ainch you,' one replied. 'An

incendiary bomb's got going over at one of your boss's fields,' he said, gesturing with his shovel. 'We're gonna put it out afore it takes hold.'

Before he had time to object I'd grabbed a shovel, hitched up my skirts and jumped in the back of the truck.

Seconds later we were backing into the field.

There wasn't any time to lose. The shattered bomb was alight and the grass around it was already on fire. Left for much longer, it would be no time before the whole field was on fire. God knows the devastation if it spread to the village.

'Come on, boys,' I cried, digging my shovel deep in the steaming pile of manure.

For half an hour we worked steadily, racing from the truck to the bomb and shovelling manure onto the blaze. When it ran out we forked up great cowpats and threw them straight onto the flames too.

Talk about thrilling. I suppressed a little chuckle as I thought of what Miss Whitehead would say if she saw me now. The Norland had never taught me the correct handling of a cowpat, after all!

Soon more and more villagers and ARP wardens had joined us and together we worked shoulder to shoulder.

I thought of Norland's other motto. 'United we stand.' When we had learnt it all those months ago in the lecture rooms of Pembridge Square I had no idea that it would take on such meaning.

Finally, with sweat pouring down our faces, we finished. Disaster had been averted.

By the time I reached Mother's, I was exhausted, smeared in sweat and cow dung but absolutely elated.

Don't get me wrong. Nurseries were lovely places and being a Norland nurse was all I had ever wanted but it didn't mean I didn't yearn for a bit of adventure, and a change from time to time.

Mother's face was a picture when she saw me. 'Darling,' she gasped, when she opened the door. 'What have you been up to?'

Rita and Sally sat round open mouthed as I recounted my adventure and I half wished I'd sneaked a bit of shrapnel away to give to them. It would be better than buried treasure.

Mother rewarded my efforts with an extra big portion of pudding. Her legendary Queens Pudding that I'd feasted on throughout my childhood had now been replaced with Poor Knights pudding, the same thing but made with stale breadcrumbs.

By now food wasn't just strictly rationed, it was against the law to waste it. Not a scrap was thrown away and stale bread-crumbs went into everything.

After an afternoon spent shovelling cow dung onto bombs that pudding tasted like the nectar of the gods.

On my way home I happened to glance back over the fields. I had seen quite enough drama for one day but what I saw made me stop dead in my tracks.

The city of London was on fire . . .

7

We're All in it Together

Friendship – loyalty – staunchness in the face of danger.
The Sea of Adventure, Enid Blyton

NO SOONER was the Battle of Britain beginning to end than the Blitz had begun. The landscape around our village is fairly flat and sometimes, on a clear evening, you can see the lights of London twinkling eighteen miles away. But tonight there was no twinkling. London was on fire.

The skyline was lit up with an intense orange glow. I could barely imagine the ferocity of those fires, that I could see them so clearly from all these miles away.

I stood stock still in the field, hardly daring to move a muscle, the only sound the pounding of my heart in my chest. I watched the scarlet flames billowing into the early evening air and grieved for the many thousands of courageous souls battling for survival in our capital.

The great barrage balloons that loomed like giant whales over the outskirts of London, could not prevent the destruction.

Soon I was joined by others and we stood staring in dismay, watching in silence.

Finally, as the dusk gave way to night and the fires burned even more ferociously, I turned and ran for home.

'You should have seen it, Mother,' I said breathlessly, as I let myself into the kitchen. 'The city's on fire.'

Mother's face fell as she set down a cup of tea in front of me. 'Poor souls,' she whispered.

We had heard about the nightly bombardments of London but nothing could have prepared me for the sight of it. Since the 350 German bombers filled the skies of London six weeks previously on 7 September, the first night of the Blitz, thousands of people had died. The ten-hour raid on that first night alone killed 436.

Night after night the Germans came. For seventy-six consecutive nights, London was bombed. Central London had copped it. The Strand, the West End and Piccadilly were attacked. St Thomas's Hospital, Buckingham Palace, Lambeth Palace and the House of Commons were all hit.

St Paul's Cathedral stood out, according to one observer, as 'last, loneliest, loveliest, apart . . . in a desolation comparable to Ypres' where my father had fought in the Great War. Even my old place of work, Great Ormond Street, had been bombed. Thank goodness all the sick children had been evacuated by then, but the ward I had once worked on with Princess Tsahai had taken a direct hit.

I'd squeezed my eyes shut and shuddered when I read about it in Father's *Evening Standard* a few days before. Just twelve months previously I had worked there in blissful ignorance of the horrors that lay ahead. Now it barely seemed to matter whether you had your cuffs on when you addressed your seniors. Small, everyday worries paled in comparison with this carnage.

The hospital might in fact have been completely destroyed had it not been for the heroic exploits of one elderly stoker.

William Pendle was a veteran of World War One. Like my father, he wasn't intimidated by the German army.

When the bomb hit the hospital it burst the gas and water mains. Instead of running to the nearest shelter the sixty-seven-year-old waded through waist-deep water and managed to turn off the flooded boilers, just before they exploded. The fact that the hospital stands today is down to him.

William Pendle, like many other courageous and resilient souls, embodied the new phrase, 'Blitz spirit'.

'Britain can take it,' announced Churchill. The victims of the Blitz discovered a new solidarity, shops stayed open, people continued going to work and the mass panic, riots and confusion that Hitler had prophesied weren't happening.

Civilians and ARP wardens worked round the clock, digging out the trapped, injured and dead. Firemen, like Spitfire pilots, became heroes for their seemingly relentless ability to keep working and the operating theatres of London's hospitals soldiered on in the basements.

Emergency food offices and 'Londoners' Meals Service' were set up to provide for homeless people who had lost their ration books, shops and kitchens to bombs.

Even the famous showgirls at the Windmill Theatre danced their way through the Blitz. The theatre became famous for their motto: 'We Never Closed'.

But further to the east of London, the people who were really suffering were the poor working-class, living in and around the docks.

In the crowded tenements and terraced houses with no outside space, they had no shelter at the bottom of the garden to run to, as I did at the Beaumonts'. They were sitting ducks for Hitler's bombs.

The day after witnessing the fires I returned to work but found myself in a sombre mood. I carried on my duties but my mind kept drifting back to the sight of those flames raging into the night sky.

I thought of little Elsie from Bethnal Green, whom I had

cared for at Hothfield, and I felt my heart shudder. Her mother was somewhere in that raging inferno, if she was alive at all. The poor Bethnal Greenies. What was to become of them now?

I remembered reading the letter Miss Edith Taylor, who ran the Bethnal Green day nurseries, had sent us just before the outbreak of war, to tell us about how the mums had gone to see *Me and My Girl* at the theatre. 'The entertainment was greatly enjoyed and we arrived back at Whitechapel at 9.20 p.m. with the mothers dancing "The Lambeth walk" home,' she'd written. Now, a year on, those same spirited mothers would be running for their lives as incendiary bombs split open the skies.

My fellow Norlanders were pounding the bomb-ravaged streets. I'd read of one Norlander's experience in the *Norland Quarterly*, which amazingly, Miss Whitehead still managed to write and send out, though it became the Norland bi-annual because of paper rationing.

A Miss K. Marshall wrote, 'I have been looking after bomb-shattered people in a shelter in a very poor part of London, which has suffered badly from the raids. I had misgivings as to how we should be received as nurses had not been taken to this shelter before. I wondered whether people would take no notice of us or rather resent us. The night was pitch dark but a kind warden led me by the hand and took us down some cracked stairs to the shelter. We arrived blinking like owls in the light. I need have had no fears. About six children rushed at us and seized us by the hand shrieking, "Here's the nurse, let's try on yer tin 'at, Nurse."'

The London child is certainly not shy, nor are his parents for that matter. Fifty people were lying round the benches. All ages between eighty to six weeks, the latter a sweet little person fast asleep in a carry cot, made out of a box lined with American cloth and given by the warden. I think the wardens are beyond all praise.

Everyone's cheerfulness is amazing and everyone is so wonderfully adaptable. They settle down in their little corners. The men play darts, the women knit. The children fall asleep on the damp, grubby, wet floors and never complain. One woman told me she hadn't been to bed for six weeks.

Last night a bomb fell too close for comfort, then another so close the shelter rocked. That one totally demolished the house next door. I expected that to leave people nervous and shaken but they sing 'Roll out the barrel' to drown out the noise of the bombs.

Most wonderful of all I have not heard of one person speak hatred of the Germans, nor of wanting to hurt back. With wonderful people such as these one can hope for peace on earth and goodwill amongst nations, in spite of the present horrors.'

Her letter moved me so. They say times of fear unite nations. This country has never, and I suspect, will never again see such spirit and such camaraderie among the classes.

The bombs, like so many wartime experiences, were a great social leveller. People became just that – people – and sympathy and understanding overruled snobbery. The class divisions of the interwar years were replaced with a 'we're all in it together attitude'.

But the Blitz spirit wasn't just to be found in the cities. It spread the length and breadth of Britain, infusing towns and villages with renewed vigour. Here in Appleton it was well and truly alive and kicking. Us villagers were the backbone of Britain.

Despite the bombs these were good days for Britain and we all knew it. Morale was high and Churchill's speeches roused us up.

Our Baptist church, which I attended every Sunday morning with Mother, Father, Frank, Iris and the children, was packed with worshippers, and everyone chatted after the services.

Villagers went about their business with a stoic air of defiance.

When the Germans dropped a stick of nineteen bombs near the high street, neighbours simply patched up the damage and got on with things. It was pure chance whether you would be the unlucky one or not, but for as long as you stayed lucky, you kept going.

People that had never previously spoken now stopped to chat, and petty arguments and silly feuds fell by the wayside. What good was it praying for peace as the bombs rained down, then squabbling with your neighbour?

Mother and Father were thriving with their new happy family of evacuees, though Mother was still fuming with little Rita's mother, who, despite promising she wouldn't ever do it again, had turned up on the pretence of visiting Rita for a few days, only to do a bunk to meet her latest man.

'She doesn't deserve that little girl, I tell you,' fumed poor Mother.

As for Sally, her guarded violet eyes never left my mother, as she pottered round the kitchen after her.

Little Rita was made of more robust stuff and now she'd come out of her shell she wasn't intimidated by anything. Whenever naughty Basil was home from boarding school he would steal her doll, which she'd named Jesus.

'Rita Fowler, I have Jesus,' he'd tease. 'Jesus has been very naughty today and he needs a spank.'

'Me no Fowler, me Ratcliffe,' she'd scream, ripping her doll out of his hands and belting him round the head with it.

'Don't hit Jesus.'

Mother and Father still insisted on the ritual of their Sunday afternoons together. The evacuees just played out in the garden; there simply wasn't a fear that they would be snatched or anything bad would happen to them.

Even the nursery at the Beaumonts' seemed more relaxed, with Iris coming to spend more and more time with her boys after tea, while I sewed or knitted and allowed them space to bond.

The calm couldn't last, of course. We were at war after all. The incident with the last bombs, coupled with a landmine dropped nearby, made Frank realise that the war was getting a little too close for comfort and it was decided we should all be evacuated to somewhere safer.

At the beginning of November, 1940, Frank drove Iris, Peter, Benjy and me down to our new home in a small village in Devon, before kissing his wife and sons and returning to Appleton.

I didn't really want to go, and neither, I suspect, did Iris, though naturally, she never said as much to me.

I told my mother that we were leaving. It felt like a rotten time to be so far apart from my parents.

'We're in safe hands with your father and his patrol, don't you worry about us, you just look after those little boys. They're your concern now.'

She was right of course. I was loath to leave Mother, Father, dear Sally and funny little Rita, but I was a professional nanny now and my priority had to lie with the safety of the children in my care.

I had to go where the job required me to.

Unfortunately, the job required me to go to the middle of nowhere. It wasn't just my family I would be missing, it was the sense of being in the thick of things.

Frank had taken a house in a village on the northern edge of Dartmoor, miles from anything. There was barely a soul about. At any other time its isolated beauty would have appealed to me, but with all the adventure going on elsewhere I longed to be closer to the action. Now I'd got used to the raids, even they didn't hold the fear they once had. I had changed and I wasn't the only one.

It was an instrumental time in the advancement of British women. Our status was undergoing profound change. War offered up countless opportunities. Women were leaving their homes in their droves, taking off their skirts and pulling on trousers and overalls. They were driving ambulances, working in ammunitions factories, taking on the men's jobs. Even our future Queen, the then Princess Elizabeth, was a subaltern in the Auxiliary Transport Service.

The public couldn't get enough of the so-called Spitfire women, the 164 female pilots of the ATA (Air Transport Auxiliary). When not in combat these women were transporting new or repaired planes to the war zone.

Women were getting their hands dirty for the first time and were no longer seen, as my mother always had been, as the gentler sex. Their new activities offered emancipation unimagined by my mother's generation. It made quite a change from dusting, or baking puddings!

When they weren't working it seemed that most women, in the cities anyway, were drawing seams up the back of their bare legs in pencil, slicking on red lipstick, rolling their hair and hitting the dance halls. One heard of the new crazes that were sweeping London: the jitterbug, swing, boogie-woogie and big-band jazz. Hitler may have described jazz as 'barbaric and bestial music of the sub-human Negro exploited by Jewish capitalists,' but Londoners took to it with a passion. People filled the dance floors in their droves to forget their cares by dancing to it.

Officers on leave escorted their ladies to the Lyons Corner House, where Mother had taken me before the war, to watch the eight-piece band play 'The Rose of Tralee'.

If women weren't kicking up their high heels on the dance floor they were going to the cinema to watch Hollywood stars like Clark Cable, Cary Grant and Jimmy Stewart.

Carmen Miranda in *Down Argentine Way* and Joan Crawford in *Strange Cargo* provided escapist entertainment.

I'd seen photos in Frank's *Evening Standard* of women done up to the nines, tottering through bomb craters in high heels and red lipstick. Churchill had stipulated that a well-groomed feminine appearance was a 'morale booster' for both sexes in these times of strife, and women were flaunting their femininity.

A live for the moment and seize the day attitude prevailed. I'd even heard of young women having illicit affairs. War was freeing women who had been brought up repressed, and they were embracing the new relaxed atmosphere. I suppose there is no greater aphrodisiac than imminent danger and being starved of male company.

Sadly, none of this was the case for me. I hadn't exactly been living the high life in Appleton either, but down here in Devon, the pace was so sleepy that I had the time and energy to reflect on the things I was missing out on.

Make-up and heels were banned from the nursery and there wasn't a man around these parts for miles, not unless you counted the odd weather-beaten farmer, much less a dance hall or cinema.

Just mile upon mile of endless moorland, two young children and an increasingly bored and frustrated mother.

I adored children and my love for Benjy and Peter was now beyond question but what was my destiny? I was no longer a teenager; I was twenty now, my passage into womanhood had been marked by the endless thud of bombs. What did my future hold, where did I fit in to this new way of life that was sweeping the cities? I worshipped my charges but I yearned for adventure, too. Seems I wasn't the only one.

Eventually, Iris cracked.

'It's just so quiet around here,' she stormed. 'I can't bear it any longer. I'm calling Frank to come and get us.'

By the time we returned to Appleton six months later in May 1941, the Battle of Britain and the Blitz were more or less over. Hitler's air force had been redeployed to take part in the invasion of Russia.

Civilian deaths were placed at 43,000. The youngest casualty recorded was that of an eleven-hour-old baby. Eleven hours old! What a heartbreaking statistic. Can you imagine the agony of giving birth to a precious baby only to have him die in such a savage way just a few hours later?

My mind again turned to the Bethnal Green nursery. How many of Elsie and her gang were now orphaned and homeless? Eighty tonnes of bombs had fallen on Bethnal Green alone and Stepney lost 40 per cent of its housing! The East End was a scene of devastation, with large areas derelict and depopulated.

I was needed, now more than ever. Maybe my cause wasn't to drive ambulances and my fate was not to be found on the arm of a GI?

Like a sign from above, fourteen days after the Blitz ended, I was made an official Norland Nurse, further to my year of satisfactory work with the Beaumonts. I was no longer a trainee. Surviving the Battle of Britain and the 110 bombs that had hit the village had been some student training ground!

It was ironic. As more women were leaving the safety of the home and their families, I was now more embedded in the home than ever.

Just as I was beginning to really embrace my life in the nursery, especially now that I was fully qualified and back in Appleton, where I could participate in the war effort, I got a bit of a shock. Something else had happened in our absence, something that was causing quite the stir, in particular amongst the young ladies. The Canadian Artillery Regiment had rolled into the area and was stationed in the grounds of a beautiful local manor house. They were here to train and prepare for the D-Day landings, and their presence had temperatures raised and pulses racing.

Everyone, including me, was utterly hooked by the handsome Canadians. For villages starved of young men, this sudden influx of dashing young soldiers was better than Christmas. These tanned, confident young specimens oozed sex appeal.

I remember the first time I saw their green trucks rumbling up the high street. There must have been ten of them hanging out the side of the truck in their smart, dark-green collar and tie uniforms and their perky little hats.

Their macho swagger and charisma acted like a calling card; by the time they had parked up at the end of the high street they were being mobbed by local girls, who swarmed round them as they handed out sweets, cigarettes and dazzling smiles.

Another two put on an arm-wrestling show, much to the delight of the assembled girls.

'Ainch you strong,' cooed one.

'Have a feel of these babies,' bragged one of the arm wrestlers, flexing his biceps in her face.

'Ooh, it's as 'ard as metal,' she giggled, running her hand down his sleeve.

Where did these girls get their confidence from I wondered?

I was far shyer than that and kept my head down as I pushed Benjy and Peter's pram towards their truck. After all, despite my fascination with the reports of dance halls, and my yearnings for adventure, my contact with the opposite sex had so far been confined to the odd flirtation with a choirboy. I'd led such a sheltered life and could never match the village girls' confident flirting and vigorous hair tossing.

By the time I drew level with the truck I felt quite hot

under my starched Norland collar. I could virtually smell the testosterone oozing off them.

Just then, one stepped in front of my pram and dazzled me with a mega-watt smile. Oh my, he was handsome. His piercing eyes seemed to penetrate right through me.

It's funny. I always remember people's eyes and this young man had the most gorgeous deep-brown ones.

'Good morning, Ma'am,' he drawled, tipping his cap at me.

Suddenly I felt quite flustered and didn't know where to put myself.

'Morning,' I squeaked.

'Cute kids,' he said, with another of those smiles, pinching a delighted little Benjy's chubby cheek.

'Oh, not mine,' I blustered.

As I scurried on my way he winked at me, and a funny little tingle ran up my body. I was still blushing by the time I pushed the boys' pram home.

Iris saw my face and smiled slyly, her blue eyes flashing dangerously.

'Met the Canadians have we, Nurse Brenda?'

I said nothing.

'I have some of the officers coming for dinner as a matter of fact,' she went on.

Trust Iris to get in on it and start entertaining the troops. I might have known.

The officers, when they were arrived later that evening, were no less charming than the rest of the troops.

Iris had gone to town and soon she was laughing gaily as she pressed cocktails into their outstretched hands.

We all sat down to one of Cook's magnificent meals.

'Your home is really beautiful, Mrs Beaumont,' said one officer, drawing back her chair for her.

She positively glowed under the compliment.

'Our little Brenda met some of your soldiers today,' she said, smiling wickedly.

'Just watch out. Ma'am,' warned the officer, looking at me. 'Some are married with children or have sweethearts back home in Canada.'

I was mortified. I wasn't about to go and start an affair with one of them.

I said nothing.

What was it Thomas Jefferson said? 'When angry count to ten before you speak; if very angry, count to one hundred.'

Well, I counted to ten, then excused myself and returned to the place where I felt comfortable. The nursery. My world.

It wasn't just the opposite sex that was enthralled by our glamorous new visitors. The local kids and evacuees were forever trailing round after them, staring in awe as they staged their endless arm-wrestling matches.

A London boys' school by the name of Strand Grammar School had been evacuated to a nearby town, but some of the sixth-formers spent their days hanging out with the troops. The soldiers even erected a homemade boxing ring near their camp and the local children and evacuees would compete as 'paperweights' or 'dustweights'.

How exciting it must have been for these young boys, who ran errands and became unofficial dogsbodies for their new idols. Unbeknown to anyone at the time, these innocent friendships were to prove explosive. A few years later they helped to spark a military alert, at the time of the D-Day landings no less, with members of MI5 arriving to question the boys' headmaster on allegations of being a spy. It was an odd scenario, but then, war does indeed do strange things.

The fifty-four-year-old headmaster of Strand Grammar School, one Leonard S. Dawe, contributed crosswords to the *Daily Telegraph*, in his spare time. On occasion the sixth-formers would help him compile them, and come up with clues. Newspaper crosswords have always been popular but never more so than during the war, when people helped pass the time spent in air-raid shelters by filling them in.

Whilst some members of MI5 were whiling away their idle moments in the month before the planned D-Day invasions with the help of the *Telegraph* crossword, they were stunned to notice vital code names that had been ascribed to the sea-borne assault, appear in the puzzle.

The answer to one clue, 'One of the USA' turned out to be 'Utah'. Innocent enough, but not in May 1944, when it was the code name for the beach assigned to 4th US Assault Division.

Then, on May 22 1944, came the clue 'Red Indian on the Missouri'. Answer, 'Omaha'. Code name for the D-Day beach to be taken by the 1st US Assault Division.

Five days later, MI5 spotted, with what must have been growing disbelief, the clue 'Big-Wig' to which the answer was 'Overlord', the code name for the entire D-Day operation! On 30 May an answer was Mulberry – code name for the floating harbours used in the landings. Finally, on 1 June, and just five days from the first D-Day landings, members of the counter-espionage service must have been floored to see that the solution to 15 Down was Neptune, the codeword for the naval assault phase.

They wasted no time in pulling in Leonard Dawe, the author of all these puzzles, for what surely must have been the most intense questioning of his life. The only possible conclusion appeared to be that he was a spy, tipping off the Germans. He later recollected, 'They turned me inside out.'

He eventually convinced them of his innocence but it was still a mystery. Only years later did some of the former sixth-formers, who aided Dawe in compiling the crosswords, come forward and explain that they learnt the words from the

Canadian troops based in the area. 'The soldiers talked freely in front of me because I was obviously not a German spy,' recalled one former Strand schoolboy.

Back then, no was one aware of the brewing espionage scandal, and a lot of laughter came from the camp. The Canadians quickly became a much-loved fixture among the locals of many surrounding villages. Their charm certainly rubbed off, not just on schoolboys, either, as there were eleven weddings between local girls and Canadian soldiers.

I watched these comings and goings like a bemused bystander, and strange feelings swirled inside me. Not jealousy, no, something else, curious dismay perhaps. When it came to men I was so innocent it wasn't true. I knew nothing of the opposite sex. I wouldn't have known what to do with a handsome soldier even if I did find myself alone with one, and I was too timid to find out.

In the evenings the cheekier children would hide in the long grass around the camp while some of the soldiers took their new lady 'friends' into the fields for some hanky-panky. They'd wait until the soldiers were better acquainted with the object of their affection before launching a surprise attack from their hideout, whooping and dancing round the couples before making a run for it.

I only heard tell of it, mind you, because of course, come evening time, I was always to be found in the nursery. By myself.

Every evening was spent in the same way; knitting, sewing, washing and scrubbing soiled nappies in great buckets of soapy water or ironing. My job wasn't done until I had finished all my chores, and usually these could only be completed after the boys had gone to sleep. I was rarely done before 10.00 p.m. and I could hardly go out after that, especially not when little people would be waking me up at 6.00 the next morning.

We didn't get – nor expect – much time off, not like today's modern women. I tell you this not to invite pity or sound like a martyr; that was simply the way it was and our expectations didn't extend beyond that. Being a nanny is a fairly isolated life, at least in terms of adult company, and you don't go into it if you expect a full and busy social life. There is only so much you can fit into one half day off a week, after all.

Little wonder that so few Norlanders married. A formal survey conducted in 1935 showed that only 25 per cent of nurses married.

Socialising below stairs or with one's employers was unthinkable and many of us found ourselves alone with our charges for the majority of the week.

There was an unstated implication in Norland during the Thirties that personal fulfilment was to be found in serving your family and being the very best nurse you could possibly be. Becoming a nanny is a little like giving yourself to the Lord: you have to do it with your whole heart. And for the most part, I did. Apart from anything else, there were simply more pressing things to worry about.

By summer 1941, it wasn't just food that was rationed. Clothes rationing was introduced and the basic annual ration was sixty-six coupons, with a dress typically costing eleven coupons and a coat thirteen.

Fortunately this did not affect me much as I wore my Norland uniform six and a half days a week. I had to give up twelve coupons in exchange for my uniform, but this was a small sacrifice.

New nurses in training were hit hard, mind you. The Board of Trade fixed the uniform values at eighteen coupons for a cloak, eight for a dress, four for an apron, and did not recognise the necessity for collars and cuffs. The Norland decided that for the first time ever, nurses could wear the long sleeves of their dresses rolled up. Nurses without collars and cuffs, sleeves rolled up? This must have been a bitter pill for Miss Whitehead to swallow, but these were trying times and the Norland had to show they could adapt.

If I did need new clothes I, or Mother, could always run up a new dress. There was nothing we couldn't make do or mend, with old scraps of material. Learning to sew at Pembridge Square was a very useful skill that proved especially handy in wartime. My charges didn't want for clothes, as I used to knit them the most delightful little striped woollies or sew them little shirts. Neither did any of the evacuees. Thanks to a huge shipment of donations from around the world after the Blitz began, an evacuee could be dressed in a pullover from Canada, socks from Australia, shoes from America and a coat from New Zealand. The world was truly a small place during the war.

Fashions were changing around Surrey though. Some of the more daring ladies were wearing trousers; perhaps they were hoping to look a little sporty and chic like Katharine Hepburn. I would never dare, mind you; Mother would have had a blue fit if I wore anything other than a skirt or dress. Ladies simply didn't wear trousers. In fact I didn't wear my first pair until I was in my seventies, and even then not often. Mother did allow shorts with pleats in them on camping trips, on occasion.

As the bombs began, blessedly, to die down, things in Appleton grew calmer; that is until the peace and quiet of the nursery was shattered one morning.

I was changing Benjy's nappy when I heard an ear-piercing scream. Whirling around I saw Peter sat on his potty; his little face the picture of pain.

'Sweetheart,' I gasped. 'What on earth is wrong?'

It was then that I saw his willy was in his hand. He'd been playing around, as three-and-a-half-year-old boys do, and somehow he'd managed to get the foreskin rolled right back and it was stuck fast.

'My winkie hurts,' he roared.

Oh crumbs. The Norland taught me for every eventuality except this one.

Dashing downstairs I picked up the phone and rang the doctor's surgery.

'It's Peter,' I said to the receptionist. 'He's got his foreskin stuck.'

Not five minutes later, the GP was bounding up the stairs, his black leather bag in hand. He took one look at Peter, who by now was quite red in the face.

'Hmm,' he frowned. 'We need to do something about this now. Get him on the nursery table.'

Sweeping aside my knitting, I lifted Peter off the potty and onto the table. Poor little mite was howling in pain.

Seconds later the doctor had administered chloroform, with a cloth over his face.

Peter's little body slumped back on the table.

The doctor moved with astonishing speed. Whipping his scalpel out of his bag, he took Peter's penis in his hand and with a few deft cuts had circumcised him . . . right there on the nursery table. I couldn't believe my eyes.

Bewildered Peter came round to find his willy wrapped in blood-soaked gauze.

I had to break the news to a bemused Iris later, when she visited the nursery for tea. She was relieved that Peter was going to be perfectly fine, of course, but she stayed no longer than usual and there was still nothing but that chilly kiss on the forehead, for either of her sons.

It was me who cuddled little Peter when he cried over the foreskin incident, me who whooped with delight when I saw Benjy's first teeth break through his gums and me who watched his first faltering steps in the garden with pride. Both boys ran to me instinctively when they hurt themselves and needed a cuddle.

I dare say they loved Frank and Iris and they in turn loved their new adopted sons, but really the only time they spent with them was an hour or so a day. The boys' entire lives and day-to-day care was in my hands. I had grown to love them dearly, but my bond with Benjy was absolute. I suppose when you've shared a child's first milestones, you feel your life is intertwined with theirs.

Benjy's little legs were nicely chubby and he was blossoming into a cheeky, happy little boy. But as he approached his second birthday and Peter his fourth, my time with them was coming to an end.

As ever in wartime, events moved rapidly and something was always round the corner to make you realise that your life was never really under your control.

By December 1941 all single women aged eighteen to sixty-five that weren't already contributing, were to be conscripted into the war effort, whether they liked it or not. They had to take up work either in the services, nursing, factories, transport, or the Land Army. Five million women were needed to help fill the roles that the men, fighting on battlefields, had left behind.

The National Service Number Two Act made history because it meant that Britain was the first nation in the world to conscript women.

At this stage the law only applied to single women, married women were exempt, but all women were made to feel uncomfortable if they weren't doing their bit. Posters carried by parading factory girls read: 'Don't queue with the shirkers, join the women workers' and women were told at recruiting rallies, 'If you know anyone who is not working, make them feel darn uncomfortable by giving them the lash of your tongue.'

Iris's days as a lady of leisure were up, and so was my time in her household. It was considered selfish, reckless even, for a woman to employ a nanny to do a job she could quite easily be doing herself, and in any case, Iris may have been exempt from conscription, but I wasn't. War was about to open up a whole host of opportunities. Or so I thought.

I marched along to nearby Leatherhead to register.

En route all sorts of fantastical and exciting possibilities whirled around my mind.

Perhaps I could join the RAF, learn to fly a plane like those brave Spitfire pilots who'd captured my imagination ever since I saw them shoot down a German? Or get my hands dirty driving an ambulance or an army truck.

The sky was the limit . . .

'Impossible,' snapped the bespectacled clerk with whom I had just shared my ambitions.

My dreams burst like a balloon.

'But why?' I asked.

'You have a skill,' he said firmly. 'You are a trained nurse-maid. Do you know how many evacuees there are in this country?'

Not off the top of my head but I could see where this conversation was going.

He was right, I must have been mad to think I could learn to fly a plane. My thoughts drifted back to the Bethnal Green-ies and to little Rita and Sally. I had to stay focussed on why I had trained with the Norland in the first place.

What was it that Miss Whitehead had drummed into us over and over?

'The future is made by the children for whose characters and training you are responsible. Your contribution and examples are valuable.'

There was no point lamenting the fact that I wasn't going

to drive ambulances. My contribution was more powerful and needed than ever before. Construction not destruction. I couldn't fail my charges now. The children of this dreadful war needed stability and love.

Soon after my meeting with the conscription clerk I received notification of my next assignment. Scanning the letter, my eye fixed on the signature of my new employer.

Lady Francesca Smythe-Villiers of Granville House in the village of Little Cranford.

I gulped. Who'd have thought it? Little Brenda Ashford mixing with the aristocracy.

What was I to call her? Francesca? No, that wouldn't do. Lady Smythe-Villiers, or even Your Ladyship? My tummy did little flip-flops of nervous excitement.

I did so hope she was nice, some of these Ladies had some funny ways as well I knew after hearing about Lady Lillian.

When it was time to kiss little Benjy and Peter goodbye I found myself sadder than I could ever have imagined.

I kissed and hugged them tightly.

'Be good boys for your mummy, my darlings,' I whispered.

Bill offered to drive me to the station in the Rolls and as the car pulled off down the drive I turned to wave a last goodbye to my charges through the back window.

Peter was waving furiously and smiling but Benjy's little face wore a worried frown as he stared bewildered after my departing car.

I sighed heavily. So many changes already for him, how I hoped his life would settle down and he'd get the stability he so desperately needed.

But as we sped to Leatherhead train station I could never have guessed at what was coming his way next. Something unspeakably awful and tragic had been unfolding, right under my very nose.

Testimonial

Nurse Brenda leaves of her own accord to take up work in a war nursery. We are very sorry to lose her as she has always proved to be a very capable and conscientious nurse. She was kind and patient with the two boys (aged two and three years) and also took great pains in their training. In short she was very satisfactory in every way and she leaves with our genuine regret.

January 1 1942

8

Crumpets and Coal Fires

> Hush-a-bye baby, on the tree top,
> When the wind blows the cradle will rock;
> When the bough breaks, the cradle will fall,
> And down will come baby, cradle and all.
> English eighteenth-century lullaby

THE BOTTLE-GREEN Daimler was the only car waiting at the station car park, and leaning against its gleaming bonnet, with a copy of *The Times* tucked neatly under his arm, was her driver.

Mr Worboys, His Lordship's chauffeur, was dressed immaculately in a dove-grey suit and peaked cap.

'Brenda Ashford,' I presume, he grinned, revealing a gap between his crooked teeth a mile wide.

He was not by any stretch of the imagination a good-looking man. His face was weather-beaten and his skin more pockmarked than a bomb-shattered London street, but everything about him invited friendship and trust.

Two bright blue eyes shone out of his craggy face.

'Come on then, Nurse Ashford,' he said, with a wink, opening the door for me. 'Hop in. We can't keep Her Ladyship waiting, now can we?'

He hoisted my trunk into the boot, leapt behind the wheel and then we were off, whizzing down the narrow country lanes. As he drove, Mr Worboys kept up a running commentary.

'His Lordship owns all the land for as far as you can see,' he said, sweeping his arm theatrically over the landscape. '2,500 acres they reckon's 'is parish.'

Great swathes of farmland stretched out to the horizon. Did Lord Smythe-Villiers really own all this? What a lucky man. In the spring sunshine the landscape looked absolutely stunning. I'd never seen so much lush green pasture, such beautiful woodlands.

His Lordship's property was deep in the heart of the West Country. Field after field of corn and maize swayed gently in the breeze and beyond that, herds of fat cows grazed contently.

In some of the fields young women toiled away wearing fawn breeches and green jumpers, their faces smeared with mud and sweat. As they worked they sang and laughed.

All day long we work and sing,
We can take whatever Hitler brings,
Give us a shovel and we'll get the job done,
We won't stop 'till this old war's won!

'Land girls,' explained Mr Worboys. 'They weren't so welcome with the farming folk to begin with. That's centuries of farming tradition you're messing about with, letting a load of flippety young girls loose in the fields, but they've proved their worth and now they all rub along together.'

I stared a mite enviously at these young women. I'd read that more than a third came from London and the industrial cities of the north of England, and now conscription had swelled their numbers to 83,000. Each land girl was paid 28 shillings a week (equivalent to £42 today), a very low wage, but food, board and lodging were provided with the job.

How wonderful it must be, to be let loose in all this beauty and fresh air, away from the bomb-shattered cities.

'We're lucky us village folk,' said Mr Worboys. 'We live off the fat of the land in these parts. You won't starve, Brenda, specially not up at Her Ladyship's.'

Soon we were driving through a picture-postcard village and Mr Worboys was parping his horn and waving at passersby, who stared curiously into the car at me.

'This is Little Cranford. You'll never be lonely 'ere you know,' he chuckled. 'Word will have already reached the furthest farm that Her Ladyship's Norland Nanny has arrived.'

If a Hollywood location agent had come looking, they couldn't have found a prettier picture of a quintessential English country village. Nothing bad could ever happen in Little Cranford, of that I was certain. Whitewashed thatched cottages nestled in verdant green gardens, fat creamy-coloured geese dozed in the sun and in the middle of it all stood a sweet little church and duck pond.

'Seventeenth-century, you know,' remarked Mr Worboys proudly. This village was founded by the Anglo Saxons.

'And that there,' he said, nodding towards the building next to the village store. 'Is the church hall. They have the village hop there once a month, you want get yourself down there, Brenda, and meet some of our local lads. Famers' boys most of 'em, bit rough round the edges but 'earts of gold. Reckons they'll love you, Nurse Brenda.'

With that he roared with laughter.

'His Lordship owns all the cottages in this village, in fact he owns most of Little Cranford. That's Mr Webb's place,' he said, pointing to a little worker's cottage facing the church with pink roses climbing up the side. 'His Lordship's valet. Her Ladyship moved Mr Webb from his old place down the road. He weren't right happy about that, I can tell you.'

I was just about to ask him why she would do such a thing when he was off again.

'Susan our district nurse lives over there, she's friendly with the farmer's son Bill. Bill and his father John are the tenant farmers for his Lordship and farm his land.'

'Does everyone round here work for their Lord and Ladyship?' I asked.

Mr Worboys paused and smiled. 'Comes to think of it, yes. A lot of the local women go up to His Lordship's to cook, clean and wash. My missus, Pat, is one of Her Ladyship's dailies. They keep us all occupied, that's for sure.'

As we headed out on the only road out the village I noticed there seemed to be an awful lot of children playing in and around the village streets.

'We've got evacuees coming out our ears,' said Mr Worboys. 'Can't blame 'em. This little corner of England has to be the safest anywhere. No one will drop an ol' bomb on your head here, Nurse Brenda.'

I didn't doubt it for a moment. This sleepy little backwater was a haven of quiet. I couldn't imagine I'd be ducking from flying shrapnel here, that's for sure.

'Her Ladyship oversaw the evacuation, who was billeted where and with whom,' he muttered.

'Oh, is she the billeting officer?' I asked.

'Nope,' he said. 'But she tends to oversee things.'

I wondered nervously what Her Ladyship was like. I had met her only briefly at the family's main seat some weeks before, but the interview was too brief to get a real measure of her. I'd been so intimidated by the grand surroundings I'd just sat there in awe.

She certainly seemed to have a hand in everything that went on around these parts.

'Hard to believe His Lordship owns all this,' I said.

'True. Mind you, it's not like his other place, eh Nurse

Brenda,' whistled Mr Worboys. 'That really is summit else isn't it. Hundreds of rooms, hundreds.

'His Lordship is lovely,' he went on as we bumped down a country lane. 'A nicer gentleman you'd be hard pressed to find. I takes him to the station three times a week so as he can get his train up to the 'ouse of Commons.'

'So why are they down here?' I asked.

'The big house has been requisitioned as a convalescent home for soldiers so they were forced to move to their country seat.'

And with that we came to an abrupt halt in front of one of the loveliest homes I'd ever seen. I stared at my new home in awe. Granville House, the country seat of Lord and Lady Smythe-Villiers, was a seventeenth-century manor house with a slightly wonky roof set in five acres of gardens.

It was pretty as a picture. Pale mauve wisteria curled gently round the old stone porch and swallows had made their homes in the eaves.

The golden brickwork of the house, mellowed over time, looked as much a part of the landscape as the ancient apple trees that dotted the garden.

Chickens scratched and strutted around the drive, feasting on ripe apples as they dropped from the trees.

'So beautiful,' I murmured, wide-eyed, as Mr Worboys slowed the Daimler to a halt in front of a stable block, 500 yards from the house.

The stables had been converted to house the Daimler and another car.

'Me and the missus lives up there,' he said, pointing to a flat above the stable block. 'If you need anything, Brenda, anything, just ask.'

Mr Worboys had given me a thorough run down on the village but there was still one thing about which I was none the wiser.

'What's Lady Francesca like, Mr Worboys?' I asked.

His face darkened.

'Her Ladyship? Well, how can I put this . . .'

Suddenly the door to the manor house swung open and his voice trailed off. There in the doorway was the most formidable-looking woman I'd ever set eyes on.

Lady Francesca Smythe-Villiers.

When I had first met her she had been sitting down, but now I could see she towered over me at 6ft tall. Despite being well into her sixties she had an almost regal bearing and stood ramrod straight like a statue in the stone porch.

When I glanced back, Mr Worboys had vanished into thin air. I was on my own.

Her Ladyship's slate-grey eyes were piercing and seemed to stare right down into the depths of my soul. The thin lips, hook nose and grey bun only added to the austere image.

'Nurse Ashford, are you quite well?' she said in a clipped voice.

'Good morning,' I gushed. 'I can't tell you how excited I am to be here.'

'I'm sure,' Her Ladyship replied, in a deadpan voice.

I did what I always do when I'm nervous and in the company of someone I feel to be my intellectual superior. I start to babble. On and on I went about the journey, the weather.

'Anyway, here I am and I can't wait to get started,' I blustered.

Her Ladyship's eyes never left mine for a moment and I quickly realised that hers was a face not accustomed to smiling.

'Follow me,' she said eventually. 'I'll introduce you to our evacuees.'

The upstairs, downstairs divide might have been dying out amongst the aristocratic families of England but here at Granville House, Lady Francesca Smythe-Villiers, was keeping the tradition going.

'This door,' she said, pointing to an old oak door at the end of a passageway, 'leads to his Lordship's quarters and mine. You are permitted to breakfast with us but lunch, tea and supper are to be taken with your charges in your quarters. You and the evacuees are not permitted in that part of the house. His Lordship needs peace and quiet.'

Her hard stare didn't invite any further questioning on the matter.

Our quarters turned out to be perfectly lovely. A huge old bedroom, with the most glorious views over the surrounding countryside, had been turned into a day nursery. A coal fire burned merrily in the grate and toys were scattered about the place. Two separate bedrooms had been allocated to the evacuees, one for the boys and one for the girls, and my small bedroom led off the same passageway.

My evacuees were perfectly lovely, charming little people, though I quickly realised, by the hushed silence that fell over the room when Her Ladyship strode in, that they were just as much in awe of the Lady of the manor as I was.

There were five of the poor little souls, separated from their mothers and fathers. This bunch weren't from the poor East End but from other areas of bomb-hit London and weren't half as robust as the Bethnal Greenies.

'Are you having a wonderful time?' I asked the eldest boy, who seemed to have made himself unofficial leader.

I made sure to crouch down so I was at his eye level.

Throughout my entire career I have always made sure to get down to a child's level. How on earth can you communicate with a child if you are looking down on them, much less expect them to like and trust you? Children cannot get up to your level, so you have to go down to theirs; try and understand how the world looks through their eyes.

Once I was at the same height as him I saw him relax and drop his guard.

'Yes nurse, we are,' he smiled.

Her Ladyship hovered nearby watching us with those steely eyes of hers.

John was the ringleader and the eldest at five, the other four ranged between two and five.

'It's great here,' he told me. 'There's so much to do. We've climbed trees and there's a place where you can pick strawberries and eat them straight off the bush.'

'Really, how wonderful,' I said. 'You must show me where.'

'Oh, we will,' piped up a shy little girl behind John. 'You know they have something called spring here in the country, they do, they have it once a year.'

Her blue eyes shone with such sincerity.

It would have been so easy to laugh at the little girl's innocent remark but I would have lost her trust forever so I kept my face as straight as a die.

'Well, that is just marvellous. I can't wait to explore.'

After that Her Ladyship nodded curtly, then left. The air in the nursery lightened just a little.

I stared at these sweet little souls and found myself marvelling at their spirit. They had been taken from their families to live in a strange place where they knew no one. If they could find the best in the situation then so could I.

I jolly well wouldn't let the imposing Lady Smythe-Villiers intimidate me.

The nursery was scattered with many of the popular toys of the day, little metal soldiers, not to mention books on Biggles and other popular children's literature about the war. A lot of the books, called things like 'Adventure by night' and 'Brave boys and girls in war time' were pocket-sized and specially designed to take into air-raid shelters.

I could never understand that. We were surrounded by the war, why did we have to let it invade the nursery? I made a mental note to clear them out and get the children playing other games. Biggles would be replaced with Rupert the Bear that very evening!

Later, as I helped the children get dressed and into bed, I felt so sad. Each evacuee had a small case, in which they had heartbreakingly little. Each of the girls had just one vest, one pair of pants, one bodice, one petticoat, two pairs of stockings, a handkerchief and a cardigan. The boys had even less: a vest, a shirt, one pair of pants, one pullover, one jersey, one pair of trousers and a handkerchief. Apart from a comb, some soap, plimsolls and a toothbrush, that was all their worldly possessions.

I didn't know how long these evacuees had been in Little Cranford but you could be sure when they'd arrived on the train from St Pancras, clutching their gas masks and their identity labels, they had not the faintest clue where they'd be going or when they'd see their parents again. Siblings were often separated, too. During the course of the war there were 34 million changes of address. Children were moved constantly, shunted from place to place, their fate decided by the local billeting officer.

This lot would have arrived bewildered and scared, and been promptly lined up in the village hall, where no doubt Her Ladyship would have had first pick, before deciding who was to be billeted with whom. Each billetor was paid ten shillings and six pence for the first evacuee, and an additional eight shillings and six pence for each extra one.

Having now met Her Ladyship properly, I could see how many of the local villagers would have found it hard to refuse her directions, particularly as it was Her Ladyship's houses they were living in.

Some years later I heard a headmaster's report of a local school evacuated to the west of England.

> In many cases the billeting officers are the owners of these cottages. The people living in them find it very difficult to refuse to have evacuees. They probably work for him or her as gamekeepers, gardeners, chauffeurs, etc. The feudal system is still in full swing in these districts and the cottagers dare not refuse to have children.

It could have been written about Little Cranford.

Over the coming weeks I quickly came to see that Her Ladyship was not particularly popular in the village. My goodness she was dictatorial. What Her Ladyship said, went.

There was nothing that woman didn't have a hand in. She'd moved her husband's valet from his cottage at the drop of a hat and was prone to moving people around the village on a whim. No one dared stand up to her. If she turned up on your doorstep with a command to move cottages or take on another couple of evacuees, you jolly well did!

Was it all a power game to her? To know that she could uproot families at the flick of her wrist? Hard to know, but she didn't make it easy to warm to her, that's for certain.

Even her own husband, Lord Smythe-Villiers seemed a little in awe of her. For three days a week he may have held sway over the House of Commons, but in his home it was his wife who ruled the roost.

I used to love my breakfasts with his Lordship.

Every morning I would take my seat at the table next to him.

'Morning, nurse Brenda,' he'd say. Well into his sixties, he had a gentle, soft voice, and seemed tiny beside his tall wife.

'Morning, Your Lordship,' I'd reply, beaming back at him.

Lord Smythe-Villiers was as English as a cream tea. He was descended from distinguished naval captains.

On the days he travelled to the House of Commons, where he represented his constituency as a Conservative MP, he was always beautiful dressed by Mr Webb, his valet, in a navy pinstripe suit.

Rumour had it he was also much involved in the anti-air-craft defence of London. Not that I ever dared ask him about that over breakfast. Our conversation never went beyond small talk but I loved to sit beside him in companionable silence.

Every now and again he'd pick up a dish and hand it to me.

'Don't forget your Bemax, Nurse Brenda,' he'd say. 'It'll keep you healthy.'

Bemax was a wheatgerm cereal that you sprinkled onto your breakfast as a health supplement.

His Lordship loved Bemax, in fact I rather think he thought liberal sprinklings of it on our morning porridge would be sufficient to win the war.

I would watch in fascination as, after breakfast, Mr Webb would bring in his freshly ironed copy of *The Times*.

After he'd finished his paper and coffee, Mr Worboys would bring the Daimler round to the front, and drive His Lordship to the station where the stationmaster would be waiting to usher him into a first-class carriage. It was another world.

After he left, a stream of dailies came in from the village, including Pat Worboys, the chauffeur's wife. These ladies were exempt from conscription, either because they were married, or because of their age. Instead they did no end of tasks for Her Ladyship, from cooking and scrubbing to washing all our clothes and sheets.

Her Ladyship treated these women as servants, which of

course to her they were, but I always made an extra special effort to be friendly to them. I didn't want them thinking I shared Her Ladyship's airs and graces. We were all equal as far as I was concerned.

The wonderful side effect of having so much help was that I could spend more time with the children, and I was less tired out. How joyful to be a nanny who didn't spend her days and nights with her hands plunged deep into buckets of soapy suds or tackling endless mountains of ironing. I was free from the drudgery of nursery housework. It was blissful.

Little Cranford was a veritable fairyland of sunshine and fresh air. During the day we had the most glorious time. John showed me where the wild strawberries grew and as we sat and feasted on them I'd tell stories or we'd sing songs. Sometimes we'd tramp through the fields for hours singing or playing 'It'.

Other times we'd paddle in the streams, pick bluebells and collect frogspawn. The countryside was beyond beautiful and those spring days seemed endless. Away from the oppressive gaze of Her Ladyship we could roam free and be whoever we wanted to be.

It took me right back to the roughs and my glorious childhood with my brothers.

Our days were filled with fun but of course I made sure to instruct my charges, too. It was vital that despite the horrors unfolding in the wider world, precisely *because* of those horrors, we maintain the virtues I had been instructed in throughout my childhood and at the Norland.

Once, I caught John eating his food with his hands.

'We don't eat with our hands here, John,' I chastised. 'That is what a knife and fork are for.'

If I ever caught any of the children looking sloppy they

were quickly reproached. 'Pull yourself together and pull up your socks,' I'd insist.

We always made sure our hands were washed before we ate, no elbows on the table, you ate as much as you could on your plate, never spoke with your mouth full, enquired politely whether you may be excused from the table after eating and always made sure to say please and thank you.

I was adamant that certain basic rules be followed. Never put out your tongue, never bite your nails or clean them in public, never scratch your head and avoid all other repulsive habits including spitting, cursing or using vulgar language.

Good manners were drummed into me growing up and so as far as I was concerned, my charges should be brought up with the same respect for etiquette. I firmly believe that if you show respect to others they in turn will show you respect. That includes listening to someone when they are talking, without interrupting them, and looking people in the face and smiling when you meet them. It never hurts to try and remember people's names when first introduced and use their name when talking to them. It's the little things in life that count, and kindness costs nothing. Manners are part of our national heritage and should be observed keenly. All this might make me sound like the most terrible disciplinarian but I so believe that a child is what you make them.

Balance is vitally important, too. I know how difficult it is to tread that line. Even when the children had been naughty, I made sure that I didn't spend the day solely telling them off or it would have badly crushed their confidence. I always made sure to treat John and his little friends to plenty of encouragement, praise, kisses and cuddles, especially at bedtime. Children thrive on affection and can never have too much love. Her Ladyship was most undemonstrative so someone had to make sure their emotional needs were being met.

I wondered what Her Ladyship had been like with her own children. She had three of them, all grown up and living away from home and all with terribly grand and important jobs in London. Did they ever get cuddles and kisses when they were growing up?

Who knew, but under my care I didn't want my evacuees to know a minute's loneliness or fear.

Seems my charges weren't the only ones having a wonderful experience. In the *Norland Quarterly*, which Mother posted to me, Nurse Doris Card wrote, 'I am caring for an evacuated nursery school from Deptford in London. Life is so busy. The other day, twenty three-year-olds encountered a herd of cows, you would have thought a zoo had been let loose. The children when they first arrived after many bombings were limp and would do nothing but sit by the fire. Now they play quite happily. We have few excitements, although a three-year-old did let out a styful of small pigs and we didn't know what to do first, collect the squeaking pigs or small children. Their physical health improves greatly. All the children have put on weight and one little boy whose toes touched when he walked he was so bandy has now perfectly normal limbs.'

Another nurse, a lady by the name of Lettice Birch wrote, 'I have two delightful brothers from Bermondsey. Alfie, six and Jimmy, three. Alfie is good-looking with beautiful big grey eyes. He was both father and mother to Jimmy. Jimmy is pale, plain and given to bronchitis, but he is, even after twelve years Norlanding, quite the most observant and amusing child I have ever known. My additional charge, Carolyn (Caro-lion to Jimmy to the end) is eleven months and loves to watch the boys. She has curly hair and one lock often falls over her forehead. "Cor," piped up Jimmy. "She looks like 'itler."

'On another occasion Jimmy was out for a walk with us when he observed a flock of birds flying by.

'"Aint they lovely," he said. "And all made out of eggs too." Although they came from a poor home they were far more obedient and tidy than many children I have known in well-to-do nurseries.'

Norland nurses from all over shared their wartime experiences. Some talked of the difficulties of evacuating children abroad.

A Nurse Castle and Nurse Wallace had the unenviable task of delivering fifty-two schoolchildren to their parents by sea from England to Hong Kong, dropping some off en route in Mombassa, Bombay and Singapore.

'We had two air-raid warnings before we left England and had to stay below decks for the night. What a business it was getting fifty-two children to carry their lifebelts. To make it easy we got some tape and marked each of our children's lifebelts. In the blackout at night we could feel this tape and knew it was one of ours. One of our duties was to prevent the children being a nuisance to the other passengers. We heard terrific shouting one day and found two first-class men offering six pence to the boy who could make the loudest noise for the longest time. More first-class passengers would give the smallest children sweets and soft drinks and then they would not eat their meals. Miss Castle had a bright idea. She tied a label to the wee boy's sweater, saying: "Please do not feed this child or give him anything to drink".

'When we arrived at Bombay we were so thankful to hand over our charges to their adoring parents. How we worked before arriving there and the heat, oh how we dripped! Packing up the trunks in those hot cabins and washing shirts for all the children to look a credit to their Norland Matrons. What a time. We always had our portholes shut and had to carry our lifebelts because of mine fields. We saw our destroyer hunting a U-boat. Britain is going strong.'

I was impressed and proud at the bravery and ingenuity of my fellow Norlanders.

Thankfully I didn't have to take my evacuees across oceans but I did have to get them all in the bath once a week, which sometimes felt scarcely less of a feat.

Friday night was bath night. The children were bathed once a week and the hour after tea on a Friday was hotly anticipated.

Once a week may not sound much to you, but during the war that was about the average. Everyone had a duty not to use much water and the wartime ration for a bath was just three inches of water once a week.

Hot buttered crumpets would be wolfed down as I fetched up pails of warm water from the kitchen.

Mrs Worboys would come in to help and together we would drag the huge tin bath in front of the coal fire.

Once the fire was stoked up and roaring and the bath foaming with soapy suds the fun would begin.

'Who's up first?' I'd ask. A sea of hands would shoot into the air.

'Me . . . me . . . me,' clamoured the evacuees.

In went John first, for a good rub down. A week's worth of mud and grime floated off as I scrubbed and sang 'This little piggy went to market,' grabbing one of John's toes to wash it.

'Look, Nurse Brenda,' he said, slathering foam on his chin. 'I've grown a beard.'

As he poked his tongue through the foam the rest of the children were quite helpless with giggles.

One by one they were dunked in and then out, in a little cleaning conveyor belt. By the time Mrs Worboys and I finished there were five little children all squeaky clean and wrapped in towels.

'Hard to say who's wetter,' I said, as I clambered to my feet rubbing my soapy hands on a sopping wet apron. 'Us or the children.'

Mrs Worboys, flushed red with steam, laughed.

'Right enough, Brenda.'

Once all the children were snug in their pyjamas and nighties, we'd huddle round the fire for warmth and I'd read them the adventures of Rupert the Bear, as my beloved father did all those years before.

One by one, little eyes, sleepy and toasty warm from the fire, would start to droop and close, until the floor was a mass of slumbering little bodies. The children had so much fresh air during the day that no matter how hard they tried they could never stay up past 8.00 p.m.

Together, Mrs Worboys and I would gently carry them to their beds where the sweet slumbering land of nod was waiting.

As I tenderly tucked them in under their eiderdowns, love flooded my heart. These little people were so brave. I never heard them crying for their parents or caught them being really naughty. They just got on with things. Somewhere out there in the dark, their parents were risking their lives for our country and freedom. The children must have missed them desperately and I encouraged them to write to their parents often, and tell them about all the fun they were having here at Little Cranford. In those days the phone was only for emergencies, so snail mail was the only option available to us.

Sadly, my charges' parents never visited. Not because they didn't love them. It was just too far to travel from London, too expensive and they didn't get enough time off.

How I prayed the homes these children had left behind would still be standing when they returned, and more importantly, that their families would still be intact.

During the war, 130,000 children lost a parent in active service. Goodness only knew how many orphans were being created as they slept soundly in their beds. It broke my heart just to imagine.

At the thought of orphans I remembered Benjy and Peter and made a mental note to request a call home and find out how everyone was. I hoped Peter wasn't too scarred after the stuck foreskin incident and little Benjy was feeling a little more secure after my sudden departure from Appleton.

War makes little folk resilient and children are nothing if not adaptable, but all the same, Benjy had already survived an orphanage, the threat of Nazi invasion and the Battle of Britain and he was only two. Something made me a little more protective of him than any of my previous charges. He had a heartbreaking fragility about him that plucked at my heartstrings.

The following day, Her Ladyship allowed me to make one brief phone call home.

I knew I didn't have long, and my words were spilling over themselves as soon as Mother answered. I heard the worry in her voice when she picked up the receiver, but I quickly assured her that I was perfectly fine, just missing them all.

'How is everyone?' I demanded. 'Sally and Rita keeping you busy? How's Father? Still arranging his troops? And what news of Benjy and Peter?'

'Slow down, Brenda,' said my mother, laughing. 'Everyone is very well. We haven't seen Peter and Benjy around recently, mind you.'

I didn't like the sound of that. The niggle of worry I had felt when I left them returned, a little stronger.

But Mother was bright and breezy, so I did my best to shrug it off and instead I told her all about my new job, ten to the dozen, before all too soon it was time to go, amid a flurry of my promises to come to visit soon and her urging me to take care.

I sighed as I heard her replace the receiver in its cradle. Hearing my mother's voice made me miss her all the more.

It wasn't until a few months after my arrival at Little Cranford that I was given leave and could travel home by train for a rare weekend off. I couldn't wait to see Mother and Father, not to mention Sally, Rita, Peter and my beloved Benjy.

Mother welcomed me home with an enormous hug and a steaming mug of tea. Gratefully I sank down on a chair next to the fire. Travelling by public transport during the war was never easy and one never knew entirely how long one's journey would take. I was cold, hungry and exhausted.

As I warmed myself by the fire I was brimming over with questions.

'How are Peter and Benjy?' I asked, eventually.

My mother's face fell and suddenly an awkward silence filled the space between us.

'Mother, please just tell me,' I urged.

'I heard Iris and Frank gave Benjy up for adoption.'

Disbelief then horror settled over my heart.

'They did what?' I gasped.

'I'm sorry,' she mumbled. 'I know you were fond of Benjy.'

I wasn't just fond of him. I loved that little boy dearly. A cry of anguish escaped from my lips and I put down my cup.

How dare they, how dare they do that?

I remembered his bewildered face as I'd left and the blood in my veins turned to ice. I was filled with a hopeless rage. Why would they do such a thing? It was beyond me.

Just then Mother's face fell.

'What else, just tell me Mother,' I urged.

'Well they have adopted another child so I hear, a little girl. A little white girl,' she said.

I couldn't believe they had swapped Benjy for a white child!

'Where has he gone?' I raged.

'No-one knows,' Mother whispered.

Suddenly I felt quite crushed by the injustice of it. My poor, poor sweet Benjy. Please don't let him be lying back on a bunk bed in the orphanage.

What was wrong with Iris and Frank? They had that little boy baptised into their family, had promised to love and raise him as their own. They were supposed to be a God-fearing family!

Was the idea of having a child of a different race really so abhorrent? The irony wasn't lost on me. Here we all were, fighting tooth and nail to defend our country from the Nazis and their hateful ideas about racial superiority, and yet possibly the same rancid and bigoted beliefs had been festering away in the very family I worked for.

They must have had their reasons for doing so. They weren't bad people after all. Who knows what happened after I left and what circumstances conspired to create this situation. It was after all hearsay, but it did affect me so deeply. That little boy needed love.

All children just need love, pure and simple. Is that too much to ask? Loving a child, to me, is the most instinctive thing you can do. And if you live in a community you accept who's there, and you get along with everyone, be they black, white, man or woman.

From that moment a sense of injustice settled in my heart and even today I don't think it's ever truly left me. I felt what they did so badly and I wasn't the only one. It broke the friendship between my mother and the Beaumonts.

Today Benjy would be seventy-three. Where is he now

I wonder? I hope he found the happiness and security he so desperately needed.

Benjy wasn't the only one suffering. Mother's illegitimate evacuee, Rita, the little girl she'd cared for so fastidiously and who now called my mother mummy, had gone.

'Just like that, after two years her mother turned up one evening and said she'd come to collect Rita,' said Mother.

She'd barely taken the time to write or visit and when she did she'd stayed five minutes and used the cheap rail fares allotted to families of evacuees as an opportunity to nick off with her latest fancy man.

'I don't know where they've gone or if I shall ever see that little girl again,' my mother confided in me. 'I miss her terribly.'

Not half as much as Rita missed Mother, I'd be willing to bet. I wonder if she remembers her village sanctuary and the place where, for a brief while, she found a family?

Benjy, Rita and Sally. Abandoned, ignored and rejected by their feckless parents. What messages were we sending to them, how would they grow up to behave?

What was the Norland motto? 'Love Never Faileth.' Well never again, not on my watch.

9

Stolen Kisses

The course of true love never did run smooth
Midsummer Night's Dream, William Shakespeare

BY THE time I arrived back in Little Cranford my shock had eased a little and I found myself looking forward to seeing John and the rest of the evacuees again and putting into practice my stiffened resolve to love and protect every child on my watch.

How I'd missed my little poppets and the glorious countryside I'd grown to adore. After a wonderful spring and summer in Little Cranford, autumn was brewing and I could smell it in the air.

There is nothing so precious as autumn sunshine and I could not wait to take my charges out in its beautiful golden, mellow light. To point out the dazzling show of red and gold from the chestnuts, oaks and maples, falling leaves swirling in the autumn breeze.

My mouth watered at the thought of all those wild hawthorns just waiting to be picked from the bushes, ripe apples and plump blackberries, so delicious under a cloud of cream.

I smiled as I imagined John charging through a pile of crunchy leaves in his welly boots and countless little cold hands that could be warmed by the nursery fire when we got home after one of our walks. Yes, there was much to look forward to.

The sadness that had settled over my heart since I'd heard the news of Benjy was still there but I owed it to my evacuees not to live in the past.

Mr Worboys had come to pick me up as before, and was waiting at the station with his trademark grin.

Over these past few months I'd found myself growing fond of His Lordship's chauffeur. He was a real gent and a countryman through and through. He was as loyal as the day was long to his Lordship, and loyalty is a much underrated characteristic in my book.

'Hello, Nurse Brenda,' he said warmly as I got in the car. 'There's a few little people who've missed you, I can tell you. Her Ladyship's been busy too,' he added mysteriously.

Oh dear. What had she been up to now?

On the drive back to Granville House I gazed out the window and found myself marvelling once again at the peace and solitude of the countryside at this time of war. This green and pleasant corner of England was in marked contrast to its bustling cities, which teemed with accents from all corners of the world. By now the war had well and truly gone global.

British soldiers, sailors and airmen found themselves posted to any far-flung corner of the world. My brother, Michael, was now serving with the RAF in India, after training in Canada. Christopher, David and Basil and the rest of the boys from their boarding school had been evacuated to Coniston in the Lake District and from what I could tell, were having the time of their lives.

Evacuation had done nothing to dampen Basil's sense of mischief. Indeed he had gained a new partner in crime at boarding school. He had befriended Robin Day, later to become legendary broadcaster Sir Robin Day.

Concerned that they weren't getting their full rations

of Spam they managed to get into the store cupboard and enjoyed many a Spam-based midnight feast. Perhaps a childhood spent with Basil gave Sir Robin the backbone to tackle Margaret Thatcher.

Meanwhile, as our boys went overseas, so our shores were filling up with all manner of nationalities. In London up to fifty different uniforms could be spotted, as soldiers of every creed, colour and nationality pounded the streets and filled the dance halls.

In particular, the Yanks were making a big impact. 'Oversexed and over here' grumbled some of the less charitable objectors. But I never heard tell of any bad stories, only consideration, kindness and charm. Indeed in a booklet prepared by the US war department and issued to every American soldier entering the country as a wartime guest the GIs were told: 'Britain may look a little shop-worn and grimy to you. There's been a war on since 1939. The houses haven't been painted, because factories are not making paint – they're making planes. British trains are cold because power is used for industry, not for heating. The British people are anxious for you to know that in normal times Britain looks much prettier, cleaner and neater. Don't be misled by the British tendency to be soft spoken and polite. They can be plenty tough, too. The English language didn't spread across the oceans because these people were 'panty-waists'. Remember that crossing the ocean doesn't automatically make you a hero. There are housewives in aprons and youngsters in knee pants who have lived through more explosives than many soldiers saw in the last war.'

What's more they were ordered to respect us women too.

'British women have proved themselves during this war. They have stuck to their posts near burning ammunition dumps, delivered messages under fire after their motorcycles

have been blasted from under them. They have pulled avia-
tors from burning planes. There isn't a single record of any
British woman quitting her post, or failing in her duty. When
you see a girl in uniform with a bit of ribbon on her tunic,
remember, she didn't get it for knitting more socks than
anyone else in Ipswich.'

The Yanks also endeared themselves to their numerous
fans by giving away silk stockings and cigarettes. Like them
or loathe them, they were here to stay.

Not that there was a whiff of a foreign accent in Little
Cranford or any men bearing gifts of silk stockings. Just farmers and their sons.

Little did I know it then but as the leaves turned golden on
the trees and the fruits ripened ready for harvest, the winds
of change were blowing my way, too. A man was about to
make an appearance in my life.

Back at Granville House I hugged each of my evacuees
warmly.

'I've missed you all my darlings,' I said, crouching down
to their level.

Just then I noticed a face I didn't know peering at me. A
new evacuee had arrived in my absence.

'Hello, sweetheart,' I said, with a big smile. 'What's your
name?'

The serious-looking girl gazed at me with big solemn eyes
and said nothing. Poor mite, she was probably shy.

Just then Her Ladyship swept into the nursery.

'This is Gretal,' she said. 'She's a refugee. She will be staying with us for a while. Gretal doesn't speak much English.'

So this was what Lady Smythe-Villiers had been up to. I
was heartened to see Her Ladyship's meddling was at least in
a good cause.

Gretal and her parents were Jews who had escaped from

Germany. She was just one of the estimated 10,000 Jewish children who fled Germany at the outbreak of World War Two to avoid Nazi persecution.

I never could discover any more about them, their story and how it was they came to be in Little Cranford, but the village was alive with gossip about our refugees.

Over the coming weeks I tried to reach out to Gretal but she was painfully shy and scared witless.

Soon after she arrived there was a fierce storm. Rain drummed against the windows and lightning split open the skies.

I found Gretal huddled in her bedroom hugging her knees and sobbing softly to herself.

'Oh my darling,' I cried when I found her. 'Come here. Don't be scared, thunder is only the clouds knocking together.'

But she shrank back from my touch, terror and misery flashing in her blue eyes.

Those pale eyes said it all and a million emotions seemed to race through them; pain, bewilderment, fear.

Just what horrors had this little girl seen? How unspeakably awful that this little girl, no older than five, had been forced to flee her home and her friends and all that was familiar in her life and hide out here. She was the human face of this war. The reason we were all fighting and sacrificing so much to save our country from tyranny.

Just then there was a low rumble of thunder and a howl of anguish escaped from Gretal's lips.

'Mama. I want mama.'

'Mama and Papa will come soon,' I soothed.

Her Ladyship had billeted her parents with some of the locals in the village. I knew it was no business of mine, but it struck me as so odd. Could there really be no room there for her? Her father was an educated man, a professor so I heard, and Her Ladyship seemed to treat him with a great deal of respect. Maybe they thought it best she be around other children, but Gretal obviously didn't, and cried day and night for her parents. When they did visit it just upset her further, especially when they left.

'Me go with papa,' she'd cry.

'You must stay here, Gretal,' he said softly, untangling himself from her embrace.

Gretal's papa seemed a kindly enough man but like Her Ladyship he was terribly proper. He must have witnessed unimaginable sights himself, of course, but he seemed adept at keeping his feelings locked inside. I dare say he and his wife were grateful for a safe haven and didn't want to rock the boat, but I did so feel for that little girl.

For hours after their visits she'd sit in the corner, hugging her teddy, quite alone in her misery. It was little wonder she felt abandoned in this strange country, where Lords and Ladies lived in one part of the house and children in the other.

Little Gretal had no interest in playing with John and the rest of the evacuees and always hung back, even at meal times. Even Friday night bath time, always a time of high excitement amongst the rest of the giggly gang, didn't raise so much as a flicker of a smile on that sad little face.

How I hated seeing her suffering and fragility.

I wracked my brains. There had to be a way to win this little girl over and gain her trust. I had to let her know I was on her side. Just getting down to her level wasn't enough, nor was singing her nursery rhymes or telling her the stories of my youth. The language barrier meant she simply didn't understand them.

'What is the key here?' I puzzled, night after night. I was

failing my charge and to me that was simply unthinkable. What was it they say?

Failure teaches success – try again!

But it was just so difficult. What language could I communicate to her in? One day the answer came to me. What was missing in Gretal's life? Fun, that's what.

So the next day, during our morning walk, I instigated a new game.

'Let's all pretend to make animal noises,' I announced.

John started first with a marvellous impression of a duck. His quacking soon had everyone in stitches. Then it was my turn.

'I am a lion,' I said. I tipped my head back and roared. 'Let's all roar.'

Soon the fields around Little Cranford were echoing with the sound of roaring lions.

I looked at Gretal.

A funny little sound escaped her lips. A laugh!

I roared again. There it was again. A throaty little giggle that lifted my spirits.

She never fully came out of her shell but from that day on I think she knew she could trust me. I learnt an important lesson from Gretal. Just as important as love, children need fun in their life.

My time in the countryside taught me a great many important lessons, not all of them to do with childcare.

Country folk respect the land. When you live off it you have to nurture it, and learn to follow its natural ebb and flow. Chickens weren't eaten that much during the war as their eggs were too important. Likewise the land needed to be treated like an untapped gold mine.

The countryside around Little Cranford was mostly farming land already, but any scraps that hadn't been given over to food production now were. During the war the number of acres of British soil under cultivation rose from twelve million in 1939 to just under eighteen million by the end of the war. Tractors were every bit as important as tanks, and numbers rose four times throughout the war.

At the beginning of the war, 70 per cent of our food was imported, by 1943 that figure was reversed.

Britain had to establish a new relationship with nature. Mr Middleton, one of the most popular broadcasters of the time said, 'Turn your gardens into munitions factories, for potatoes, carrots and onions are munitions of war as much as shells and bullets are.'

Land all over the country, be it small allotments, tennis courts and golf courses had been dug up to provide food. Hyde Park in London had its own piggery, potatoes were being grown at Hampton Court Palace and chickens now clucked in Pembridge Square, the smart Kensington address that housed the Norland Institute where I had done my training just before the outbreak of the war.

Even *Vogue* advised its readers: 'Our land, whether inherited acres or a council allotment, now has but one significance – food. It is the nation's larder.'

Britain was bringing in the biggest harvest of the century.

Government schemes clamped down on the black market trade in food and there were huge penalties for infringing the food regulations. The Ministry of Food issued posters and they were plastered over the village notice boards. 'It's not clever to get more than your fair share.'

Here in Little Cranford the villagers operated their own unofficial food swap system. A farmer might swap the landlord of the local pub a rabbit for five eggs, or eggs for some bread. Villagers would eat anything in a pie, mostly rabbit but even squirrel and road kill.

People rubbed along together nicely in the countryside

and no one starved. In fact, thanks to the fresh air and profusion of local vegetables I felt better than I ever had.

We all seemed to be obsessed with staying healthy. My evacuees got free orange juice and cod liver oil, which I administered daily, and His Lordship would never sit at the House of Commons without a stomach full of porridge and Bemax.

Suddenly everyone learnt how to cook and stretch and substitute. I still say I have never seen people healthier than in wartime. We didn't overeat and we watched what we put into our mouths. Emergency measures had brought about the very reform that pre-war nutritionists had campaigned for. We hardly ate sweets or chocolate, drank alcohol and we never touched processed food, apart from powdered egg and milk.

Food production was war work, vital to keep the nation going, yet despite the huge efforts of our farmers on the land, lots of people thought they had it easy and had somehow ducked out of doing their duty.

One lady whom I befriended in the village knew this attitude better than most.

Susan, the village district nurse was courting a local farmer by the name of Bill. Bill and his father John were the tenant farmers for his Lord and Ladyship. Susan was a lovely woman, real salt of the earth and fiercely proud of her man.

'Easy, as if?' she was heard to mutter on occasion. 'Anyone that thinks that should join him for a day on the farm, starting at 5.00 a.m. and not drawing breath for twelve hours, six days a week. Then we'll see who has it easy.'

I admired her loyalty immensely.

For the most part my evacuees were fit and healthy but Susan came by once a month to check on them and I warmed to her instantly. She was hard-working, and her faith in the

Lord and love for Bill were everything to her. I was most impressed with her medical knowledge and care for people.

One day Susan had a suggestion for me.

'Do you think you can make it out next week?' she asked, when she stopped off on her rounds one morning.

'I could try,' I said.

'Good.' She gave me a grin. 'The village hop is on.'

With that she pedalled off and I found myself smiling. The village hop. I was sure it wouldn't be half as grand as the London dance halls but it was no less thrilling a prospect to me. I loved dancing, lived for it in fact. When I was growing up Mother would take me for dance classes at a function room behind the local pub. It was the highlight of my week. Sadly we had to stop when Father lost his business.

'I'm sorry, darling,' she'd told me and my brothers and sister. 'We simply can't afford it.'

I was most aggrieved. 'The others don't love it as much as me though,' I cried.

My protests fell on deaf ears. Mother was the fairest woman I ever knew.

'What I do for one, I have to do for all,' she'd reply, indicating that the matter was now closed. Of course I was most put out back then, but that little lesson served me well in life. One has to be fair in all one's dealings.

Still, I did so love to dance and thought of dancing at the village hop filled me with excitement.

I don't think I'd had a night out since this blessed war began three years ago. How could I? I'd been too busy looking after my charges. But now that I had so much help from Her Ladyship's staff, there was much less for me to do of an evening. Yes, a night at the village hop would be most agreeable.

So it was arranged that I would be accompanied to the hop by a local farmhand by the name of Tom.

I'd taken care with my appearance that night, changing out of my Norland uniform and putting on a lovely cotton floral dress. I swapped my flat shoes for a pair with a slight heel and combed my hair out, but that was the extent of my beautification. I was twenty-one and I don't think make-up had ever touched my face.

Many women in those days improvised, as make-up was scarce. Some used beetroot juice as rouge and in the absence of foundation camomile was mixed with cold cream.

I wouldn't have known what to do with a tube of lipstick even if you'd been able to find me one.

'Best make do with what Mother Nature provided,' I said to myself, fluffing up my hair in the mirror.

A small knock at the back door indicated that my date for the evening was here.

Tom was a man of few words, which was just as well as he wasn't the sharpest knife in the tool kit, but he was very sweet, not to mention jolly handsome. He had lovely thick curly hair, dreamy dark eyes you could get lost in and strong muscular forearms, browned by a summer of harvesting hay bales in the fields.

Nervously he took off his cap.

'Can I accompany you to the hop, Brenda?' he said, in his thick country accent.

'Yes please,' I said, a little more eagerly than I'd planned.

He held out a hand the size of a small tractor and grinned shyly.

'You wash up real fine, Brenda,' he said, his eyes shining with sincerity.

I wasn't sure if this was a compliment, but as we walked to the village I realised Tom didn't have a mean bone in his body. We didn't manage much in the way of conversation, though, so it was a relief to reach the hop.

They may have been Jitterbugging up a storm elsewhere but in these parts it was a little more innocent. Trestle tables with a small selection of sandwiches lined the edges of the village hall and a makeshift bar was set up in the corner.

A gramophone playing dance music by Henry Hall, Jack Payne and Ambrose crackled in the corner.

'Can I get you a drink, Brenda?' asked Tom shyly.

Apart from a sip of Mother's sherry at Christmas I'd never really drunk alcohol before. I'd far rather have had a lemonade but I didn't want to appear unsophisticated. But what to ask for? Beer was a man's drink and wine wasn't really available. Gin and tonic always struck me as a glamorous drink. Iris always used to sip a G&T in the evening.

'I'll have a gin and tonic please,' I replied.

Seconds later Tom was pressing a paper cup containing a little clear, warm liquid into my hand. It was all gin and no tonic. Ice wasn't available either, not that I would have known it needed lots of it to make it drinkable.

I took a big sip and grimaced. The liquid trickled down my throat and a second later I felt like my gullet was on fire.

Goodness gracious.

'Oh I say,' I spluttered.

'Strong isn't it,' laughed Tom.

As the fiery sensation in my throat died down I felt a lovely warm glow in my tummy and soon it had spread right down to the tips of my toes.

'It's rather nice, this,' I said, taking another gulp.

'Well . . .' said Tom awkwardly. Suddenly I realised I was looking at his back retreating across the empty dance floor.

Tom had scuttled off to join all the other farmhands. The room had segregated, with all the local women and land girls standing on one side of the hall and all the men huddled on the other.

I suppressed a giggle. The women far outnumbered the men and for all the world it looked like a human cattle call, with the women eying up what hapless, terrified looking males were left.

'No matter,' I thought, taking another swig of my drink.

It was really rather good stuff this gin. Made me feel terribly happy and glowy.

By the time I finished my drink I was roaring drunk. Even my face was tingling. I giggled as I tried and failed to place a fingertip on the end of my nose. Suddenly a newfound confidence gripped me.

I had come here to dance and dance I jolly well would.

'Swhere's Tom,' I slurred to myself.

I started to cross the dance floor but the tiresome thing kept moving. Weaving my way I narrowly avoided a collision with a trestle table before planting myself in front of Tom.

'Dance, please,' I ordered a stunned looking Tom.

'You heard the lady,' grinned the man he was chatting to.

Tom did as ordered and before long we were spinning round the room together, his strong arms preventing me from falling flat on my face on the floor of the village hall.

Suddenly a hand gripped Tom's shoulder and I whirled round in surprise.

'Excuse me?' said the man Tom had been chatting to before.

'Henry is the name,' he announced confidently as he cut in, his hands encircling my waist. 'Now be a good thing and step aside, Tom.'

Tom was left standing, his mouth flapping open and shut like a stranded goldfish as Henry whisked me into his arms.

'You don't want to waste your time with him when you

could be dancing with a real man,' he whispered to me, and winked.

Well, of all the cheeky . . .

Henry danced with great gusto, his tall body leading the way. All through the song he kept up a stream of constant chatter. I'd barely finished answering one of his questions when he was asking me another. Golly, he was so interested in my life.

Henry was by no means as good-looking as Tom. He was very ordinary in fact, with pale eyes unlike the chocolate-brown ones I preferred, but he certainly had a smooth tongue.

'You're a real lady,' he whispered in my ear. 'I'd never have left you in the corner.'

Before long Tom had recovered from the indignity of being left standing and cut back in.

'Excuse me,' he muttered grimly, firmly removing Henry's arm from mine.

Back and forth, back and forth I went all night like a ping-pong ball, between Tom and Henry's arms. What a night. I had never felt so in demand.

It could have been the gin and tonic or the amorous advances of my competitive farmhands but by the end of the evening my head was spinning and I had stars in my eyes.

'The last waltz belongs to me,' said Henry, issuing me with a dazzling smile.

Succumbing to his slightly forceful charm I allowed my exhausted head to rest on his shoulder and swayed dreamily in his arms.

I went to the hop with Tom but it was Henry I left with.

As we tottered along the country lanes, the fresh night air sobering me up, I realised my hand was clamped firmly in Henry's.

It may have been a frosty autumn night, so cold and clear

our breath hung in the air like smoke, but inside I was toasty warm. The after-effects of the gin or was something more magical weaving its spell on me?

Soon we reached Granville House and on the porch we turned to face one another.

'I knew you'd come home with me,' Henry said softly, a touch arrogantly.

'Oh yes,' I laughed. 'And what made you so sure of that?'

'Because Tom and I had a bet on who would see you home, and I never lose a bet, Brenda Ashford.'

'Goodnight, Henry,' I said, smiling.

It was pitch black outside, but as I turned to close the door I saw his satisfied grin. He looked like the cat that got the cream.

As I flopped into bed, my head was spinning from the events of the evening. Poor Tom. He was such a lovely chap and I hadn't meant to abandon him but there was just something about Henry. Sure, he was cocky but I found his arrogance endearing in a strange way. He'd also been the perfect gentleman. He delivered me home safe and sound and hadn't even tried to kiss me, though if he'd tried I probably would have found it hard to say no.

The next morning, over breakfast with His Lordship, I grinned like the Cheshire cat, even my Bemax didn't taste quite as bad. And when I took my charges out for their morning walk I felt as if I was floating on air. Was this what it felt like to be in love? It was probably too soon to say, but one thing was for sure, Henry had left a big impression on me.

I felt like I'd gained entry to an exclusive club. Romance had finally come into my life and now I had men actually fighting over me. What fun!

Mr Worboys was outside the stable block, polishing his Lordship's Daimler and chuckled when he saw me.

'I daresay someone had a good time at the hop last night,' he said.

'I wouldn't like to say, Mr Worboys,' I said, but I couldn't hide the smile on my face.

That euphoric feeling lasted all day. Even Her Ladyship coming into the nursery to inspect the children didn't pop my cloud of joy.

Henry had promised to take me out again and he made good on his promise. He turned up the very next day, clutching a bunch of wild flowers he'd picked.

I was playing with the children by the stable block when he arrived. I could tell by the way he strutted up the path like he owned the place and casually placed one foot up on the upturned bucket Mr Worboys had been using to wash the Daimler with earlier, that he'd lost none of his confident swagger.

Dressed in his casual farming gear, and smelling faintly of manure, did little to diminish his appeal in my eyes.

I felt my heart start to race a little.

'You look lovely in your uniform, Brenda,' he said with a smile, looking me up and down.

I blushed furiously as the children stopped the game they were playing and looked at the more interesting new one being played out before them.

'How do you fancy being taken out for tea by me on your next half day off?' he asked. 'They do a mean cream tea in the next village.'

It wasn't much of a first date by today's standards I'll wager, but to an impressionable twenty-one-year-old back in 1942 it was better than an invitation to the Ritz.

'Oh, I'd love to,' I gushed.

'Good, I'll pick you up around three, then. Be ready.'

And then he was gone. All the evacuees stared curiously

after this cocky young man as he bounded down the drive humming to himself.

'You've got a funny look on your face, Nurse Brenda,' John said finally.

'Have I?' I murmured.

I counted down the days, hours and minutes to our date and on the day agonised over what to wear.

Mrs Worboys found me on the afternoon wailing to myself in the bedroom.

'What ever is wrong Brenda, dear?' she asked.

'It's my date with Henry. He's taking me for tea in the next village but I have nothing to wear,' I cried in despair. 'Nothing.'

I didn't own any of the silk stockings that some of the lucky girls in the cities were given by GIs, nor make-up or jewellery.

Her face flickered with concern.

'A date with Henry the farmhand?' she frowned. 'You will be careful won't you?'

But I wasn't listening. I was too busy trying to put on my only pair of nylon stockings without laddering them. By the time I was ready in a pretty red dress, I felt quite the catch.

Henry whistled when he came to collect me. 'Brenda, you look beautiful,' he said.

Then we were off, whizzing through the countryside, on the local bus.

When you're having so much fun, an hour can feel like a minute.

It was nothing fancy. Just a scone, jam and a cup of tea but by the end my head was whirling and my mind was racing. Henry had such a way with words and made me feel like the most interesting person alive.

He had big ambitions for his father's farm and wanted to make something of himself.

'I'd love my own family you know, Brenda,' he said, holding my hand over the table. 'I'd like to fill that farmhouse with kiddies.'

His eyes shone with sincerity as he stared right at me.

It was all too much, just too much. Unspeakable joy flooded through me. Little Cranford was the best place to be in the whole world right now. I felt my heart would burst with happiness.

I would probably have to leave the Norland of course but Henry would be worth it.

We hopped on the bus and held hands all the way home to Little Cranford.

Outside Granville House we paused.

'Well . . .' I said, shifting nervously.

'Well . . .' Henry smiled, his eyes twinkling mischievously. 'Sorry it wasn't dinner. When the war's over I'll take you out to a proper fancy restaurant.'

Suddenly he edged closer and I felt a hot flush snake up my chest.

'Enough is as good as a feast,' I blustered. 'I . . .'

But then I found I couldn't speak. Henry's lips were on mine, his hands tenderly clutching my face.

Oh my . . ..

I kept my eyes squeezed shut the whole while, for fear that if I opened them I might somehow break this magic spell. Henry tasted of cherry jam and smelt of autumn leaves. Never was a kiss so sweet.

As we separated, I was aware of lots of little faces watching me from the upstairs nursery window. Noses were pressed excitedly to the glass. I smiled to myself. Little folk love it when they spot adults getting up to what they consider 'naughty business'. Then another thought occurred to me. Had Her Ladyship seen us and if so, what, I wondered would she make of it? A little uneasy feeling nagged but I pushed it to one side. What business was it of hers who I was seeing?

Henry and I parted with more promises to meet up soon and I floated inside and up to my room in a delicious haze. So this was what love felt like? This was what all the fuss was about? It was a revelation.

By coincidence my walk with the children the next morning took us by way of Henry's father's farm, and there was Henry, working in the fields.

I stood and watched admiringly as he stacked hay bales onto the back of a tractor and trailer. They must have weighed a tonne but he tossed them about as if they were as light as baby lambs.

His face broke out like a sunbeam when he saw me.

'Think you can sneak out later?' he asked, leaning over the wooden fence between us.

I felt the energy pulse between us and I couldn't help but giggle.

Her Ladyship might not approve, but I'd had it with her interfering ways, and for the first time since I clung to the side of the fire escape at boarding school, my sense of adventure kicked in.

Now was my shot at romance! Why should the girls back in Appleton have all the fun? Suddenly I yearned for a life outside the nursery.

Before I had a chance to change my mind I opened my mouth.

'Yes,' I whispered impetuously. 'But where?'

There was nowhere to go. I could hardly sneak him in the house under Her Ladyship's nose, that would never do, but we couldn't stay outside either. The nights were drawing in and it was perishing cold and dark in the fields after sundown.

'We'll think of something,' he said, removing a stray hair from above my eye.

As his hand brushed my face I felt a tingle run the length of my spine.

'Till later then,' he grinned.

On the way home I puzzled my new dilemma over. I wanted to see Henry again desperately, but how? The countryside in wartime England wasn't exactly set up for romantic liaisons and I really didn't fancy puckering up in a soggy ditch.

I was still deep in thought by the time we returned to Granville House.

Mr Worboys gave me a cheery wave when he saw me.

'What's up with you, Nurse Brenda?' he asked. 'You look as if you have the cares of the world on your shoulders.'

I hesitated.

'I've met someone,' I said. 'His name is . . .'

'Henry,' he interrupted. 'I knows that.'

You couldn't really keep anything secret in the countryside.

'Problem is, Mr Worboys, we've nowhere to meet,' I sighed. 'I couldn't bear the thought of only seeing him on my half day off. Besides, by the time we've got anywhere it's time to come home again.'

Mr Worboys stared at me and scratched his head. He paused, as if he were about to say something he shouldn't.

'Well then, Nurse Brenda,' he sighed eventually. 'Her Ladyship'll string me up if she hears this, so keep it under your hat like, but it is unlucky that you young folk have nowhere to meet.

'Tonight I'll leave His Lordship's Daimler unlocked and you can meet in there. Our secret, alright?'

And with that, his lovely craggy face broke out into an enormous grin.

I could have kissed him there and then. 'Oh, thank you,' I said. 'Thank you, thank you.'

'It's alright Nurse Brenda,' he chuckled. 'I can see as how you're keen on him.'

Later, when my charges were safely tucked up in their beds, there was a small knock on the back door. I scurried downstairs.

Henry was waiting, with a twinkle in his eye.

'His Lordship's car,' I hissed. 'Follow me.'

Click. The door was unlocked just as promised.

Once inside I suddenly felt a bit scared and I realised my heart was pounding. The car smelt of leather and grown ups. This was His Lordship's car. What if Her Ladyship were to throw open the garage door? She'd be in a fearful rage if she knew we were in here.

'Relax,' said Henry confidently, making himself comfy on the back seat. 'She'll never come in here.'

The leather seat creaked as he drew me close and we started to kiss in the dark. My legs began to tremble. Suddenly I felt terribly out of my depth. I hoped Henry wouldn't get the wrong impression from our tryst in His Lordship's motor. I was a virgin and I intended to stay that way for the time being.

A live-for-the-moment attitude might have seized the rest of Britain, with people having illicit affairs left, right and centre but I had no intention of giving my virginity up on the back seat of a Daimler.

I didn't know exactly how people got pregnant but I knew the consequences of it. To have a baby out of wedlock was simply inconceivable to me and would have caused a major scandal.

Fortunately Henry was the perfect gentleman and didn't try anything. But we kissed that evening, oh how we kissed. It felt like hours. We smooched for so long I thought my lips might drop off. He kissed me with such tenderness I could have stayed in his arms all night. Nowhere felt more comfortable, safe or warm.

'I'm falling in love with you, Brenda Ashford,' he breathed in my ear.

Love and longing stirred deep inside me. I felt like a heroine in a Hollywood film.

'I . . . I . . .'

Just then a shrill whistle pierced the night air outside the garage doors.

'My Worboys,' I gasped, springing out of Henry's arms. 'He said he'd whistle at half past ten.'

Feeling like Cinderella, I kissed Henry one last time and leapt out the car.

The next morning I could barely wipe the smile off my face. My poor lips felt bruised but my heart was alive. My joy must have been infectious as the children were as giddy as a spring lambs. We played catch and ball games and even Gretal seemed to come out of her shell and join in.

While I played childish games in the sunshine, I was blissfully unaware that my handsome farmhand was playing his own darker and more dangerous game. But ignorance, as they say, is bliss and over the next six months the love between Henry and me deepened.

He played me like a fiddle and I fell for him hook, line and sinker.

I wasn't the only one taken in. Mr Worboys, bless him, left the car unlocked for us most nights and I used every spare second to meet Henry down in the fields or on my half Sundays off. There was no Baptist church around for miles, so I didn't even have to feel guilty about spending that time with my suitor.

When you are in love life seems to come alive in a wonderful way, colours seem brighter, smells more vivid, the landscape more beautiful. The year 1942 would go down in history. The year I fell in love for the first time.

Henry respected me as well as loved me, I could tell. He never put a scrap of pressure on me in the back of the Daimler and he even invited me to his farm for Sunday afternoon tea with his parents.

Sunday afternoon tea was a big deal for farming folk. They'd got their best china out and even laid the table with a clean white tablecloth. Plates groaned with home-made drop scones and thick slabs of bread with beef dripping. Leaf tea was freshly brewed and poured from an enormous brown pot. The kitchen was flooded with warmth, light and the smell of baking.

Conversation mainly centred around the farm and when this 'old' war would come to an end.

But I didn't care. Henry and I exchanged secret smiles over the drop scones. He was including me in his family, which could only mean one thing.

Golly, I was nervous. So scared in fact I'm sure my teacup rattled every time I picked it up. My tummy was churning too, so as I could barely eat a nibble of my cake. His parents were lovely people though, and when we left we made promises to meet again soon.

In turn, on my next weekend off, I took Henry home.

My parents had moved by now from Bookham to north of the Thames, to St Albans in Hertfordshire.

Mother was in a frenzy of excitement.

'Brenda's bringing home a gentleman to meet the family,' she'd smiled, when I told her.

But when Henry met her and Father, a funny thing happened.

They never said as much as they are far too polite, but I could tell they didn't like him. Just subtle little things that

Henry would never have picked up on, but something told me they didn't warm to him.

When Henry talked confidently of his ambitions for the future, Father's smile never quite reached his eyes and Mother was polite, too polite.

I ignored their cool reserve though; they would warm to him eventually. Henry was the best thing since sliced bread as far as I was concerned.

Back in Little Cranford, news of our romance had spread on the bush telegraph.

I was just folding the children's clothes away in their chest of drawers one morning when Mrs Worboys came in. I could tell by the way her mouth was twitching that she had something to say.

'I've been speaking to Her Ladyship, Brenda,' she began.

My heart sank.

'S . . . she, that is to say, we,' she stuttered. 'We're worried about you. You *are* being, well, careful aren't you? Her Ladyship doesn't really approve of your relationship.'

I bristled. How dare she? She wasn't to know that Henry and I hadn't consummated our relationship and I was as pure as the driven snow, but in any case, what business of hers was it who I was seeing or what I was doing? I wasn't her servant.

'You both must think me very naïve,' I snapped. 'Of course I am careful.'

'I'm sure, Brenda,' she soothed. 'It's just that you know nothing of life.'

She was right, but I wasn't about to tell her that when it came to sex and birth control, I did indeed know nothing. We didn't learn about the birds and the bees at school and Mother taught me virtually nothing. The only time I remember her broaching the subject of sex was when she sat me down to tell me that she used to douche with hot water as a contraceptive. The pill wouldn't be available for nearly another twenty years, so back then, that was all that was really available to her.

But even during this conversation, I still didn't really manage to understand anything about what really went on. I had a vague sense that babies came about as the result of some sort of physical intimacy, and I knew that such a thing was permissible only within marriage – I had, after all, met plenty of illegitimate babies and their poor mothers. But I was stunningly innocent. I supposed her Ladyship had guessed as much.

After that the tension in the nursery grew.

I made a point of being as professional as they come, I was a Norland nurse after all, but when she came into the room the air between us was icy and the conversation stilted. I suppose she must have resented her lack of control over me. I wasn't one of her minions she could order about at will.

But despite the oppressive influence of Her Ladyship, this was an exciting time. I adored my charges, I was in love and Britain was an exciting place to be.

In May 1943 I took stock of my life. I had been in Little Cranford for fourteen months now and I was starting to get itchy feet. I loved my charges and Henry dearly but life under the scrutiny of Her Ladyship was exhausting. I didn't want to end up like poor old Mr Webb, a whipping boy for an elderly aristocrat who couldn't let the ways of the old world go.

The evacuees were settled and happy now. My work here was done. There were children who needed me more elsewhere and adventures just waiting to be had.

I confided in Henry on my next half day off.

'You must go,' he urged. 'We will be together when this war has ended.'

He smiled and pulled me into his arms.

As I nestled into his jumper I felt a pang of regret. He was so caring, so thoughtful. Was I doing the right thing?

'Besides,' he added. 'You can come back and visit can't you.'

He was right. It wasn't the end of us. Just me and Her Ladyship.

Once I'd made the decision I felt euphoric. I told Her Ladyship at the earliest opportunity, in her quarters.

'I very much appreciate the opportunity but it is time for me to move on,' I said as politely as I could. 'I've heard a day nursery near my parents' house needs help, so I shall be joining them.'

Her slate-grey eyes narrowed as she stared at me long and hard without moving a muscle.

Outside I could hear the dailies scurrying about, polishing the floors and bagging up the laundry. They lived in fear of a dressing down from her and doubtless would be moving as fast as they could in case she opened the door.

Well you can't intimidate me now. I'm not your servant.

'As you will, Nurse Ashford,' she said finally.

Walking out of her room I felt like a weight had been lifted from my shoulders.

I was free.

It was sad saying goodbye to my charges and dear old Mr Worboys but as ever I resolved to look forward not back.

'Place won't be the same without you,' smiled Mr Worboys as he drove me to the station one last time. 'No more assignations in the back of the Daimler. Right boring it'll be,' he grumbled. 'The little 'un's will miss you too.'

'Thank you,' I said, planting a gentle kiss on his cheek. 'I'll never forget your kindness.'

Back at home I missed Henry desperately and as I had a little break before starting at my next job, I returned by train shortly after to see him.

We had arranged that I would stay with Susan in her spare room, but Henry would collect me from the station.

I simply could not wait to see him. We could hold hands in the street and not feel like we were having to sneak about behind Her Ladyship's back.

Alighting from the train I nervously played with my hair as I waited for Henry's old farm truck to come rattling round the corner.

I smiled as I imagined the sweet kiss he would give me and his cocksure smile. Perhaps we could even go to the village hop again if it were on.

I pulled my coat around me and checked my watch. Strange. He was supposed to be here twenty minutes ago. He must have been caught up with some business on the farm. No matter. I'd walk to Susan's. The fresh air would do me good.

By the time I reached her cottage, my cheeks must have been glowing as red as an apple.

'Let me in then,' I puffed, as Susan opened the door. 'It's perishing out here and I've had to walk from the station. Henry must have been delayed.'

As soon as I saw her face, I knew something was wrong. She was wearing that same angst-ridden expression Mother had the day she told me little Benjy had been adopted.

Oh no. Please not more bad news.

'Sit down, Brenda,' she said softly, pulling up a chair by the fire.

Without taking off my coat I sat down heavily and pulled it round me as if for protection.

'Is he all right?' I blurted. 'Has he been called up? Has something happened?'

'He's fine, Brenda,' she said. 'It's nothing like that.'

Poor Susan. Her gentle, soft face was stricken. Whatever the news was she didn't want to be the one to break it.

'It's just that, well, there's no easy way to say this. He's been cheating on you.'

I froze.

'What do you mean?' I gasped.

'He's been seeing a girl two villages along,' she said sadly. 'I'm so sorry, Brenda. I know how you felt for him.'

'W . . . what, the whole eight months?' I squeaked.

She nodded, as if she wanted the floor to open up and swallow her.

I felt as if I was drowning.

'No,' I cried. 'But he can't have been.'

The betrayal hit me like a punch in the chest. I thought it couldn't get worse but then . . .

'Apparently this girl found out about you and when she heard he'd been to visit your parents she threatened to sue him for breach of promise. It's the talk of the village.'

I felt like I was going to throw up. He was promised to someone else all along. All the while we were courting, he was stringing us both along.

What a silly, silly fool I'd been.

I thought of this other girl. I had no idea he was engaged to someone else, someone who probably didn't even live that far from Little Cranford. Poor girl, she had been saving herself for heartless Henry, just like me.

Her threat to sue him for breach of promise sheds a little light on the repressed times we were living in. In the cities people may have been indulging in all sorts of wild behaviour, but here in the country, saving oneself for the right man meant everything.

Henry's promise to marry this lady could be considered a legally binding contract and he obviously took her threats to sue him seriously, given that he returned to her when she made them. Perhaps she had already given up her virginity to him and, horrified to find out about me, was concerned with the damage to her reputation and loss of status.

Changing social mores have all but led to the collapse of this kind of action but back then in Little Cranford, breach of promise was taken seriously. Henry had been playing a dangerous game in stringing us both along.

I slumped back in my chair utterly defeated.

For the first time in months I saw what everyone else had seen. Mrs Worboys, Her Ladyship, my own parents. They all saw through him. They knew his cocky attitude was a front for his breathtaking deceit.

He was nothing but a scoundrel.

'Oh I'm such a fool,' I wept. 'I was prepared to give it all up for him.'

Susan placed her arms around me and stroked my hair.

'No, you're not,' she insisted. 'You loved him, he betrayed you, and he fooled us all, Brenda.'

But her kind words did nothing to ease my agony. I was utterly heartbroken.

'I thought he was the cat's whiskers,' I sobbed.

My first brush with romance had been a disaster.

As I sat in Susan's kitchen wallowing in heartbreak, the chairman of the Norland was sending out a newsletter to celebrate the Institute's fiftieth anniversary.

'In a world wholly different from that in which Mrs Walter Ward was inspired to found the Institute, we can celebrate its fiftieth anniversary confident that, it, at least, is the same,' wrote Hester Laird Wilson.

But the world around me was no longer the same. Far from it, my heart had been broken, a little piece of my soul bruised forever.

Lying in Susan's spare bed that night I stared into the dark and wondered what would become of me. If not a farmer's wife then what? It seemed that the nursery was my calling after all. I felt so cruelly let down by love that I didn't see how I could ever risk it again.

Little did I know it, but the peace and quiet of the nursery as I knew it was to be shattered forever. Coming my way was a riot of noise, dirt, disease, illegitimate babies, adultery, deserters and scandal; all set against a backdrop of some of the most lethal warfare the country had ever seen.

Oh yes. Life was about to get interesting.

Testimonial

Nurse Brenda Ashford has been here since March 9 1942. She has been nurse in charge of a small residential war nursery in our house consisting of evacuated children and one refugee child, ages about two years to five years. The numbers have varied from two to five children and for about the last six months, five children. Some help given. She is essentially a well brought up girl from a good home who desires to do what is true and right and to work conscientiously. She has had very good experience here. She is active, industrious and capable. She takes an interest in the children's health and is watchful to notice if they are not well. She is helpful and obliging and does not mind what she does. She much likes children, especially I think, the tiny ones. She leaves entirely of her own wish, as she wants to work in a day nursery near her own home. Nurse Brenda has got on very well indeed with household staff and has been pleasant with them.

10

We'll Meet Again

There was an old woman who lived in a shoe,
She had so many children she didn't know what to do!
English eighteenth-century nursery rhyme

IT WAS 7.45 on a Monday morning at the Redbourn day
nursery in Hertfordshire and all was quiet. The sickly sweet
smell of cod liver oil hung in the air and as I shrugged off my
coat it caught me right in the back of my throat.

Working quickly I bustled round the room drawing the
blackout curtains and throwing open the windows. A stream
of fresh spring sunshine flooded in and, gratefully, I gulped
the fresh air. Closing my eyes, I savoured the sound of silence.
I loved this time of the morning. The nursery was all mine
and I could gather my wits about me and brace myself for the
onslaught.

There was just time for my daily inspection. Rows and
rows of children's pegs lined the wall. Each little peg had a
boat or a golliwog emblem. I strode along making sure that
each also had the requisite little white cotton overall that I'd
hand stitched, a towel and a flannel.

Then, humming and smoothing down my Norland uniform, I threw open the door to the kitchen and lit the flame
under the huge coal-serviced copper. As it began to groan
and creak into life I heard the clanking of bottles outside. I

smiled. Martin Webb, the local milkman, had arrived in his
old blue Morris van.

Martin came from a long line of milkmen and he and
his two boys, Ray and Geoff, were part of the fabric of this
community. The Webbs had been serving fresh frothy milk
from a seventeen-gallon churn for over a hundred years, first
on a handcart, then by horse and cart and now by van. The
business had been handed down from generation to generation. The Webbs came from hard-working country stock
and were typical of the village characters that Redbourn
seemed to breed.

Situated between St Albans and Dunstable, the village used
to be a stopping point for resting horses drawing Royal Mail
coaches en route to and from London. It was a sleepy little
place where everyone knew everyone else and even though
I'd only been working here for four months, I was already
feeling at home in the close-knit community.

The job couldn't have come at a better time for me. I
needed a new focus, and the distraction of so many children
to lavish my love on was most welcome. There was still a
sharp stab of pain in my stomach every time I thought of
Henry's betrayal but I forced myself not to wallow in things.
And mostly, I simply didn't have time. My day started early,
since it took me forty minutes on the bus to get here from
where I now lived with Mother, Father and our remaining
evacuee, Sally. And once here, I immersed myself in the task
at hand.

That life still centred around the common, where chickens
and geese roamed. The village cricket team gathered there
to while away lazy summer afternoons with the soft thud of
leather on willow. Saturdays would see local boys and evacuees pitting their skills against each other in boisterous games
of football. Come winter these same boys would be helpless

with laughter as they slid along the icy paths that cut across the open space, often landing in a scrummage of flailing arms and legs.

The common was lined with rows of pretty terraced cottages, and the high street, which was the hub of the community, ran off from one side. The narrow road was lined with businesses that had been in the same family for generations, amongst them a grocer's, a butcher's, a baker's and a tailor's. It was just a stone's throw from the nursery and I could easily wander over to top up provisions. The high street was always full of hustle and bustle and I loved chatting to the village characters.

The smell of the silver-haired baker's freshly baked cottage loaves and sugary doughnuts drifted up the street, competing with the sound of the fruiterer, John, shouting out the quality of his wares.

'Come and getcha lovely pears. Nice an sorft an juicy,' he'd bellow.

His lungs were so powerful I was sure villagers from neighbouring communities could hear him.

Redbourn even had its own resident cobbler's shop, run by a smiley, dumpy man by the name of Arthur. Arthur was as deaf as a doorpost. What he lacked in auditory ability he made up for with superb craftsmanship, and everyone in the village took everything from leather shoes to footballs and horse harnesses to him to restitch.

In the middle of the high street was Bill the blacksmith's forge. His warm workshop seemed to shelter many a man hiding out from the wife, and the sinewy old blacksmith was always ready to trade gossip.

There were pubs, of course. When I walked past the Jolly Gardeners and the Cricketers they seemed to house many an old boy, permanently nursing a pint of ale with a cigarette clamped between nicotine stained teeth. Not that I went into these establishments myself. There was never time, and I couldn't bear the smell of beer, either.

At the far end of the high street there was a jam factory, which filled the whole road with a sickly sweet smell when the jam was being boiled. Next to the factory was a yard where animal hides were tanned and prepared for leather processing. One can only imagine the stench of jam and animal hide mixed together.

Two of the biggest characters went by the names of Ron and John, both of whom formed part of the duty squad at the ARP headquarters, which bordered the common.

Ron used to suffer from unfortunate mental spasms, which caused him to stargaze as if hypnotised. This would have been less of a problem, I suppose, had his day job not been delivering groceries. When his eyes started to go in the middle of a delivery he was a danger to himself and the public alike, as the morning he ran into the wall of the disused gas works, scattering apples far and wide proved. He also had a penchant for soldering, and running out of things to solder one night at the ARP headquarters he busied himself sticking darts into the kettle so he could mend it. A tray of sausage rolls usually kept him distracted.

Then there was John. John was a baker with a stammer.

One night John was on patrol when he heard someone approach through the darkness on a bicycle.

'Who g . . . g . . . goes there, friend or f . . . f . . . foe,' he stuttered.

Getting no response he threw his walking stick at the 'enemy'. There was an almighty crash.

'I'll give yer friend or foe if I gits me 'ands on yer,' bellowed a voice in the night.

Centuries of unchanged tradition had been observed and

celebrated by these characters, from May Day through to Michaelmas.

The friendliest was always the milkman, though.

'Morning, Brenda,' said Martin now, with a beam. 'Lots of lovely milk and butter for the children today.'

He unloaded vast pats of glistening unsalted butter and jugs of creamy full-fat unpasteurised milk, collected straight from Fish Street Farm a few fields away, just hours earlier. It wasn't until a few years after the war that legislation was passed to ensure that all milk was pasteurised. Back then the milk was as fresh as it comes and it was the milkman's job to collect it, bottle it, deliver it and wash up the bottles afterwards. The taste was just heavenly and it had a head of cream on it four inches thick. The poor people of the village used to buy skimmed milk for a penny a pint.

'That'll keep 'em nice and 'ealthy,' Martin said, with a grin. I was sure he threw in extra for the children as there always seemed to be so much.

'Wish my evacuee boy would eat better,' he said, shaking his head and mopping his brow. 'He seems to survive off bread, spread with brown sauce. I don't reckon he's ever eaten with a knife and fork before.'

Martin and his wife Lily had two evacuees billeted with them at their farm, Walter and Billy. Walter was from the East End and Martin was forever telling me how utterly bemused he was in his new surroundings. 'I don't think he's even seen the moon afore you know,' he whispered one morning. 'He seems terrified of it.'

I could have stayed trading stories with this loveable old milkman all morning but there were jobs to be done. Glancing at my watch I realised it was 8.00 a.m.

Outside, the babble of voices grew steadily louder . . . and louder . . . until it seemed to reach a fever pitch of noise.

The morning stampede had begun.

Suddenly the door burst open and a stream of little folk and their mothers, brothers, sisters or grandparents, whoever happened to be dropping them off, came pouring through in a great tidal wave of human life.

'Ello Brenda love, 'ows yerself?' called out one evacuee's mother as she pushed her little son Johnnie through the door. 'I fink 'e's got nits again.'

Little Johnnie stood scratching his head with filthy finger-nails as a steady stream of snot trickled from his nose.

'Go on yer li'l bleeder,' she said, shoving Johnnie through the door. 'Ta'ra all.'

I groaned inwardly. Not again. We'd only just got rid of the last infestation. There wouldn't be a child in the nursery that didn't have them by lunchtime.

A village local, an elderly man in his eighties, dropped off his grandson. The mother would already be hard at work on the early shift assembling war machines at a nearby factory.

'His mother'll collect,' he said, giving me a grin. 'Just doing my bit.'

One by one they streamed in through the door. Bleary looking mothers clutching bewildered babies and grubby faced toddlers, exhausted staff, volunteers, and excitable children.

It was a riot of snot-filled, nit-laden noise and chaos.

We would be flat out for the next ten hours until the nursery closed at 6.00 p.m. Breaks would have to be taken whenever and wherever they could, it was all hands to the pump in this place.

I had never in all my life worked anywhere like this day nursery.

Every morning most of the children had to be bathed, dressed in their nursery overalls, fed breakfast or at least milk, and that was before the day had even begun.

Whilst bathing one child it would inevitably be necessary to rescue a would-be escapee or fend off another child's curious exploration of someone's face. Some little tyke, still slippery from the soapy bubbles, would make a desperate nude dash for the door.

'I'm like the little old lady who lived in a shoe,' I'd think, giggling helplessly to myself.

At times it was simply too chaotic and I despaired of the workload. How would we ever make it through to tea time, I'd wonder? But somehow we always did. It was utterly exhausting, though, and by the time my head hit the pillow it was always spinning. But as the weeks had whizzed past I'd realised I didn't care. I was loving every smelly, chaotic second!

It might have come a year or two too late but finally the government had recognised the need for war nurseries to be formed up and down the country.

'If anything good has come of this war, it is the fact that at last the need and the value of day nurseries has been forced upon [the nation]. A woman cannot be expected to pull her weight in a factory if she is worrying about her children all day,' said Lady Reading, Chairman of the National Society of Day Nurseries.

She was right, nursery nurses were invaluable in enabling mothers to be released for war work, and now, purpose-built nurseries like ours here in Redbourn were popping up all over the country. They were the forerunners to the ones that are everywhere today but back then nurseries were relatively unheard of.

With the agreement of the Ministry of Labour, the wartime day nurseries were funded by the Ministry of Health, which supplied the capital and some of the maintenance costs. Local authorities set up the nurseries and contributed to their running costs through their Maternity and Child Welfare Committees. Ours was brand new and had been built right on the village common, sandwiched between the scout hut and the boys' school.

We had about thirty children who were divided between the baby room and another larger room, for three to five year olds.

The children were a mixture of evacuees and locals. Their mums were all out hard at work, either in Luton at the Vauxhall factory making armaments, Brocks Firework Factory in Hemel Hempstead, which now made star shells that exploded in the air to illuminate the ground and reveal the position of the enemy, or the Sphinx factory in Dunstable, making parts for Spitfires. An old silk factory in Redbourn was also a big employer of local women. It had long since stopped producing silk and had been closed for years but now a London tea firm had moved in to escape the blitz and was keeping the locals busy packing tea and coffee.

For mums who had stayed at home to look after their children or perhaps had jobs in service, this must have come as an almighty shock, but despite the long hours they worked I only ever saw happy, cheery faces at the nursery doors. Perhaps they relished the opportunity to have a break from their children and earn a bit of extra money.

To look after these thirty children there was me in the baby room, a frosty matron by the name of Mrs Bunce, two lovely smiley young junior nursemaids in their teens named Beryl and Betty, a nursery school teacher in her thirties called Joy, who ran the three to five-year-old nursery room and an evacuee cook called Mrs Ratcliffe.

We also had an elderly lady volunteer from the village who'd come in and help out, a kindly soul named Pat, with long silver hair to her waist and a face as wrinkled as a walnut.

We were a mixed bunch, some with years of training under their belt and some with none, but despite this we all rubbed along together marvellously. The more experienced staff helped out the younger untrained girls and we all got along famously, with one exception.

Sometimes when two ladies meet, the dislike can be instantaneous. And so it was with me and the disapproving Mrs Bunce.

Mrs Bunce had trained at a rival college to Norland, St Christopher's, and I rather suspect she took against me because Norland was perceived to be the superior and better known institute. It didn't matter what I did, from bathing the children to washing nappies, she knew a better way.

'I think you'll find, Brenda . . .' became Mrs Bunce's catchphrase. After dealing with her Ladyship at Little Cranford I could handle a village know-it-all, but still, the rivalry between us was bubbling just beneath the surface at all times.

That morning, as the nursery began to throb with life and Betty, Beryl and the rest of the staff bowled in with a cheery greeting, I realised someone was missing. The officious Mrs Bunce. She was usually here by 7.30 a.m. prompt and by 10.00. I started to get an uneasy feeling.

'Anyone seen Mrs Bunce?' called Joy, poking her head in the baby room. 'The weekly food order's got to be made and a fella from the council's coming for some invoices.'

'Not a trace of her,' I said. 'Most mysterious.'

Finally, at 10.30, a man from the council came by. I happened to be at the door when he arrived.

'I'm afraid Mrs Bunce isn't coming back,' he said. 'No reason. We're appointing you as deputy matron, Brenda, until we can find a replacement. You can start now. Your salary will be fifteen pounds a week.'

'B-but I don't want . . .' I stuttered. My voice trailed off as the door slammed behind him and he beat a hasty retreat across the common.

Just like that I found myself promoted.

Oh crumbs. I hadn't signed up for this responsibility. Running a nursery of this size was like nothing I'd ever done before.

'Congratulations, Nurse Brenda,' said the cook, walking up behind me. 'You must be chuffed to bits.'

But I wasn't chuffed to bits. I was horrified. All I wanted to do was look after my babies, but now I had to run the place.

Whatever happened to the mysterious Mrs Bunce, I shall never know, but back then there simply wasn't time to dwell on her disappearance. It was sink or swim!

'Pull yourself together, Brenda,' I scolded myself. 'How hard can it be?'

Over the coming months I began to see *exactly* how hard running a nursery was during a war.

A typical day went something like this.

Oversee the bathing and dressing of thirty children, prepare and feed breakfast, administer cod liver oil in a storm of protest, comb thirty heads for nits, check children for lice, apply cream for impetigo, prepare prams for babies' walks, toddlers' playtime, boil wash woollies, nappies, cot sheets and clothes, fill bottles, prepare lunch, serve lunch, clear up, get children down for naps, break up fights, clean up, order weekly food, manage rations, issue means-tested invoices and nursery bills, mending, shopping, administration, tea time, story time, play time, watch out for Doodlebug rockets flying overhead, change thirty children into day clothes, oversee home time, scrub nursery from top to bottom. Draw blackout curtains and lock up.

Phew. No wonder the day went by in the blink of an eye. Once I'd been made deputy matron, the months flew by as well. With every passing week I would wait for a new matron to turn up and relieve me of my duties but strangely, no one ever showed up. After about six months I began to realise that no one would. I was now the new matron of Redbourn day nursery, whether I liked it or not.

It makes me so cross when I think how childcare workers' role in the war is often overlooked. One hears so little of our daily efforts.

Hundreds of thousands of mothers could go to work safe in the knowledge that their little ones were being cared for. We women workers, be they land girls in the fields, ladies in factories, the women driving ambulances or trucks, worked our socks off. Blood, toil, tears and sweat were given by every single woman from every single class and background.

But while the war raged on around the world a smaller, but no less explosive little battle was being played out in the nursery.

Ever since the evacuees, who were mainly from the docks of the East End, had arrived at the village scout hut fresh off the train from St Pancras, they had made a big impact on the village. Those that didn't come from the docks lived on the Peabody Estates in Shoreditch or Stepney. These people knew a thing or two about community and after a few scraps to begin with, blended in seamlessly with the locals and enriched village life enormously.

All the evacuee boys had colourful nicknames like Leftie, Swannie and Spanner. Maybe the village boys with nick-names of their own such as Podge, Fisty, Stallion and Mr Patch – so-named because he missed a patch when potato picking – recognised fellow characters in their midst because they were welcomed with open arms, albeit with plenty of teasing.

Football united them and Podge and his mates pitted their

skills against Spanner and his team in huge matches on the common, sometimes as many as thirty a side.

The back slang the evacuees spoke bamboozled the local lads. By putting the letter from the back of a word at the front and adding an 'a' they created a whole new language that they used when they didn't want the natives to understand them. The local lads gave as good as they got though and ribbed them mercilessly when they caught them hunting for eggs in the trees.

There was widespread disbelief at how little the evacuees knew of country life. Martin the milkman was stunned when he heard tell of one little boy instructing his younger brothers and sisters not to touch a drink called milk for it could kill them. Fortunately Martin's excellent milk won them all round and must have done them some good, as this boy's younger brother went on to captain Tottenham Football Club and play football for England.

Despite their cheek the evacuee boys were very respectful of their elders and always tipped their caps to the police, vicar and the doctor, as well as to me.

But there was one person I couldn't warm to, no matter how hard I tried.

Gladys Trump was the mother of five-year-old Jimmy, an evacuee from the poorest slum district of the East End. Single mother Gladys was fiercely protective of Jimmy and her eleven other older children, so protective in fact that she had insisted on being evacuated with 'er boys'. She'd packed in her cleaning job and got on the evacuee train with them.

I hadn't realised that simply upping sticks and coming with your child was an option, as in all my previous experience the parents had stayed behind in the cities and continued with their jobs or whatever activity they had been conscripted into. But knowing that large parts of the East End were now nothing but smouldering bomb sites, I wondered if Gladys's home was even standing. One thing was for sure, she was absolutely not going to be parted from her vast brood. To her credit, Gladys had got herself a job in a nearby factory and was really making a go of it in Redbourn, but though I respected her in many ways, I also found her infuriating beyond belief. Not since Mrs Bunce and I had locked horns had I been engaged in such a battle of wills.

Gladys was an imposing woman even though she was no more than 5ft 2in. She had beady dark eyes that glared at me through a cloud of cigarette smoke, which wafted up from the fag permanently welded between her thin lips. Gladys had had a hard life and it showed on her face. She must have been pretty once but now her face was weather-beaten and pinched, ravaged by a lifetime of raising twelve children on her own.

As I saw her push open the nursery door that morning my heart sank. She spotted me and straight away I saw her thick jaw tighten and start to twitch.

Uh oh. I was in for a tongue-lashing and I knew precisely what it would be about. The first time Jimmy and Gladys turned up, I had mentioned that he, like all the other children, would be bathed every day. She had reacted as if I were suggesting he be boiled alive. On that occasion I had relented and let Jimmy attend without his bath, but Joy had told me that the other children teased him for being smelly.

When I bumped into Gladys in the village a couple of days later, I told her we were looking forward to seeing Jimmy again, but that he really would have to have a bath. Gladys caused a terrible stink about it and we hadn't seen Little Jimmy for well over a month. Now it seemed they were back.

Pushing her face so close to mine I could smell the rotten odour of stale nicotine and last night's ale, Gladys let rip. 'Oi,' she hissed. 'Make sure my Jimmy don't ave a bleedin bath today alright. E'll catch 'is death a cold.'

Drawing myself up to my full height I said as politely as I could muster, 'Jimmy needs a bath, Mrs Trump. All the children here are bathed in the morning.'

Her eyes glittered dangerously as she leant back and crossed her arms. They were so big they were like legs of mutton.

'I'm tellin' yer, he ain't 'aving no bath, or yer'll ave me to deal wiv.'

With that she cackled loudly, revealing a row of rotten brown stumps for teeth.

As she stomped off I took a deep breath through my nose and exhaled slowly out my mouth.

After dealing with Mrs Whitehead and Lady Villiers I wasn't about to be scared off by the likes of Gladys Trump. Taking Jimmy's hand I marched him through the nursery to where Joy was standing. She was just finishing off bathing a few other children in the vast white stone sink.

'Joy. Help me undress Jimmy, will you? He needs a bath.'

Poor little Jimmy. He didn't protest, in fact he looked rather pleased to be relieved of the weird assortment of garments he was wearing. Damp little trousers were held together with a safety pin and his flimsy top was ripped and filthy.

I gasped when I saw his body. He was pitifully thin, and his scrawny little torso was covered in angry looking pus-filled blisters.

'Little treasure,' I said, trying to soothe him.

I didn't like the look of that one bit. It looked like impetigo, a highly infectious bacterial skin condition. I made a note to call Nurse Sybil Trudgett, the district nurse in these parts who came to the nursery regularly to check over the children.

Poor Jimmy was filthy dirty. I don't mean the sort of dirt

that floats away in water. His skin was almost dyed brown by ground in dirt and he smelt, oh how he smelt.

Ignoring the acrid smell of urine, Joy and I gently washed him. We'd never get him totally clean but we could get the worst of it off. In later life I heard of some billetors dunking evacuees from the slum districts in sheep dip and shaving their heads to rid them of dirt and lice. Well I wouldn't stand for that here. I wouldn't fail little Jimmy. These children needed to be respected; they were the future generations of citizens who would rebuild the world after this awful war was over. Jimmy included.

Wrapping his shivering, scrawny little body up in a towel I helped Joy dry him off and change him into his clean nursery overalls.

Bless him. His little blue eyes shone with gratitude. His face, now it wasn't caked in dirt, looked so young and innocent.

'Fanks,' he said, with a sniff. A ferocious woman might have been raising him but he was a little sweetheart.

'Now for your medicine,' I said, smiling.

His nose wrinkled up in disgust.

'Don't worry,' I laughed. 'It's only cod liver oil. All the children have to have a tablespoonful each morning. It'll keep you nice and healthy.'

Jimmy joined the line of other little children waiting for their daily dose.

I tried not to laugh as each child reacted the same way. Faces grimaced and noses screwed up in disgust as the fishy oil trickled down their throats. Seconds later drops would dribble back out down their chins and down the front of their overalls. No amount of boiling in the old copper would ever get the fish oil stains out of those now.

I could hardly blame them. Kathleen and I used to dread having to take it as children, in fact poor Kathleen, being a sickly baby, was slathered in a mixture of cod liver oil and malt then wrapped in cotton wool. I'll never forget the smell. Still, what couldn't be cured must be endured, for everything else there was cod liver oil. David still takes his daily dose today!

Next it was Jimmy's turn.

He eyed the spoon suspiciously, like it was an unexploded bomb.

'I don't wanna,' he cried.

'Come on,' I said brightly. 'Upsey daisy, hold your nose. Swallow hard and down she goes.'

Spluttering, he gulped hard and shuddered.

'Bleedin' 'orrible,' he muttered.

'Language, Jimmy,' I said.

He hung his head, and then looked at me with big solemn eyes. 'Sorry, Nurse.'

With that he went to join the rest of the children who were having their hair combed for nits.

Since little Johnnie had brought nits back they'd gone round the nursery like wildfire. In the days before modern lotions and potions, we just had to comb each child's hair daily. It was a long and laborious task and no sooner was one child nit free than another would be reinfected. We fought a losing battle with them.

Just then a high-pitched scream echoed through the nursery, followed a second later by a wild-eyed Pat racing through the room.

'What on earth?' I gasped. I thought the roof had come off.

'My hair,' screamed Pat. 'My hair. They're everywhere.'

The poor woman clawed at her waist length silver hair with her bony hands.

'I've got nits everywhere. I can feel them crawling on my scalp,' she shrieked.

She was beside herself. The sight of this elderly lady screaming like a banshee had the children in fits of giggles.

'Beryl and Betty,' I snapped. 'Take Pat outside and comb
her hair through, will you.'

'Now now, children,' I said, clapping my hands and
attempting to restore order. 'Outside to play at once, please.'

Returning to my small office I sank into my chair and
let my head rest on the desk for a second. Between Gladys
Trump, the children and the nits, I was wrung out, and the
day had barely begun.

The upside to all this work was that I really was too busy
and tired to dwell on my heartache over horrid Henry. I
hadn't heard much from Little Cranford since I left. Susan
kept me updated a bit, though, and apparently Henry and
his fiancée weren't very happy. Little wonder. Threatening
to sue your intended for breach of promise is hardly the best
start to married life!

That evening, when every child had been collected,
there was just one little one sitting on his own in a chair at
reception.

Jimmy.

'His mum's late again,' said Joy. 'Factories close at half past
five but I reckon she tootles off to the pub.'

'You get off, you have a bus to catch,' I said.

Turning to Jimmy I sighed. What was I going to do about
this woman? She knew the rules, all children to be collected
by six. We all had buses to catch and homes to go to.

When she finally arrived, Gladys and I glared at each other
and she left with Jimmy without saying a word.

All night Gladys played on my mind. There was no doubt
she loved her son but to me she was morally degenerate.
What kind of woman allowed her child to get so dirty he
smelt of urine and contracted skin infections?

The next morning I opened the door and who was standing there, casting a dark shadow over the doorway? Gladys Trump herself.

Cold, calculated fury flashed over her face and her clenched knuckles were turning white.

'Ow dare ya,' she hollered. 'It's a bleedin' disgrace.'

Her face grew redder as her voice got louder. Little flecks of spittle flew from her mouth onto my face.

'Whodya fink you are? He aint never had a barf in his life. He don't need a barf now. Keep yer 'ands offa 'im.'

'I won't make any apologies for bathing your son, Mrs Trump,' I said, trying to keep my cool.

'Well, I've put a stop to yer little game so I 'ave.'

With that she shrieked with laughter and stomped off to the munitions factory.

I shook my head as I watched her bowl her way across the common, scratching her head and scattering chickens as she walked.

Utterly infuriating.

'Of all the . . .' I muttered.

'Er, Brenda,' piped up Joy. 'You'd better come and have a look at this.'

I turned around to see Joy hopelessly tugging at Jimmy's raggedy little shirt.

'She's only sewn his clothes onto him.'

She had too. Jimmy's shirt, vest and trousers were all sewn together with rough, clumsy stitches.

What on earth?

If this woman wanted a fight, a fight she would have.

'Unpick them, please, and then he can have his bath.'

And so the battle between Gladys Trump and me raged on, with both sides refusing to back down.

We bathed him, she sewed him into his clothes, I warned

her not to be late, she carried on turning up at whatever time suited her.

I just could not for the life of me understand why this woman didn't want her son to be bathed or cared for. At this point I was beyond caring. I had enough on my plate. I was so busy with the day to day running of the nursery and spent most of my time ordering supplies, managing rations and overseeing things, tasks that didn't come naturally to me, I might add. I didn't have time for a silly game of one-upmanship with a fishwife of a woman.

Sadly, Jimmy wasn't the only one. A lot of the evacuee children were almost as filthy. They'd come in on a Monday morning after a weekend with their mothers, their poor bottoms red raw and covered in nappy rash and sores.

I'd well and truly had it with these women. As far as I was concerned they were thoroughly irresponsible.

I thought I'd seen it all when I saw Jimmy's roughly sewn together clothes, but I was soon in for another shock. The Norland might have taught me a good many things, including how to cross stitch, steam a pudding and above all, how to keep little people scrupulously well cared for, but it hadn't really opened my eyes to the ways of the world.

Over the common from the nursery there lived a lady, whose name I shan't divulge to protect her identity, who was happily married to a local man. They had two children together and when war broke out the husband was called up and sent overseas to serve in Belgium.

In his absence an evacuee family, including the mother and various aunts and uncles, moved in next door. The family of twenty-two all managed to squeeze into a tiny little cottage, how they managed I shall never know. But the oldest of them was himself a young man called up to join the troops abroad. He had done so for a short while but had soon discovered the army was not to his liking and promptly deserted. In the four years since the war started he had deserted that many times. Even numerous spells in an army prison had done nothing to curb his fleet-footed ways.

When this man wasn't deserting he would take up with his neighbour's wife. This lady and the deserter had gone on to have *five* more children together.

The affair and the illegitimate children were the talk of the village. What her poor husband would make of it all when he returned to find that in his absence his wife had acquired another family was anyone's guess.

In the meantime her youngest children were under the care of the Redbourn day nursery. When her littlest tot needed breastfeeding we simply took him over the common to be fed by his mother, who would nip home from the factory, and then bring him back to the nursery.

One morning it was my turn to take the baby for his 10.00 a.m. feed. Collecting him from the baby room, I gently swaddled him in a warm blanket and made my way across the common.

'Lets see if mummy's already home, shall we?' I said, planting a little kiss on his head.

'Anyone in?' I called, creaking open the front door.

No answer.

Picking my way over the children's toys scattered through the hallway, I made my way gingerly up the narrow, creaky cottage stairs.

As I climbed I became aware of a strange noise, a sort of frantic scuffling.

At the bedroom door I paused and knocked. 'Baby's here for his feed,' I called.

The door swung open and missus was sitting up in bed, naked with a thin sheet drawn over her. She looked awkward and tense.

'Hand him over then,' she muttered.

Suddenly my eyes were drawn to the floor.

There, poking out from under the wrought-iron bedstead, was a pair of legs. The legs were in a pair of army fatigue trousers and heavy laced brown boots.

Oh very subtle.

So this was the child's father, the deserter, cowering under the bed.

She saw my eyes flicker down to the floor and she glared at me. An uneasy silence hung in the air. I handed the child over, not a word was said, and I got out of there as fast as I could.

As I walked across the common back to the nursery I shook my head in wonder. I didn't know how these women did it.

She wasn't the only one, by any means. Adultery was rife. I'd heard lots of talk of people having affairs and illegitimate children were popping up all over the place. The brief encounter became a common experience as servicemen and women and civilians sought comfort where they could find it. I suppose every day you were alive in such conditions was a gift, and made people behave in ways they would never normally.

I looked on at this behaviour in curious dismay. Now I'd seen it first hand. I knew it was not one's place to look down or judge people, and we were living in extraordinary times after all, but was it so hard to remain faithful? I thought of Mother and Father, still devoted to each other after years of marriage. They would never dream of cheating on one another.

That night, still perturbed by the sight of the deserter under the bed, I was in no mood to be trifled with.

Come half past six, who should be sat there at reception, still waiting for his mother to collect him? Yes, you've guessed it. Jimmy.

Right! I had warned that woman time and again not to be late, in fact I'd even gone so far as to tell her I'd leave him outside if she wasn't punctual. Well, she'd pushed me too far this time. I'd call her bluff so I would.

Gently buckling Jimmy into his buggy, I wheeled him out to the front of the nursery and pulled the door closed behind us. I left him there and took up my hiding place next to the porch. I couldn't be seen but I could keep an eye on Jimmy from my vantage spot.

'I'm right here, sweetheart,' I whispered.

I daresay Jimmy was used to strange comings and goings as he didn't even bat an eyelid, just swung his little legs from the buggy and played with his toy car.

I settled in to wait.

Presently the figure of Gladys came swerving round the corner and gently swayed up to the nursery. She was humming a little tune to herself, probably still flushed from the warmth of the pub, but when she saw Jimmy she stopped dead in her tracks.

My heart pounded as I waited for the explosion.

Wait for it.

'Jimeeeee,' she screeched, in a voice so high-pitched it was almost off the human radar.

There it was.

The fag dropped from her lips as a terrifying scowl crossed her face. Her eyes bulged as she let rip with a stream of obscenities. My goodness the language. She was still softly cursing to herself as she wheeled Jimmy up the road.

The next morning I braced myself. A night's sleep had done little to temper her rage.

Jabbing me with a nicotine-stained finger she let me know exactly what she thought of me.

'It's a bleedin' disgrace. Whodaya fink you are?'

On and on she went.

'I warned you I would do it if you were late and what's more I shall do it again,' I said as calmly as I could with an irate East End mother bellowing in my face.

Do you know, after that I never saw Gladys Trump again. From that day forward she sent one of her elder children to collect Jimmy. It was a blessed relief. No matter that they always pinched whatever was hanging from the washing line when they collected him, at least I didn't have to contend with her again.

A few days later we had a visit from one of my favourite Redbourn village characters. Nurse and midwife Sybil Trudgett, aka, Trudge, was a familiar sight pedalling through the village streets on a bike that must have weighed the same as an army tank. She wasn't the slimmest of ladies, which was probably just as well as she needed her stout frame to propel that beast of a bike up and down the common.

Nurse Trudgett had probably delivered every baby born within a ten-mile radius. She must have been well into her fifties, and where she got her tenacity and cheerful resilience from I'll never know, given that she seemed to spend every hour god sent on her rounds. It went some way to explaining why she'd never had her own children.

One could tell she was coming by the way the evacuee boys on the common stopped whatever they were doing to raise their caps and stand clear. She was just the sort of efficient woman who commanded instant respect.

Since taking over the running of things I'd got to know Nurse Trudgett well. The nursery was means-tested and the mothers paid what they could afford. The only person who could possibly advise me on whether to charge them one penny or seven shillings was her. She knew everyone and everyone knew her. A woman like her was as vital to the lifeblood of the village as heating and water are to a home.

She had an affinity with Redbourn that flowed through her body, from the grey hair on her head right down to the tips of her hobnailed boots.

Now, seeing her large figure hove into view, I popped the kettle on. Nurse Trudgett liked her tea strong and brown.

'How are we all today?' she called out as she bustled in.

'Lovely to see you,' I said. 'Couple of impetigo, a tonsillitis, chicken pox and a suspected German measles case for you.'

'Marvellous,' she said, with a grin. 'Keeping me busy as ever I see.'

After I'd shown her Jimmy's impetigo and she'd prescribed a perfectly horrid mauve cream to spread over his boils, we settled down to chat over tea. I confided in her my despair over Gladys Trump.

Nurse Trudgett listened patiently as I ranted over the state of Jimmy. She nodded her head when I told her he was sewn into his clothes, and just the merest flicker of a smile played on her face when I told her about hiding behind the porch.

'Well you and her have been having fun and games,' she said finally, folding her hands neatly on her lap.

'What else am I do?' I cried, throwing my hands up in despair. 'The woman is impossible.'

She smiled and instantly her weather-beaten face softened.

'I understand, Brenda. Really I do. But you know, you mustn't be so hard on women like Gladys.'

'But Jimmy's filthy and she's always late . . .' I insisted.

'That may be,' said Nurse Trudgett, her voice growing a little firmer. 'But what you have to understand is that she has raised twelve children more or less single handedly in a tiny two-bedroom flat in the Peabody buildings in Stepney. Those buildings are notorious, they are infested with bugs and in all honesty should probably have been bulldozed years ago.

'You cannot imagine the poverty. Picture the scene, Brenda,' she urged. 'Thirteen of them in a dirty tenement flat. There are no facilities in those places. The only lavatory is at the end of each balcony, next to a single tap. There are small children everywhere, sometimes naked from the waist down to save on washing.'

I felt my attitude towards Gladys soften. I remembered that when she arrived in Redbourn I had a grudging respect for her tenacity. She had after all kept her family together under the most miserable of circumstances.

'She loves those children fiercely, with an intensity that you and I who are not mothers could never understand. They are her life! Why do you think she's here? She's doing the best she can,' insisted Nurse Trudgett, aware she was finally getting through to me.

'But a bath,' I protested weakly.

'The only bath they have is filled with coal,' she said. 'Besides, Gladys doesn't wash her children because she genuinely believes they will catch their death of cold. That belief is engrained in her. That's why she was furious when she realised you had bathed Jimmy.'

'I . . .' my voice trailed off lamely.

'She hasn't enjoyed the privileged upbringing that you and I have, Brenda. Not everyone is lucky enough to be born into comfortable houses with money in the bank.'

I thought of rambling Hallcroft, my childhood home, with its many bedrooms, hot running water, rose bushes and huge garden backing onto wide open fields.

I smiled as I thought of how Father used to bring back brown paper bags groaning with sweets on a Saturday afternoon, of the way he mowed the lawn to look like railway tracks and spent hours playing trains with us. Or his little trick of arranging the fruit on our plates to look like smiley faces.

He and Mother had lavished us with love and time and built us the most idyllic home in which to spend our childhood. Then I tried to imagine the squalid, filthy overcrowded flat of Jimmy's childhood. The gulf between my start in life and Jimmy's could not have been wider.

Shame and humility washed over me. How could I have been so impossibly judgmental? I'd grown up and then trained in a different world to these East End folk, a rarefied and privileged existence where etiquette, wealth and standing ruled. I hadn't extended my view of life beyond the wrought-iron railings and quiet gentility of Pembridge Square.

Imagine wealthy Iris Beaumont, who so casually gave her child up, coping in the slums without her chauffeur driven Rolls Royce. A woman who adopted two children, then instantly distanced herself from them by hiring a nanny to raise them. For all her faults, her raucous behaviour and her foul mouth, Gladys loved the bones off her children. She would sooner carve off her own leg than dream of giving one of them away.

'You know, Brenda, the more I see of life the less I am surprised by it,' sighed Nurse Trudgett. 'Each generation has their own ways of raising their children and to them it is right. Old country folk round here used to wrap their children in waxed brown paper at the start of winter to keep them warm. And every year a Romany gypsy family comes through these parts in a horse-drawn caravan. They stop to help with the fruit picking and they are respected and welcomed in the village. They are good people.

'I remember going out once to attend to a birth, the mother was a beautiful gypsy lady with hair to her knees. The birth was peaceful and full of love. After I'd delivered the baby they put her to sleep in a little cardboard box under the bed.

Some people might frown upon that but not me. I daresay that baby was more loved and cherished than most.'

Suddenly I thought of the Norland's insistence on lining up the babies' cots outside in the snow during the coldest winter in forty-five years, so they could take their naps. That might also be counted a little bizarre, but the intention was just as sincere as that of the gypsies, the country folk and the East End mums.

I may have joined Redbourn day nursery naïve in the ways of the world and a little narrow in my outlook. But thanks to the kindness and understanding of this lovely lady, I left it with a broader perspective, and I hope a little more understanding.

Later in life I was thrilled to hear that Nurse Trudgett had been awarded the MBE in 1954 for her work in the community, and rightly so. This unique woman delivered 2,500 babies over her career and kept a community healthy and happy. Nurse Trudgett's compassion opened my eyes. I never did see Gladys again after our last showdown, but I like to think my newfound insight would have made me softer towards her. She had an enormous effect on me, indirectly. I was certainly more compassionate towards other people as a consequence of having met her.

With all the excitement and noise generated by the older children it would be all too easy to forget the babies I spent most of my time looking after, but there was one little girl whose story particularly touched my heart.

Juliet was just a little tot of no more than two when her mother dropped her off at the nursery. She was the prettiest little thing, with soft blonde curls and a smile like a sunbeam. Whenever she saw me she would throw open her arms, bounce up and down in excitement and flash me an adorable gummy smile. How could I resist such a lovely invitation to a cuddle? The paperwork could wait, I always made time for a hug with Juliet.

Tragically, her older brother, aged eight, had been sent to live in an institution and probably sterilised on account of the fact that he had Down's syndrome. Nowadays the medical world knows far more about the treatment and care of people with Down's syndrome and you would never dream of institutionalising and sterilising a child with Down's, but back in the 1940s it was a more ignorant age.

It was probably a hangover from the eugenics ideology of the nineteenth century that people with 'less desirable traits' should be prevented from having children by placing them in gender separate institutions. Horrifyingly, some of the first victims of Hitler's euthanasia programme were children with Down's syndrome, not that we knew that back then in 1943.

Juliet's parents, first cousins, were bereft at having to give up their beloved son.

'I just couldn't cope,' the mother confided in me, one morning soon after Juliet started.

'He was so strong and he would hit me,' she whispered. 'One day he barricaded himself in his bedroom by pushing the wardrobe against the door.'

She never said as much, but I knew she and the father were praying little Juliet didn't have the syndrome. That poor woman looked haunted and she doted on her little girl.

'I do so hope Juliet will be all right,' was as much as she would say.

'Don't you worry,' I smiled. 'She will be fine.'

After that I always made an extra special effort to spend a bit of time with Juliet and lavish her with cuddles. She was the most affectionate child I'd ever cared for and her face would light up when I walked into a room.

'She's got a soft spot for you I reckon,' chuckled Joy, when she saw us.

After about six months of her being there I was in the baby room one day when I heard a funny noise. I looked down and saw Juliet, sitting on the floor of the nursery where she usually played happily with her toys. Instead of babbling to herself, she was sitting ramrod straight, her back was rigid and she was shaking.

'Darling,' I said, bending down to pick her up, 'are you all right?'

The episode, if you can call it that, passed in no time. She seemed fine after that, and I thought no more of it until a month or so later the same thing happened again. Only this time it was far worse. Her poor little body was in spasms and her face went bright red as she shook. I tried to uncurl her fists but they were clenched shut.

'Juliet, can you hear me,' I cried. Finally she collapsed exhausted into my arms.

Terrified, I called Nurse Trudgett and she cycled over immediately. She examined Juliet and then promptly called out the doctor. The doctor made a thorough examination of Juliet, who was by now fully recovered and beaming at the stern man with the stethoscope like he was Santa Claus.

The diagnosis was swift.

'Looking at her facial characteristics, skin tone, family history and behaviour I would say she has Down's syndrome,' he said, frowning.

My heart sank. What would her poor mother say? Fortunately I wasn't there when the diagnosis was passed on; I don't think I could have borne witness to her heartbreak.

I often wonder what happened to that sunny, adorable, lovable little girl after she eventually left the nursery. Of all the children I have ever cared for she was the one with the most love to give, which just makes her possible fate all the more tragic.

Characters like Jimmy, Gladys Trump and Juliet continued to make my life in Redbourn a constant source of wonder. The place consumed my every waking thought; it was like working inside a bubble. After I'd got the bus home, mother would put my dinner on the table and it was much as I could do to wearily raise the fork to my lips. All too soon I would be heading to bed. My life revolved around the nursery, quiet evenings at home and Sunday morning worship, with no social life to speak of.

I was just twenty-two and in a position of huge responsibility for one so young. Consequently I allowed the job to take over. Being conscientious I so wanted to be professional and not let the reputation of the Norland down.

My life within the four walls of the nursery ruled out any chance of finding a boyfriend. I was simply too busy, or too ill, to socialise. Hardly surprisingly, during my time at Redbourn I contracted everything the children caught. That nursery was a breeding ground of germs and my poor immune system took a battering. I even gave German measles to my brother Christopher while he was on leave to go abroad.

Outside on the village streets, however, people were beginning to relax a little as the fear of German invasion subsided.

On 6 June 1944, thirteen months after I began working at the nursery, the Allied invasion of Normandy took place. Those same cheerful young Canadians who had won the hearts of Appleton villagers all those years before, during my first job, were now heroically sacrificing their lives on the beaches of Northern France.

Bulletins rang out from wireless sets all over the village. 'Here is a special bulletin. D-Day has come. Early this morning the Allies began the assault on the north-western face of Hitler's European fortress.'

But despite its success, the dangers were far from over.

A week after D-Day, on 13 June 1944, the first V1 pilotless plane crossed the English coast, and during the following month thousands were launched on war-weary England.

On 8 September, four years after the Battle of Britain, the longer range V2s began to fall out of the autumn sky. It was too late for the Germans to win the war, but once again we found ourselves in the line of attack.

There were ten thousand casualties in the first week of the V1, or Doodlebugs as they came to be known, but it was the V2s, which gave no warning, that were really sinister. Unseen and unheard they plummeted to earth delivering one tonne of high explosive at a speed of 3,500 feet per second. The 'V' stood for *Vergeltung*, or retaliation.

As our troops advanced throughout Europe, the Germans retaliated by raining down these hateful missiles.

These unmanned invaders from the skies terrified me. They truly were the ultimate weapons of terror warfare. I was outside in the playground the first time I encountered one of them. I became aware of a strange droning noise overhead just as it abruptly stopped. A V2 rocket!

I felt sick with terror.

I'd been warned that when the engine cuts out, that's when the bomb is ready to begin its descent. Where it fell was anybody's guess.

I stood stock still in the playground, ice-cold panic pumping through my veins.

'Everyone inside now,' I bellowed.

The staff, sensing the urgency in my voice, gathered Jimmy, Juliet and the rest of the boys and girls together and ushered them back inside, where we quickly hid them under the tables. The children thought it a marvellous game of course, but us adults were all scared witless.

We stared at each other, our faces white as flour.

I was tense as a coiled spring, waiting for an almighty explosion. It never came, but the fear of waiting and the silence as we waited for it to drop, was unbearable.

This happened a few more times as these hateful machines of war passed over our heads. Fortunately none ever exploded in Redbourn but the anticipation aged us no end. That was the only thing that I remember being really scared of throughout the war.

Ironically, as these rockets left people paralysed with terror, our thoughts were already turning to peace. Thanks to D–Day it was widely believed we were winning the war and most knew these rockets were Hitler's futile last-ditch manoeuvre in retaliation for the Allies' advance throughout Europe. At the same time, the blackout gave way to a halfhearted dimout and we wearily took down the blackout curtains.

Soon after the rockets began, another strange noise filled the skies over Redbourn. The village was alive with news of the day the horizon turned black. I hadn't witnessed it but many of the villagers had become aware of a strange droning sound, different from the hated rockets. Staring out their windows they were flabbergasted to see hundreds of British RAF planes towing gliders fly overhead.

One by one, villagers trickled out of their cottages until soon the common was filled with silent on–lookers, craning their necks skywards, an uneasy feeling growing in the pits of their stomachs.

'It was obviously an invasion force,' one local told me. 'But for where?' 'The skies were black with planes,' muttered another.

We didn't know the exact scale of it at the time but some

truly horrendous battles were being fought by our boys in Europe. The last year of World War Two was our country's darkest hour. Tens of thousands of sons, husbands and brothers lost their lives. Precious few survivors of these battles walk amongst us now.

One person clearly moved by this was Martin the milkman. His eldest boy, Ray, twenty-one, had joined up and was serving with the 1st Airborne Division. Martin tried to maintain his sunny disposition when he delivered the milk but his face was pinched with worry and his poor wife, God bless her, took on a haunted look.

Somehow, in some way, we all felt responsible for Ray. The Webbs were so popular in the village and young Ray was 'one of ours'.

It was widely believed that Ray's division had gone to Arnhem. As part of Operation Market Garden, paratroopers were dropped in the Netherlands to secure key bridges and towns along the Allied axis of advance. The British forces were quickly hampered by unexpected resistance, especially from the 9th and 10th SS Panzer Division. Arnhem was the scene of some horrific and fierce fighting and from the bulletins we heard on the wireless, we knew it was a resounding failure for the Allies. Three quarters of Ray's division had been killed in combat. The whole village prayed for Ray's survival.

A couple of weeks after the skies had turned black I heard a furore out on the common. Glancing out the window who should I see striding along the road but Ray himself! It was a moment of sheer joy for the village. People rushed out of their homes to applaud him. Ray was one of the lucky ones and it's a miracle he survived.

I watched with a lump in my throat. With his dark hair, chiselled features and Errol Flynn moustache, he was so handsome. He got a hero's welcome, particularly from the young ladies of the village, who positively swooned in his presence.

The village was buzzing after Ray's return and we all prayed like we had never done before, for a swift end to this war. Two months later, barbed wire started disappearing from Britain's beaches, and Father and the rest of the Home Guard were stood down from duty.

Finally, the following May, 1945, came the moment we had all been waiting for, VE Day. Victory in Europe. A huge cheer erupted from the boys' school next door and bulletins all over the village rang out with the triumphant news. The following letter was sent to schools up and down the country and pinned on notice boards in the village.

Today as we celebrate victory, I send this personal message to you and all the other boys and girls at school. For you have shared in the hardships and dangers of a total war and you have shared no less in the triumph of the Allied Nations. I know you will always feel proud to belong to a country which was responsible for such a supreme effort; proud, too, of parents and elder brothers and sisters who by their courage, endurance and enterprise brought victory.

Signed George R.I.

London went mad with joy, people screamed and shouted, perfect strangers embraced. Revellers danced the conga, a popular new import from Latin America, the Lambeth walk and the hokey cokey.

Churchill appeared on the floodlit balcony at Buckingham Palace with the King and Queen, while the princesses were allowed to party with the celebrating crowds below. On every street a sea of red, white and blue flags and bunting fluttered triumphantly.

In Redbourn, Union Jacks were hung at every window and people finally looked less careworn and more relaxed. Even the deserter must eventually have crawled out from under his mistress's bed! Martin the milkman and the villagers organised a huge afternoon of races, games and tea on the common. John, Ron and Podge celebrated alongside Spanner and the rest of his gang with egg and spoon and sack races followed by tea with lashings of jam.

I spent my VE Day more quietly. I went home to be with my family. I had survived incendiary bombs, flying shrapnel, doodlebugs, betrayal, a broken heart, German measles and ferocious East End mums. The war was over. I was shattered.

What a terrible price we paid for victory. A total of 67,100 civilians were killed during the war, 7,736 of whom were children. Then there were the hundreds of thousands of brave servicemen and women who lost their lives fighting to secure our freedom.

In the 100 days between VE Day and VJ Day, Churchill was replaced by Clement Attlee, which surprised my father no end.

Many felt Churchill was the person to lead us in war but not in peace.

On 15 August 1945, VJ Day, once again the Union Jacks of Redbourn were dusted down and returned to windows and the villagers sang and danced in the high street. Bonfires were built on the common and rockets released. Unfortunately one hit the thatched roof of the Chequers pub. The firemen weren't able to put out the inferno and the next morning the gutted shell looked a little sorry.

I stayed home again with my parents and listened to the King's Speech.

'Let us join in thanking Almighty God that war has ended throughout the world, and that in every country men may now turn their industry, skill and science to repairing its frightful devastation.'

'Amen to that,' agreed Father.

My father's affection for the King was now even stronger after he and the Queen had stayed in London and held their heads up high. Their presence and their visits to the bomb sites of the East End were invaluable for morale. When Buckingham Palace was hit, the Queen said, 'I'm so glad we've been bombed. Now we can look the East End in the face.'

A few days later we attended a church service at our local Baptist church, as we did every Sunday morning, to give thanks for the ending of this terrible war. We had been remarkably lucky, as a family. My brothers were for the most part too young to be involved in conflict, and my father was too old. We had escaped the fate of so many of our fellow citizens, who were killed on British soil.

As for my siblings, Michael was demobbed from where he was stationed with the air force in India and the rest of the boys came home from the Lake District. Kathleen was working as a midwife in Woking and thanks to the war was a virtual stranger to me. I was looking forward to getting to know them all again!

The all-clear had sounded for good, the strains of 'We'll meet again' were to be heard everywhere and the age of post-war austerity had begun. What now for the village and the nursery?

Twelve evacuee families loved village life so much they decided to stay on. They were embraced by the local community and became a welcome part of it, settling down and raising their families in Redbourn. Even today an old boys and girls reunion is held with ex-evacuees occupying a table known affectionately as 'cockney corner'.

Not so for Jimmy and his mother, who decided to return to the East End.

When it came time for Jimmy to leave, he flung his arms around me.

'Fank you nurse Brenda. I'll never forget ya.'

My heart soared.

'Nor I you my little treasure.'

He may have been filthy, thin and pale when he arrived but I like to think he left me rosy cheeked, happy, well fed and clean – the perfect child. Who knew what the future held for little Jimmy?

Unrelenting poverty in a tiny two-bedroom tenement flat? Even if his home was still standing, it was set in a bomb-ravaged wasteland. Still, knowing Jimmy he'd be all over those bomb sites, quickly becoming ruler of his strange new playground.

Over at my parents' house life was all change, too. Soon after the war ended I came home from the nursery one day to find my mother utterly distraught.

'Lady Lillian is insisting that Sally return to live with her,' she cried.

'But how can she?' I protested. 'Sally has lived with us for years.'

Call us naïve, but as Sally had been with us for six years with scarcely a visit from her Ladyship, we assumed she would be with us forever. She was one of the family now, a happy healthy seven-year-old. We had even enrolled her in a local Catholic school as per Lady Lillian's wishes.

'She can and she is,' sobbed Mother. 'What's more I'm not allowed to visit. Her Ladyship has consulted a doctor who thinks it best Sally make a clean break of it and not have contact with us, as it will confuse her.'

As I hugged her I realised my mother was bereft.

'I loved that little girl as a daughter,' she whispered.

Saying goodbye was a painful and bewildering experience for all involved. Sally blamed herself.

'When I saw her putting on make-up on a visit once, I told her my mummy doesn't wear make-up. She was angry. Is this my fault?'

Sally's lip was quivering as she spoke.

'Of course not darling,' gushed Mother. 'She's your mummy and she wants you home.'

Mother folded little Sally into a last hug and wept her goodbyes.

We never saw that little girl again.

As Mother returned to the house I felt so scared. What would she do now without her little Sally to care for? What would women all over the country do now their roles had changed? Return to a life of domesticity? 'And where do we go from here?' was the title of a *Vogue* article on the future of women after the war. So many had found liberation and acceptance in wearing a man's uniform during the war, giving it all up would be a bitter pill to swallow.

In 1945 divorce rates were double what they were in 1938. Women had tasted freedom and they didn't want to return to the kitchen. (Amazingly, though, I heard the lady who had all the illegitimate children with the deserter was forgiven by her husband when he returned. Not only that but he even helped to raise all the children as his own. What a forgiving fellow! He was regarded as a saint by the village.)

Whatever women wanted, the remaining years of the Forties and the Fifties represented a backwards step for their emancipation. There was desperation to see society return to normal and women going back to their old domesticated role was part of this. One factory manager even said in a report, 'This girl has so taken to machinery that she'd like to become an apprentice and go right through the works. This of course is not possible on account of Union agreements. A woman's place is in the home.'

He wasn't alone in his feelings.

Things were all change for me, too. Wartime nurseries declined due to the withdrawal of Ministry of Health funding and so Redbourn day nursery was put into the care of the local authority. This spelled bad news. The children were leaving in their droves, full-time care not being needed anymore, and the staff were losing their enthusiasm. Who could blame them? We all felt like we were just going through the motions.

I so wanted to leave, but to do what? Britain was a much-changed place. The British nanny was dying out, a symbol of a disappearing way of life. One by one, private colleges to train nannies were closing. In 1945 the National Nursery Examination Board was founded, and laid down national standards of qualification. NNEB courses were introduced into new colleges of further education. The new state run colleges threw open the profession to girls whose families could not afford private training.

More and more families began to employ cheaper au pairs and untrained help. Post-war austerity was already biting and social changes meant that employing a nanny in a uniform wasn't seen as prestigious in the way it once was. In three years' time the NHS would be formed and mass antenatal care organised for the first time.

Meanwhile the Norland's headquarters at Pembridge Square had been sold off, the lecture rooms and work rooms where we had toiled, ironed, sewed, knitted and polished our prams now lay empty. Miss Whitehead had resigned in 1941. No more children's laughter echoed round the grand old house.

The Norland moved from Bideford in Devon to Chisle-hurst in Kent and like so many other businesses, was engrossed in financial survival. Economy became the order of the day.

In March 1946 I could stand it no longer and handed in my notice. The nursery had lost its soul and I my enthusiasm for it, but I owed it a huge debt of gratitude. What a journey of discovery I had been on. The East Enders and this little community opened my eyes to the world. Thanks to them, the bombs and betrayal, I had changed. I was no longer a naïve young girl, but a strong woman. I could look forward with my head held high and say I did my duty. I did my little bit to help secure the safety and freedom of our children.

The world was changing, but could I change with it? Was I still needed and wanted? Could I keep the pram wheels rolling? Now that the bombs had stopped raining down were there any children in need of protection, love, stability or just a lap to sit for a cuddle?

For me the route was obvious. My faith in Jesus had always been strong in my life, even when I'd been a directionless child who'd found company in the warmth and safety of the Girls' Brigade. It seemed natural that I would be drawn back to religion in some way.

Feeling lost, I was only too pleased to take up an offer that had come my way.

Mary was an old friend of mine whom I had met through the church, and, hearing I was at a loose end, she invited me to join her on a religious conference in Hildenborough, Kent.

Religious camps, or rallies as they were known, were springing up all over Britain. They were extremely popular in the post-war years and offered direction to thousands of youth. For young men and women who had seen their homes bombed, their loved ones killed, and survived countless brushes with death, these conferences offered hope and peace in uncertain times.

And so it was that I found myself travelling to Kent with Mary. On the way she told me whom we'd be meeting there.

'My brother Branse is going with his friend Bill,' she chattered excitedly. 'You'll like Bill, he's lovely. Very bright, he's studying theology at Cambridge University.'

Apparently Bill and Branse were great friends and had both flown Spitfires in the RAF during the war.

'Terribly brave both of them,' Mary went on.

Her voice dropped a decibel or two.

'Do you know, when they were out on a secret sortie somewhere over Europe in their Spitfires, they experienced something that made them convert and decide to give their life to the Lord.'

'Gosh,' I gulped, my eyes growing wide. 'Converted in the skies. I wonder what happened to have given them such a profound moment.'

'Who knows,' whispered Mary. 'They would never dream of discussing it.'

I tried to imagine what they must have experienced out there in the dark, huddled in their cockpits.

Such brave men.

I wasn't disappointed when I met them.

'Hello,' said the softly spoken, blonde haired young man, shaking my hand earnestly. 'I'm Bill.'

'Hello,' I murmured, savouring the warmth of his hand in mine.

Oh my. Bill was quite lovely, delicious in fact.

He radiated a goodness and a gentle sincerity I'd never come across before.

For the rest of the day we barely drew breath, chatting till the sun went down. I talked about my work as a nanny and he told me about his studies at Cambridge University. I'm quite sure he was far more intelligent than me but he was so interested in everything I had to say, and kind, gentle and considerate.

I never found out what happened that day in the Spitfire but whatever it was, his love for the Lord was now beyond question.

One evening I watched him out of the corner of my eye during a prayer meeting. His eyes were closed and a look of utter peace washed over his face as he silently mouthed the prayers.

I marvelled at the strength of his faith and bathed in the gentle aura of serene reverence that surrounded him. He was nothing like cocky, boasting Henry. This was a man at peace with himself and the world.

This was a man I could truly fall for.

Testimonial

Miss Ashford was appointed as nursery nurse at Redbourn Day Nursery in May 1943. In September 1944 she was promoted to position of Assistant Matron. She has proved herself to be most capable in every way, conscientious, loyal and faithful in dealing with parents and staff and her work is of the highest standard. I would add that she has been in complete control of the nursery.

County Hall.

Nurse Brenda Ashford

> We'll never forget you.
> *Mary Poppins*, P.L. Travers

TODAY I am ninety-one and I look back on a wonderful, rich and rewarding life crammed full of adventures and love.

And what adventures! From ducking flying shrapnel to caring for illegitimate children and running war nurseries with rockets whistling overhead.

During World War Two I encountered everyone from German Luftwaffe pilots, draconian hospital matrons, the doyennes of England's oldest nanny school to East End mums and Lords and Ladies, but surviving the war is only part of the story.

I've had my heart broken and battered, been betrayed and bombed but I've kept smiling throughout. Being a nanny is not for the faint-hearted, you know! It's a calling not a career, that's for certain.

But I owe my profession a debt of gratitude.

Looking after babies and children has kept the sparkle in my eye and the spring in my step. They say caring for children keeps you young. Perhaps that's why I didn't retire until I was eighty years old, meaning I am proud to say I've been a nanny for sixty-two glorious years. Surely that makes me Britain's longest serving nanny?

There has never been a dull moment. Children have moved me from extremes of despair and heartache to sheer joy and helpless giggles.

Perhaps the most emotional job I ever had began in the late 1940s. I watched a little girl being born. She emerged blinking and bewildered from the womb. I had the honour of being the first person to tenderly cradle her little body and the privilege of being her nanny for nearly eight years. I was there when she cut her first tooth, dried her tears when she bumped her head and saw her take her first faltering steps into the world.

Sadly, I was also present at her funeral after she died aged sixty in 2007. I witnessed the full circle of life from birth through to death.

What has that taught me? That our journey through life is fleeting and we none of us are masters of our own destiny. We owe it to ourselves to live each day on earth as if it is our last.

But as ever in life, heartache can be followed by happiness.

My last job was perhaps my proudest moment. Aged eighty, I was thrilled to find myself caring for the babies of a woman I cared for when she herself was a baby. My 'grand charges' Felix and Jemima, are now thirteen and twelve respectively, and their mother Susanna is forty-six, and I'm proud to say I looked after them all. To me, they're the family I never had. To them I'm just Nanna.

I never dreamt when I graduated from the Norland Institute aged eighteen that I'd still be looking after babies aged eighty! Which just goes to show that if your heart is full of love for little children your body will keep on going.

I never did find true love or have a child to call my own. I'm afraid Bill found a stronger love in the arms of the Lord and there wasn't time for me to find another man. There were simply too many babies who needed my love.

Yes, I sacrificed my dreams of finding love and having my own family to care for the offspring of others but I have not one regret. For every single one of the hundred or so children I have cared for has flooded my heart with love and personal fulfilment. The one thing that has motivated me above all else and driven me on year after year, baby after baby, is the desire to replicate the happy childhood I enjoyed, in homes throughout the land.

With each family I worked for I realised what I loved more than anything was getting them on their feet and creating the happiest home life I possibly could. Sprinkling a little of the magic that I had experienced in my own blissful childhood was most gratifying.

I have puzzled many times over the ingredients for the perfect recipe for a happy home. It needs to be a place with parents who worship their children. Throw in some stability, a dash of routine and respect. Sprinkle with some fun and imaginative games and stir well.

A vital ingredient in this recipe, I have concluded, is the mother. As long as the mother is happy the household will be happy. That was where I came in. I would go into the home prepared to do anything that a mother would do, be that the night feeds, housework, winding a fussy baby, or taking baby out so mother could sleep. By supporting the mother through smiles, gentle encouragement and hard work, she'd be up and about and on her feet in no time.

The thrill of seeing a happy mother and in turn a happy, warm household was beyond measure.

And that's all I have tried to do, really. It's not so complicated.

I've seen childcare trends come and go but the only thing any mother need really do is give her whole heart over to love. If she does this, the rewards will be endless. After all, the world would be a much happier place if people tried to fill their houses with love. Some people just need a little reminding, that's all.

In sixty-two years I hope I have imparted a little of that love, magic and wisdom.

I am still in touch with many of the children I cared for and every year at Christmas and on my birthday I am rewarded with many letters and photos from my 'babies' all grown up.

These days my life is a little less eventful. I live in sheltered accommodation and I still find it a surprise to be called Brenda. I'm so used to being called Nanny, you see. But I have the memories of a thousand cuddles from chubby arms. Those smiles and the magical sound of a child's laughter will keep me going for a few more years yet.

I dare say that as a Norland Nurse I could have worked for royalty or diplomats, and travelled the world. But I didn't. I'm proud to say I stayed on British soil and did my duty. I did my little bit to help secure the safety and freedom of our children, and I found love by the bucketload along the way.

The Norland motto, 'Love Never Faileth', has always been my guiding light. I hope I never have failed a single child.

Afterword

Nana was my rock. She was always there for me, when I was tiny, when I was growing up and when I was old enough to know better. Never questioning, always supporting. Her total love and kindness to me were that of a mother. I never knew any different. And so it has always been and is still now, and the most lovely thing for me is that my children love her just as I have always done. Truly inspirational, with a love of babies that enabled her, even at the age of eighty to get up in the small hours to care for them. She just has a way with them that is impossible to put into words, they just respond to her. 'I can't' is not in her vocabulary. Always there to help and love, through good times and bad.

Susanna Morris

Extract from Volume Two

Every saint has a past and every sinner has a future
Oscar Wilde

IT WAS a most intriguing request and one I knew I couldn't possibly ignore.

'I really am in the most urgent need of help for my wife,' said the gentleman's voice on the other end of the phone. 'Meet me at Fortnum and Mason in London's Piccadilly and I shall explain more over tea. I will be wearing a bowler hat and carrying a cane. Good day to you, Nurse.'

The Norland had arranged my first interview for private work since the wretched war ended nearly a year ago. After handing in my notice at Redbourn Day Nursery, I was most eager to get back into a private household. The time I spent looking after evacuees and local children was the most eye-opening and rewarding of my career but since the end of the war the nursery had lost its soul, and I my enthusiasm for it. I couldn't wait to work one-on-one with a family that needed my help.

As for my own family, Mother, like so many other women returning to a life of domesticity after the war, was struggling to readjust without her beloved evacuees.

Father was concentrating on building up his textiles business, with the help of my brother, Christopher.

Michael was starting to train for a career in the theatre and Basil was working abroad for a timber firm. David was just sixteen and trying out his first steps in this new era.

The baby boom was beginning so, as a midwife, Kathleen was rushed off her feet delivering babies in Surrey.

Thanks to the war all my siblings were virtually strangers to me. Now it was March 1946 and post-war Britain, like her people, was a much-changed place.

The glamorous GIs that had enthralled all our young ladies had returned to America and their families. 416,800 American soldiers were killed fighting in World War Two and our friends over the ocean were reeling from their losses every bit as much as us.

Economy and survival were the order of the day as women and returning soldiers struggled to find their place in the world. But what sort of world remained to many of them? The answer was uncertain. There was a major shortage of jobs and housing.

We had beaten Hitler's army but his terrifying attacks had left behind a sobering legacy. Once glorious buildings crumbled to dust, closed streets and blown-out houses empty and devoid of life could be seen all over the land. Pavements in the cities were pockmarked with bomb craters and Keep Out signs on bombsites acted like a magnet to naughty children seeking out thrills.

But there was also optimism amongst the rubble. We had survived. We owed it to those that had lost their lives for our freedom, to restore our great cities, our nation, ourselves. Part of winning this war meant acceptance of sacrifices and a willingness to rebuild our country from the ashes up. There was everything to do.

And so it was that I took a red double-decker bus up London's Piccadilly in still smart Mayfair, to meet this desperate gentleman and answer his call for help.

I too must look forward, not back. With state-run colleges opening up everywhere to train nursery nurses, employing a private nanny in a uniform was not as prestigious as it once was. No, I should feel most grateful for a position in a house, however difficult it may be.

Liveried doormen graciously swung the door to Fortnum and Mason open for me.

War may have altered England a great deal but some traditions would never die out.

Hitler dumped 18,000 tonnes of explosives on London during the war but Fortnum and Mason at 181 Piccadilly had survived. Afternoon tea here was a British institution and I was pleased to see the place was thronged with customers nibbling dainty sandwiches and sipping tea.

Had Hitler really believed he could replace our beloved cucumber sandwich with stollen and bratwurst?

Once inside a welcoming rush of warmth hit me.

Smartly-dressed waitresses darted about the place carrying tea trays piled high with fresh leaf-tea brewing in bone china and plates of little cucumber sandwiches with the crusts cut off.

It reminded me of when Mother and I had gone for tea at Lyons Corner House all those years before, as a treat for being accepted by the Norland.

How different a person I was now! But then, war had altered us all no doubt.

I caught sight of a lone gentleman with a cane resting against the white linen tablecloth. Dressed smartly in a double-breasted dark suit and cravat, he looked like a well-to-do banker or merchant.

As soon as he saw me, he smiled, took off his bowler hat and rose to his feet.

'Miss Ashford?'

'Mr Sacks?'

'Yes indeed,' he said warmly, pulling back my chair for me. 'I can't tell you how grateful I am to see you.'

Soon I found my plate piled high with sandwiches and a delicate little cup full of the most delicious smelling tea pressed into my hands.

I took a sip and eyed the cakes that our waitress had brought to the table. Sponges and scones that looked as light as gossamer sat tantalisingly atop a white doily.

We'd never had anything as refined as that at the day nursery. I smiled as I pictured little Jimmy's face if someone were to set down a plate of such delicacies in front of him. I dare say it would have been demolished in the blink of eye.

Rationing was still in full swing despite the end of the war, indeed bread was more tightly rationed now, in 1946, than it had been during the war years. It could still be bought however, if you had the money to pay for it, which judging by his smart appearance and the leather briefcase by his chair, Mr Sacks obviously did.

Remembering I was a professional, I tore my gaze away from the mouthwatering afternoon tea and looked Mr Sacks in the eye.

'Do tell me about your situation and then I can see whether I can be of assistance,' I said, with a smile.

'My wife Carolyn has four children, two boys aged two and a half and four and a half, and baby twins, one boy, one girl, born just a few weeks ago.'

'Gracious,' I exclaimed. 'You do have a houseful.'

'Quite honestly, I don't know how she's coping,' he said. 'She is exhausted. '

Suddenly I realised he too had dark circles under his eyes.

'Oh, you poor things.'

He sighed dramatically as he took a bite of his cucumber sandwich and then chewed thoughtfully.

'On top of which, poor Carolyn's father is gravely ill, on his death bed really, so we need to move in with him.'

His voice dropped to a whisper and he glanced left and right. I leant in closer.

'We rather suspect his nurse is manipulating him. He has altered his will and left everything to her,' Mr Sacks muttered. 'So the move is of the utmost urgency as I'm sure you can appreciate.'

My eyes grew as wide as saucers.

'Oh absolutely, I understand,' I said nodding my head vigorously.

That poor, desperate couple. Baby twins, two children, a house move, a dying relative and a fraudster to contend with. If ever a family were in dire need of help it was surely them! I had decided to accept the job before he even offered it to me.

'We'll need you right away, Nurse Ashford. You will take the job, won't you?'

No sooner had I nodded my head than he stood up, put on his bowler hat with a flourish and beamed brightly.

'Marvellous. The salary will be £15 a week and you can report to my wife tomorrow.'

With that he strode from Fortnum and Mason, hailed a cab and vanished into London's bustle.

I sat back in my chair, my head still spinning from the speed of my new appointment. Hurriedly, I finished my cup of tea, eager to get home and prepare to meet my new charges.

It was only later as I packed my suitcase and uniform ready for my new job that I realised.

He hadn't paid for our tea! Little did I know it then but I was about to become embroiled in a most peculiar world.

An invitation from the publisher

Join us at www.hodder.co.uk, or follow us on Twitter @hodderbooks to be a part of our community of people who love the very best in books and reading.

Whether you want to discover more about a book or an author, watch trailers and interviews, have the chance to win early limited editions, or simply browse our expert readers' selection of the very best books, we think you'll find what you're looking for.

And if you don't, that's the place to tell us what's missing.

We love what we do, and we'd love you to be a part of it.

www.hodder.co.uk

@hodderbooks

HodderBooks

HodderBooks